Between th

Between the Two:
A Nomadic Inquiry into Collaborative Writing and Subjectivity

By

Ken Gale and Jonathan Wyatt

*To Nell,
with love
Toretta -
xox.*

*Dear Nell
best wishes*

**CAMBRIDGE
SCHOLARS**

P U B L I S H I N G

*from
Ken
xx
March
2010*

Between the Two: A Nomadic Inquiry into Collaborative Writing and Subjectivity,
by Ken Gale and Jonathan Wyatt

This book first published 2009. The present binding first published 2010.

Cambridge Scholars Publishing

12 Back Chapman Street, Newcastle upon Tyne, NE6 2XX, UK

British Library Cataloguing in Publication Data
A catalogue record for this book is available from the British Library

ISBN (10): 1-4438-1637-X, ISBN (13): 978-1-4438-1637-3

TABLE OF CONTENTS

FOREWORD

BRONWYN DAVIES,
PROFESSORIAL FELLOW, MELBOURNE UNIVERSITY

This is a beautiful and astonishing book. The authors take up and develop the concepts that Deleuze created when working with others like Guattari, Foucault and Parnet, precisely in order to make possible the experimental and deeply moving writing found here in this book. No longer difficult-to-grasp abstractions (as they were when Jonathan and Ken first took them up), the Deleuzian concepts they work with here take on an intensely lived materiality within the flow of words between these two men talking and writing.

Jonathan and Ken tell the story of, or more accurately, they live within the writing of, their developing friendship with each other and with Deleuze. They enfold each other and unfold into their relations with each other, and also with those human (and non-human) others around them. I found myself, as reader, drawn into the folds and plateaus of their relationality, first as an outsider looking in, curious about what it was they were allowing me to see, then slowly taking up my existence within the *space-in-between* that was generated in their writing. They write about writing as an act of love, and I as reader, found myself embraced in that love. I found myself in love with and immersed in their words, with their struggle, with the space-in-between they were creating.

Understanding the concept of the space-in-between is important for entering into (and being undone by) what it is that Ken and Jonathan have generated here in this writing. It involves the dismantling of two separate subjects whose essential selves pre-exist the writing, and who are separated by an unbridgeable gap or space between them. Although the specificity of each still exists (and perhaps even exists more vividly), with each of their separate histories and separate social and spatial contexts, the focal point, the source of energy and change, is the movement-in-between, in which each becomes someone in relation to the other—each exists in the unfolding relation with the other, and in the *lines of flight* into the not-yet-known that open up between them.

Central to the generation of this space-in-between are the capacity for listening, and the use of writing as a method of inquiry. Jonathan and Ken demonstrate in their writing to each other, both their finely tuned capacity for listening and also the struggle to listen--the difficult and complex task of listening—each finely tuned into his own affect, each finding words to speak the specific truth of that moment of being, each able to speak, to be so tuned in, precisely because their separation from the other is undone in the mutual acts of writing and listening.

In this moment of being, where affect and words and connection work to make the moment and the movement-in-between possible, a *haecceity* or thisness, opens up new possibilities that lie beyond that which any separate "I" might grasp. In this present-day over-controlled, over-surveilled neoliberal world, such moments and movements are profoundly important. We can (almost inevitably) become the rule-following products of elaborate surveillance systems, obedient to the endless, never sufficient production of whatever the system demands of us. Or we can do the kind of work that is being done here to open up new and exciting, life-generating possibilities. In this Deleuzian universe, the "I" is no longer the central agent. In its place is the *body-without-organs*, the body whose borders are not bound by skin, whose agentic possibilities lie not in their individuality, but in their relation to others (including non-human others), and in lines of flight that open up new thought, and new modes of being.

One of the many reasons this book works so well is that it includes the moments when things do not go well, when they don't understand each other, when they don't "get" Deleuze, when they can't hear each other. These troubled and troubling moments enable the reader to enter the struggle to know differently *with* Jonathan and Ken—rather than being bowled over by their erudition and their beautiful writing, rather than being envious of and baffled by their perfect relationship. In this sense it is a profoundly pedagogical text, a text that opens up the Deleuzian concepts for use, and that opens up the practice of collaborative writing as a method of inquiry.

Methodologically the book is significant, combining Deleuzian concepts with collaborative writing as a method of inquiry, and drawing on collective biography, in order to make visible the break with the positivist, evidence-based inquiry so beloved of neoliberal managerialists. It shows instead how a new and complex philosophy can be explored in practice, giving rise to new insights, new lines of flight, new ways of being. Ken and Jonathan don't *tell us* about Deleuze and his concepts, they bring Deleuze to life in their own documented practices in such a way, that we as readers can also bring them to life in our own everyday life and research practices. Innovative research methodologies are paid lip-service by current neoliberal managers, but they quail before actual instances of it, wedded as they are to measurement and to the already-known. For that reason this is a courageous book, since there is a good chance that those with control of research funding will not be able to comprehend its significance. For that reason, perhaps more than any other, we should be provoked to explore what it is that is revolutionary here, and what we might learn from it.

Pedagogically this book is profoundly important. It shows a new way of teaching—through affect, voice and relationality brought together in one moment, and one movement. It potentially frees student and teachers from the isolation, competition and powerlessness that are the hallmarks of neoliberal education systems. To make visible and comprehensible how we exist in relation, how new ideas and ways of being become possible within those relations is probably the single-most important contribution that can be made to educational philosophy and practice at this point in history.

Jonathan and Ken escape, through this work, all the constraining, containing categorisations that might have held them fixed. They cannot be read within any of the old clichés of gender, or nationality, or age, or sexual preference. Their lines of flight dismantle these narrow categories, and in their place offer an ongoing *differenciation* of themselves-in-relation, not just in relation to each other, but to those others they encounter, including the readers of this book. This book is a profound gift to every reader. I predict that it will be read from cover to cover, and then read again, for the pure pleasure of it, and also for the possibilities for life that it opens up.

—Bronwyn Davies
July 2009

ACKNOWLEDGEMENTS

We both have a number of people to thank for their insights, advice, encouragement and interest:

Our companions amongst the group associated with the Centre for Narratives and Transformative Learning at the Graduate School of Education, University of Bristol, some of whom have accompanied us to the annual Congresses of Qualitative Inquiry (about which much more in the book) and/or been associated with the doctoral programme at Bristol: Viv Martin, Artemi Sakellariadis, Ying-Lin Hung, Tim Bond, Dave Bainton and Jackie Goode. Jackie would be the first to describe herself as a 'hanger-on' to this group, but there has surely never been a better hanger-on. She was there right at the beginning, reading our first collaborative writing and sharing her observations over dinner at Radio Maria.

Tami Spry, Ron Pelias and Larry Russell: for being there with us these past couple of years and for, in a sense, taking up with us something of what we try to do in this book.

Bronwyn Davies and Susanne Gannon for being our companions in working with Deleuze and collaborative writing.

Kim Etherington and Andrew Sparkes, for their rigorous, perceptive and positive examining.

Rebecca Nestor at the Oxford Learning Institute and Sheila Pregnall at the Oxfordshire and Buckinghamshire Mental Healthcare Trust, who, over more than six years, have provided consistent, always positive, always present support for Jonathan.

Ken's colleagues, friends and students in the Faculty of Education at the University of Plymouth for their influence, ideas and support during the writing of this book.

We both could never have completed this book without members of our families, many of whom figure in it: Tessa, Joe and Holly and Katy, Reuben and Phoebe. They have inspired us throughout.

Finally, we cannot say enough about Jane Speedy, our erstwhile doctoral supervisor, whose unwavering support, sustained and sustaining enthusiasm and energy and warm friendship has contributed so much in making this work possible.

Thank you all.

INTRODUCTORY SPACES

WRITING SPACE ONE

WHAT IS THIS BOOK? WHAT IS IT FOR?

Between the two, between-the-twos

This book has developed out of the joint dissertation that we produced collaboratively while undertaking the Doctor of Education programme at the University of Bristol, UK between 2004 and 2008. When we originally decided to write together, we were motivated to enquire into our different writing styles. We tell more of this story later[1]. In our first writing[2] we reflect upon these different writing styles: on the one hand there was Ken, the serious-minded, inquisitive thinker, engaged in conceptual analysis, eager to inquire and to present ideas in a dense and detailed 'academic' style; and, on the other, we found Jonathan, the storyteller, exploring the subtleties and nuances of the heart through narrative accounts of loss.

This interest in styles was our first intersection, the point at which desire was sparked, a desire that soon pushed, pulled, teased and taunted our writing in different directions. As we began to write with and to each other we began to be aware that we were writing in a different way. As Deleuze describes his work with Guattari,

> "You know how we work–I repeat it because it seems to me to be important–we do not work together, we work between the two." (Deleuze & Parnet, 2002, p.13)

This passage, as a way of describing what we do, is central yet intangible, the heart of our *body-without-organs* (Deleuze & Guattari, 2004b). As we were writing the final stages of this book, Jonathan wrote to Ken, in an annotation to an earlier draft,

> "Between the two–it's become so important to us and yet at times I don't quite know what it means."

---

[1] See Who Are We? Of Multiplicity and Connection, pp.12-24
[2] See Inquiring into Writing, pp.50-66

This somewhat troubled remark encapsulates the emerging nature of our work together. As the living, breathing heart, our 'between the two' is also elusive and mercurial. We are still trying to search it out, our epistemological sensibilities creating our intrigue, our intellectual wonder, at what this is. We search for its *logos* and trouble ourselves with the use of elaborated codes, plying our trade as writers and applying words from our lexicon. But this shifting spectre of essence that troubles us is constituted by the hegemony of the Kantian noumenon: it *must* have body, it m*ust* have form, it *must* be a thing in itself. The desire to define, to express the all-embracing denotative utterance, can have pre-occupying effects; the need to colonise meaning becomes obsessive. Foucault (2002) warns against such inclinations, suggesting that they encourage fabrication, knowledge construction and the creation of their own objects of inquiry. In such a way we think we come to know what 'between the two' is; we give it a meaning; we make it a thing. This is what we have learned, what we have been taught. Our intellectual selves have taken on board the nature of the academic pursuit: we need to know what it means. We need to pin it down, to establish it, to be able to say, 'This is what it means'. After all this time writing together, we are still sometimes troubled by those all-pervasive epistemologies that provoke us to search for foundational knowledge. We have learned to need to know.

But in this book we are learning to work between the two of us. We have shifted the emphasis of what we do away from the logic of rationality and reason toward what Deleuze calls a *logic of sense* (Deleuze, 1990). We have *sense* of what this writing is but we are unsure of what it *means*. The 'between the two' that we have worked within has provided a space in which our writing is *becoming*: it "implies movement, agency and continuity" (Etherington, 2004, p.15). As MacLure (2003) might put it, the space between the two of us is "the gap across which desire might spark" (p.3). Or, to use another figure from the work of Deleuze, it is in the space between us that our writing has *stuttered*. Deleuze uses the word 'stutter' to describe a form of expression that we see as being creative and which is bound up with the use of language as performance:

> "This is what happens when the stuttering no longer affects preexisting words, but, rather, itself ushers in the words that it affects; in this case, the words do not exist independently of the stutter, which selects and links them together. It is no longer the individual who stutters in his speech, it is the writer who *stutters in the language system (langue)*: he causes language as such to stutter. We are faced here with an affective and intensive

language (langage) and not with an affection of the speaker." (Deleuze, 1994, p.23)

Deleuze's figurative use of stuttering provides us with a way of describing not only the becoming of our writing but also the dynamic nature of our relationship, and in so doing exemplifies the intricate and changing multiplicity of this book. We write, we respond, we re-write, we comment, we re-order. This very paragraph is stuttering. Its impediment is its life: we are constantly producing meaning and changing it. In our state of becoming we are writing both for and against ourselves; we stutter all the time.

We work via e-mail–we live many miles apart, Jonathan in Oxford, Ken in Plymouth–exchanging writings as email attachments in a form of *interactive interview* (Ellis & Berger, 2003). Mostly, we take turns, one of us responding to the other. We have come to term these sections of this book, after Deleuze (Deleuze & Parnet, 2002), as our *between-the-twos*. Our between-the-twos have evolved: one of us might 'spin off' from our own writing, taking what Deleuze might call a *line of flight* (Deleuze & Guattari, 2004b; Deleuze & Parnet, 2002), so two or more, in a series, will be sent before the other responds. In some writing spaces our between-the-twos experiment with form, drawing from Richardson's proposal that working with form offers different avenues of inquiry (Richardson, 2007, 1997a). In Therapy and in parts of Alterity 3, we use play script and fiction respectively; in Alterity 2 we offer poetry. In each case it is possible (if not always easy) to identify our individual voices in these alternative between-the-twos; our voices change, metamorphose, the one into the other or into something different.

Our fictions have not yet allowed us fully to inhabit other bodies: although other characters are present, 'Ken' and 'Jonathan' are always there. We have not yet fully let go of ourselves.

The first person plural, the 'we', of this book is both of us, Ken and Jonathan–or Jonathan-and-Ken-ing, or Becoming-Ken-Jonathan. This voice has entered our work towards the end of the process. Each of us has taken responsibility for spaces where we use this voice, writing a first draft that the other has then read, commented upon and/or added to. Writing these spaces has been different to our between-the-twos. Writing this, here, now, for example, feels a different process. *This is Jonathan writing, at this point in this space thinking as much as I can of how 'we'– our 'Becoming-Ken-Jonathan'–see/s this; and I feel that I am positioned facing towards you, the reader, with Ken alongside. No, within.* It is possible to indicate, within each 'we' space, whose hand has held the pen, so to speak, but that would be only one response to the question of who wrote it. Increasingly, as we note during this book, our senses of self have become fluid: stutterings, movements, verbs, becomings through writing. Even when one of us is writing we both are writing.

Our writings are often not linear. They follow lines of flight, they sometimes go unexplained, and they might evoke and sometimes revel in the ambiguity of many meanings. As Deleuze writes about his work with Felix Guattari:

> "We were never in the same rhythm, we were always out of step: I understood and could make use of what Felix said to me six months later; he understood what I said to him immediately, too quickly for my liking– he was already elsewhere. From time to time we have written about the same idea, and have noticed later that we have not grasped it at all in the same way." (Deleuze & Parnet, 2002, p.13)

We have grown into this writing. Increasingly we have found that our writing is both a method of inquiry (Richardson & St Pierre, 2005) where, as we write between-the-twos, we discover and construct new meanings and sensitivities, and a lived, embodied experience: writing becomes us. We are both researching through (and into) writing and becoming through writing. The dense multiplicity and interconnectedness of the work of Deleuze provides us with an articulation of our between-the-twos and the becomings that these involve. The figurative nature of a Deleuzian logic of sense suggests that they can be seen to operate on what he refers to as a 'molecular level'. He argues that this molecular level takes over from the merely animal or the merely human.

> "(T)he affects of becoming-dog, for example, are succeeded by those of a becoming-molecular, micro-perceptions of water, air etc. A man totters from one door to the next and disappears into thin air: "All I can tell you is that we are fluid, luminous beings made of fibres (sic)." All so-called initiatory journeys include these thresholds and doors where becoming itself becomes, and where one changes becoming depending on the "hour" of the world, the circles of hell, or the stages of a journey that sets scales, forms, and cries in variation. From the howling of animals to the wailing of elements and particles." (Deleuze & Guattari, 2004b, p.274)

Our intention is that our between-the-twos operate at the "thresholds and doors where becoming itself becomes".

So, what is this book? What is it for?

This book as rhizomatic writing

We draw upon the work of Deleuze to provide us with an appropriate figure that will give sense to the way in which the form and content of our book unfolds. The figures created by Deleuze reject the arborescent structure that books traditionally use: the tree with its branches and leaves reaching out for light (enlightenment) and its system of roots around the central tap root probing down into the earth searching for stability, working to establish strong foundations. In place of this traditional model, with its central core and firm trunk-like body, Deleuze proposes, through the application of principles of multiplicity, connection and heterogeneity, a model of the *rhizome*.

"A rhizome ceaselessly establishes connections between semiotic chains, organisations of power, and circumstances relative to the arts, sciences and social struggles. A semiotic chain is like a tuber agglomerating very diverse acts, not only linguistic, but also perceptive, mimetic, gestural, and cognitive: there is no language in itself, nor are there any linguistic universals, only a throng of dialects, patois, slangs, and specialised languages. There is no ideal speaker-listener, any more than there is a homogenous linguistic community. Language is... "an essentially heterogeneous reality". There is no mother tongue, only a power takeover by a dominant language within a political multiplicity. Language stabilises around a parish, a bishopric, and a capital. It forms a bulb. It evolves by subterranean stems and flows, along river valleys or train tracks; it spreads like a patch of oil. It is always possible to break a language down into internal structural elements, an undertaking not fundamentally different from a search for roots...a method of the rhizome type... can analyse language only by decentering it onto other dimensions and other registers. A language is never closed upon itself, except as a function of impotence." (Deleuze & Guattari, 2004b, p.8)

The figure of the rhizome is central and recurrent in the work of Deleuze and provides a valuable means of understanding the synthesis of form and content to be found in his work. Deleuze and Guattari's *A Thousand Plateaus* is an example of a rhizomatic book, where, instead of a series of chapters delineating the logical progression of the book from introduction to its conclusion, it takes the form of an 'open system' of plateaus.

"It does not pretend to have the final word. The author's hope, however, is that elements of it will stay with a certain number of its readers and will weave into the melody of their everyday lives." (Massumi, in Deleuze & Guattari, 2004b, p.xiv)

It is possible to enter and leave the book at will and not follow an enforced linearity. We intend our book to be rhizomatic, to be–to an extent–an 'open system', in that there are links and connections across 'writing spaces' (as indicated by footnotes). The linear order in which we present it (about which more below) is one, but not the only, sequence in which it is possible to read it.

This book as a *body-without-organs*

The spirit of the rhizome and its structural implications can be found in another important figure that Deleuze, drawing from Artaud, evokes: the *body-without-organs* (Deleuze, 1990; Deleuze & Guattari, 2004b). This figure helps to exemplify the way in which the form and content of our book has emerged.

> "The body is the body / it is all by itself / and has no need of organs / the body is never an organism / organisms are the enemies of bodies." (Artaud, in Deleuze & Guattari, 2004a, p.9-10)

Deleuze uses the body-without-organs (BwO) as a means of rhizomatically expressing freedom, of releasing the potential of the body from the constraints of habit, character and affect. In this respect the BwO involves an active experimentation with the unrealised potential of the body, perhaps through the destabilisation and transgression of traits, features and ways of doing that have tended to construct the body in particular ways, limiting its potential within a recognised organisational form. The BwO exists beyond the organism:

> "We come to the realisation that the BwO is not at all the opposite of the organs. The organs are not its enemies. The enemy is the organism. The BwO is opposed not to the organs but to that organisation of the organs called the organism." (Deleuze and Guattari, 1988, p.158)

We can think of the body-with-organs as having extension or being extended in place and time and the body-without-organs as expressing the intensities that exist in and between these organs in this space and time. What is crucial to us in using the BwO as a figurative representation of the way in which our book works is that Deleuze sees the potential of the body as being realised through multiplicity and connection. As we follow lines of flight and flee from the forces that might be seen to constrain us, we engage in nomadic inquiry; we are becoming *nomadic subjects* (Braidotti, 1994), territorialising spaces and allowing

"(T)he BwO (to reveal) itself for what it is: connection of desires, conjunction of flows, continuum of intensities. You have constructed your own little machine, ready when needed to be plugged into other collective machines." (Deleuze & Guattari, 2004b, p.179)

So we understand the BwO as not rejecting the organs that might be seen to constitute it, but rather as rejecting the type of organisation that encourages it to exist in particularly narrow, fixed and stable ways. This writing is experimental, it is transgressive; it expresses a desire to be curious, to destabilise and to trouble the givens of accepted discourses, knowledge constructions and ways of thinking and doing. We are encouraged by the multiple, connected, social nature of the BwO; it seems that the becomings of our between-the-twos exist on *planes of immanence* (ibid.). It is on and within these planes of immanence that desire, the desire to produce, to enable and to create, exists. Our desire is productive. It is this that encourages us to think about our book as a BwO as an intensive nomadic inquiry in and through writing, which follows a logic of sense, working rhizomatically with sensation as a means of inquiry, transgression and creativity. Unlike the organism which establishes concepts and ideas as organs in fixed and established ways, we see our writing as both creating and containing multiple, interconnected assemblages, *haecceities*[3], within a logic of sense and sensation, as the basic units of our work.

In using the thinking of Deleuze as a way of dissolving the binary of form and content we are also drawn to the work of Pelias (2004), who talks of a "methodology of the heart" as a means of displaying the

"(R)esearcher who, instead of hiding behind the illusion of objectivity, brings himself (sic) forward in the belief that an emotionally vulnerable, linguistically evocative, and sensuously poetic voice can place us closer to the subjects we wish to study." (Pelias, 2004, p.1)

We are also attracted by the embodied nature of Pelias' approach that seeks to "foster connections, opens spaces for dialogue, and heals" (ibid, p.2). We feel, therefore, that the 'body' we present as the culmination of our work together up to this time, is not simply a 'body of knowledge' but a living, breathing testament to our work together. We hope that this book sets off other lines of flight, intersects with other worlds and creates concepts which then dissolve in the emergence of other fields of thought and feeling. It is our view that, in making a proposal for a methodology of

---

[3] We offer an extended take on Deleuze's figure of haecceity on pp.91-93

the heart, Pelias' work corroborates that of Deleuze and the figure of the BwO. In an early section of his book entitled *Part 1- The Missing Body: A Sentence Concerning What is Absent in Scholarly Writing*, Pelias responds to his title by posing the inducement: "We could say the heart" (p.2) and provides a number of different images of the heart: "the one exposed, raw, deep inside the operating theatre's ribs...the symbol of desire...the swollen orb...that voracious fruit that cannot be picked" (pp.2-3) and so on. He continues with his inquiry into the "missing body" in a similar vein by posing a number of suggested ways forward and, for each, suggesting different ways of looking: "or, perhaps instead, we could say the hand", "or we could say the groin", "or we could say the bones" (p.3) and so on. The playfully ironic way in which Pelias builds up these dimensions, these levels of inquiry, offers a powerful deconstruction of the formal conception and organisation of the body and in so doing provides a clearly illuminated representation of the BwO. In his writing he encourages us to see the heart, the groin, the bones, etc. in multiple ways. He offers multiple opportunities for re-constructing the body, for experimentation and transgression: a methodology of the heart, a beating heart that lives in the intensive reality of a body-without-organs, responding to multiple vibrations and rhythms in sensitive and ever-changing ways.

This book as (writing) space(s)

We borrow the term *writing space* from hypertext literature (e.g. Bolter, 2001; Joyce, 1987; Kolb, 1994; Moulthorp, 1992), and from the hypertext software Storyspace (Bolter et al., 2001) in particular. In hypertext writing, readers have choices to move, rhizomatically, from one passage of text to a number of others and back again, or off in a different direction, should they wish. These passages of text, 'writing spaces', suggest to us a liminality, a sense of in-between places, intangibilities, which are congruent with what we seek to achieve.

We have used electronic tools, including our primary *modus operandi* of using email to exchange our writings as attachments. We are with Cavallaro (2000) in wishing to destabilise the stereotypical boundary between the mysticism and irrationality of the narratives of *mythos* and the rational, scientific and measurable world of *techne*. We feel comfortable with her assertion that

"(Therefore) technology is informed by mythology, insofar as it is an *artistic* practice, and mythology is informed by technology because *construction* is its fundamental purpose." (Cavallaro, 2000, p.42)

We are drawn to the innuendo of fiction that exists in Foucault's constructivist use of *fabrication,* where that which is made is also made up. We wish to emphasise the technology of hypertext as a creative metaphor for Deleuzian conceptualisations of *rhizome* and *nomadic.* The term 'writing space' also helps to encourage a shift away from linear to associative thinking (Morgan, 2000).

In this we are drawn to the structural and conceptual antecedents of Deleuze and Guattari's *plateaus* (2004). We are alert to Foucault's (1986) view that:

> "The present epoch will perhaps be above all the epoch of space. We are in the epoch of simultaneity: we are in the epoch of juxtaposition, the epoch of the near and far, of the side-by-side, of the dispersed. We are at a moment, I believe, when our experience of the world is less that of a long life developing through time than that of a network that connects points and intersects with its own skein." (Foucault, 1986, p.22)

We are also aware of Gibson's (1984) view that the *cyberspaces* we populate and inhabit are consensual realities, where meanings, identities and knowledge are continually being discussed, negotiated and contested. Our inquiry seeks to dissolve the binary of inner and outer space, characterised by the world of the internal and the external, the subject and the object. So, later in this BwO, as we write about the 'actual', 'real' places where we write, we begin to find ourselves, in the writing, characterising these 'places' in terms of our feelings and our emotions[4]. Where we write becomes what we write; what we write becomes where we write. So, as nomads, we write and we inquire, we find ourselves transgressing the boundaries and certainties of the *logos* of *striated space* and opening up an irreverent and metamorphosing patois in the *nomos* of *smooth space.* Here we are working with Deleuze and Guattari's (2004b) notion of smooth space characterising places of becoming, where our movement, our wondering and our wandering, our process, perhaps, is given precedence over our arrivals. We wish to offer a *poetics of space* (Bachelard, 1969) in which we find ourselves re-visioning our worlds and creating a shifting but welcoming landscape of inquiry. We find these *heterotopia* (Foucault, 1998a) in our nomadic inquiries. They become us and in them we become: as we are drawn by their 'utopian' allure we also draw them.

---

[4] See Our Writing Places, Our Writing Spaces, pp.40-47

This book as story

We see this book as many things: as rhizomatic, as a body-without-organs, as exploring the space(s) between the two of us. We talk of following lines of flight, of wandering, of following a logic of sense in our investigations of subjectivities. We are nomads and we suggest, too, that the reader might also read us nomadically.

However, we have grown conscious that the pieces of writing we present here tell a story. As we re-read and re-draft our writings we become increasingly conscious of, and affected by, a sense of our developing relationship over time. We have come to see our writings differently as we have revisited them in the context of completing our dissertation, producing this book and looking to what might lie ahead for the two of us. Such a view of our relationship, therefore, is not linear, but is located, as Freeman (1998) describes,

> "(In) a mode of time that is rather more like a circle or spiral, embodying a dialectical movement from present to past and past to present, at once. This movement is in turn conditioned by the future as well, in the form not only of hopes, expectations, and so on, but of the projected self that both emerges from and gives form to the landscapes of one's history." (pp. 42-3)

We have, in short, as we have read each other and written again about what we have read, become aware of our performance of narrative (Smith & Sparkes, 2008). A narrative of us. A number of narratives of us. A number of narratives of the writing of us.

This sense of our narrative performance(s) is symbolised in two interconnected ways: by our decision to present our between-the-twos in chronological sequence and in the use that we make both of introductions to those writing spaces and of text boxes to interrupt them. The introductions and the text boxes serve as our *chorus*: commentaries on the 'action' of the unfolding drama, drawing the reader's attention to what we notice in our writing, in our story, from the perspective of a different moment in time.

So, this book is our story. Not a modernist, linear story, but a multiplicitous, layered story, one into which we invite you in the hope that you, as readers, will, in turn, become our writers (Richardson, 2000a).

WRITING SPACE TWO

WHO ARE WE?
OF MULTIPLICITY AND CONNECTION

Our reflexive desire in this writing space is to offer an(other) insight into the 'we' of this book, to enable the reader better to hold us as the embodied writers who work together on this book; to lay open something of our *prejudice* (Gadamer, 1980), the conditions whereby we arrived at this experience.

This is a story of how we came to be writing these pages. We did not simply appear, fixed, as the writers of this work. We have history. This is a "writing-story" (Richardson, 1997a): one tale of how this book came into being, how we "gave birth to ourselves" (Cixous, 1991, p.31). Fittingly, for a project that has been undertaken through the exchange of email attachments, it is the content of our emails themselves that we employ to relate this narrative.

'Who are we?' is a complex question that we wish, first, to trouble.

The question concerns who and not what we are (Cavarero, 2000).The what is easier, but duller; more identifiable but less telling; more commonsense, but reductive. The what–we feel its seductive pull–would tell the reader that, for example, we are Ken, in his 60s, Dad to Katy, Reuben and Phoebe, a university lecturer, sea-lover; one who loves to laugh and to dance and who laughs and dances in love. And Jonathan, counsellor and staff developer, coming up to 50, father of Joe and Holly, husband to Tessa, and land-lubber. The whats are endless, they tend towards the static, and they never satisfy: Ken reads and does philosophy, has always written diaries, and enjoys the music of PJ Harvey, The Rolling Stones, Prince, The Pixies, Leftfield, The Pogues, The White Stripes, Timarawen, Sun Ra, Mink De Ville, Faithless, Eddie Cochran, and Groove Armada. Jonathan lives for his one coffee a day and his twice a week game of five-a-side football, listens to (rather than reads) novels, wrote a diary for a few years in his twenties, and plays the French Horn occasionally–and so on. There are always further whats.

The meaning of 'who' is elusive.

We have come to see who as being always in process. In our writing we have come to place more emphasis on the *how* than either the who or the what. 'How' is the action of the 'who', the verb; the doing, not the emphasis upon the 'person', the noun, the status. We have spent time railing against the nouns that are incumbent, obsessing about the *doing* of the writing, its embodiment, its refusal in its performative form to be of the person, in a representative sense, but about also our process, our body-without-organs.

We wish also to consider the meaning of 'we'. Are 'we' Ken and Jonathan, the humanist individuals? Do they constitute the 'we' of this story? We would argue to the contrary, that this book's 'we' embodies an understanding that we are "in a constitutive relation with the other" (Kottman, in Cavarero, 2000, p.ix). This is a book written by Ken-and-Jonathan or, rather, Becoming-Ken-Jonathan: a process, a becoming, a body-without-organs, grass that grows between (Deleuze & Parnet, 2002), in smooth spaces (Deleuze & Guattari, 2004b). This diminishes neither our uniqueness nor our embodiedness. On the contrary, there are no intersects (Klein, 2005) without distinctness, no between-the-twos without the one and the other; and for grass to grow between there have to be the rocks that flank it. We take up these questions, of what we mean when we say 'who' and 'we' throughout the book.

So how are we able to respond to the question, "who are we?", given our questioning above? In embracing a Deleuzian notion of becoming and of always being in motion, we warm to Cavarero's (2000) invitation to narrative, to endeavour through narrative to open the Becoming-Ken-Jonathan for view, in all this narrative's partiality and situatedness (Gannon, 2006), all its transience and doubt. "(N)arration reveals the finite in its fragile uniqueness, and sings its glory." (Cavarero, 2000, p.3)

We tell this narrative, of how we came to be writing together, implicitly, through our email correspondence over the years leading up to this book.

Our writing for this book has been produced primarily through the exchange of writings as attachments to emails. Elsewhere the emails themselves have remained invisible: here we bring them stage front. Our collaboration has been born out of and sustained by these emails and the writings they have carried.

The emails that follow were exchanged without a sense of ever having a wider audience. Rather than attempt to *tell* the reader who we are, we allow ourselves–our process, our 'how'–including that which is most obscure to us, our birth (Cavarero, 2000), to appear through these writings. Comments for clarification are added in italics to the email text. Other comments, written with hindsight, are in boxes.

By way of introduction to the first set of emails, we would like to take you to a cold February morning in Bristol, in the southwest of England, in 2004, when, with some twenty others, we began our first unit on the University of Bristol EdD programme. In the round of introductions, and not having met before, we each told the group that our respective families had guinea pigs. We remember that Jonathan reported how his guinea pigs were a source of irritation to him (all the clearing out, their lack of recognition of him as the one who fed them and kept their home clean), and that Ken might have mentioned how endearing he found his; but we can't be sure that this is how it was. Maybe those sentiments were expressed at a later time, but guinea pigs were certainly a first connection.

On the second day of the unit we 'found' each other further: we were two of a group of three that wrote together–in response to a paper about loss (Speedy, 2005)–and that shared its writing on the final day to its peers. Christine (Chris) was the third group member. Our (Ken and Jonathan's) email correspondence, which Chris was initially part of, began some three weeks after the end of that doctoral unit:

***

On Tuesday, February 24, 2004 10:19am, Jonathan wrote:
Hi Chris and Ken,
I hope that you're both well, and enjoying the reading and thinking (and writing?) about our assignments.

I am planning to use the experience of our collective response to Jane Speedy's piece as the focus of my paper. *(Jane Speedy was a tutor on this unit.)* I think that the theoretical focus will be on issues of evaluation of narrative research, reflexivity and positioning, and also on questions of what constitutes narrative research (was what we did narrative research in its own right?). I am a bit vague on this at the moment as you can tell!

There are also ethical issues, which is what has prompted me write to you. How would you feel about my using the material that you each contributed? I would like to present it in some form (in landscape? Or in a different way; I'm not sure yet).

I have yours, Chris, but I don't have Ken's: if you are ok with this may I have a copy? And does either of you have the flipchart with our collective 'conclusion'? I didn't pick it up.

Let me know what you think. Many thanks.
Jonathan

The next day, Wednesday 25 February 2004 at 10:54am, Chris responded:

Hi Jonathan
I'm most impressed that you have already worked out what you're going to do for the assignment. I had to use all last week for paid work stuff and am just getting my EdD files out this morning! I'm quite happy for you to use my material, no problem. I gave the flip chart sheet to Kim (*Etherington–a course tutor*) to hold up for us in the session, so whether she kept it or not I don't know, but I didn't think to keep hold of it. If you can't retrieve it perhaps we can try to remember what we said?
Good luck! Regards,
Chris

And Ken responded an hour later, Wednesday 25 February 2004, 11:51am:

Hi Chris, Hi Jonathan
Like Chris I am very impressed that you have managed to make a start on the assignment Jonathan. I have spent a great deal of time thinking about it but, like you Chris, have had to be involved in my day to day work stuff that I haven't managed to put pen to paper or to come up with any good ideas as yet.
I am happy that you use my material Jonathan: in many senses it partly belongs to you and Chris anyway because it came out of a situation in which a great deal of sharing and inspirational learning was taking place. If it wasn't for you...!

> An early indication of between-the-twos and of multiplicities, perhaps.

I will have to type it for you, as my handwriting is pretty illegible: I am hoping to find a 'window' on Friday morning and will e-mail it to you then. I am pleased that you might be able to do something with the material...who knows we might get a joint narratives research project out of it later down the line!!

> Ken seemed aware of possibilities even at this point.

Do you have e-mail addresses for the whole group? I don't seem to have. It's good to be in touch and hope to hear from you both again.
Best wishes
Ken

A few days further on, on Monday 1 March 2004 21:38, Ken wrote to Jonathan:

Hi Johnathan,

> We notice in these early emails how Ken regularly has trouble spelling Jonathan's name...

I have attached the 'written up' piece for you. It was quite interesting to write it up as I hadn't looked at it since we did the exercise together: I found a few fresh ideas lurking around my psyche, which I leapt upon, not having formulated a coherent idea for my assignment as yet!

I hope that the attachment is useful and I wish you luck and good fortune in writing your assignment. I am planning to start mine next week when I have shifted a backlog of marking. It would be good to hear how your assignment goes and to keep in touch. I hope that things are well for you.
Best wishes
Ken

On Thursday April 8, 2004, at 12:40pm, Jonathan sent writing to Ken and Chris:

Hi Chris and Ken,
I've had a first go at the essay and thought I would send it to you both. If you have time - and I know that you'll be up to your eyes in your own assignments, amongst other things - I'd value knowing what you think. Any feedback welcome. But, please, don't feel obliged - if you can't, no problem.
Thanks.
Hope it's all going well with you. If you want to run anything past me I'll be more than happy...

> A first invitation to a reciprocal exchange of writing.

All the best,
Jonathan

Ken read Jonathan's writing and responded, on Wed April 14, 2004, at 21:33pm:

Hi Jonathan,

> We began here to correspond as a pair rather than as a three…

I sat down tonight and read your assignment. I really enjoyed it on a number of levels and I feel good to have been a (small) part in its development.

It's almost mundane to say that I think that it is a really good 'academic' piece (that word that keeps dogging me!) I think that you should feel confident that it will achieve good marks at this level. I really like the way in which you have managed to blend so many important but different things together into a piece of writing that feels coherent, really well structured and very readable. You have pulled it all together through the careful and sustained use of a strong and passionate argument.

However, it wasn't just those things that made me like your writing. It was so full of life, whilst, paradoxically, addressing death. Reading your work, I was struck for the first time by the fact that you and Chris talked about the death of a father and a mother and that it was my mum and dad whom I had introduced to the group, through the photograph, who play such a significant part in my life generally and in being on this course in particular.

> We wrote together about fathers and mothers in Gale and Wyatt (2008b) and write about fathers in 'Alterity 3'.

I felt exactly as you described in your writing: should I be here? What's the point? Is it worth it, all this time and money? I really liked the way in which you brought that into your writing.

Thanks for letting me read your work: I think that it is really good and I certainly enjoyed reading it very much. I haven't copied these comments to Chris but will do if you think that it is OK or that it is a good idea.

Best wishes to you
Ken

> Years later, we sign off with 'best wishes' much less frequently but we are still unable – as men? – to find an acceptable alternative.

In May 2004, we attended our second unit–on autoethnography–following which we exchanged emails with Chris about how we were progressing with our assignments. Jonathan wrote his about the death of his father (Wyatt, 2005a) and sent a draft to Chris and Ken in July. Chris responded warmly soon after.

Having not heard back from Ken, on Monday, August 23, 2004 at 9.53am, Jonathan wrote:

Hi,
I've been thinking about you...concerned that you've gone quiet...
Hope you're having a good summer and that the writing went/is going well. Get in touch when you're ready to. Would be good to hear from you.
Best,
Jonathan

To which Ken replied three days later, Thursday 26 August, at 22:28:

Dear Jonathan
Thank you for keeping in touch. It was so kind of you to write after I had left it so long before I contacted you. I can't begin to say why I haven't written for so long but I have searched myself and know that it is not negligence. I had a real struggle to write the last assignment; not because of the writing itself but because I was really busy. When I actually found the time I actually enjoyed writing but it was really stressful trying to find that time.

I have just read your assignment and I can't tell you how moved I felt to read what you wrote. My dad died suddenly when I wasn't there: I was 30 miles away on a beach with a friend, laughing, playing, swimming, kissing, oblivious to what was happening to him. When I arrived home and heard my Mum's desperate voice on the phone telling me that he had simply died I cracked. Like you I had a crystal moment in a petrol station, driving to see my Mum and him. Tears pouring down my face, everything around me was vibrant, full of life, Cornwall on a bright sunny afternoon - I couldn't believe where I was or what was happening, it was all so sudden.

I think that in many ways you have been very brave to write what you have written and to put it out into a public place. I feel very touched and grateful that you have allowed me to enter this world through your writing. On a more mundane note it dragged up all kinds of thoughts about autoethnography and assessment and validity and all the things that we talked about at the last weekend of the course. I would like to have shared with some of the small group discussions that you had during this time.

I will send you my assignment but it feels rather small alongside what you have written and sent to me. Thanks for your patience and friendship. I look forward to seeing you in Bristol for the next unit; perhaps we could have a coffee one day or a drink after one of the sessions.

I hope that you had a good holiday. I have managed to spend lots of time on the beach and in the sea with my family and friends.

> The beach and sea are powerful images in Ken's writing, and in his life.

Best wishes to you
Ken

There followed brief correspondence about summer holidays and about meeting up in Bristol, then, on Sunday August 29th 2004, Jonathan responded, in turn, to Ken's autoethnographic writing:

Hi again Ken,
I've had a good read of your essay. Thanks. It was great to get more of a picture of your working life. I particularly like the parts where you are in conversation with the group of students and with the individual student (who sounds really interesting, by the way). I felt drawn into the struggle (as I perceived it) for you to hold on to your role as teacher and to carry sensitively the authority that's given to you by students both administratively (re essay criteria) and intellectually.

It struck me that it is difficult to carry that role, and the authority that goes with it, in a way that allows students to experience doubt enough, but not so much so that the chaos becomes overwhelming. (It reminds me of the counselling role that I have where people often want me to tell them what to do; it's hard, but important, to resist it, but to do so carefully.) I thought that you came over as being open but not woolly! (Which is hard to crack, I think.)

I also enjoyed the way you related these stories to the literature and theoretical concepts. They're fascinating and helpful, I find, but slippery, too: I have to keep asking myself, say re. the 'fold', now what's that about?

Picture it; try to make it stick...but I keep having to go back to it. That's good, though.

> Ken's confidence with theory and Jonathan's newness to it has been part of our dynamic.

So, thanks again. Enjoy the break from doing EdD stuff. It'll soon be the pre-reading for November's unit (Understanding Ed Research - you're doing it too aren't you?).
Hope the guinea pigs are thriving.
All the best,
Jonathan

> Exchanging writing as attachments, and responding to them, was becoming the currency of how we related.

On Saturday 4 September, 2004, at 14:29, Ken responded:

Hi Johnathan
Good to hear from you again.
Many thanks for your comments on my assignment: I really think that you grabbed a number of things that I was trying to deal with in my writing, so it is reassuring that they also came out in your interpretation of what I was trying to do. I really enjoyed reading your assignment and as I said to you before your writing evoked powerful memories and feelings surrounding the deaths of my parents. Your writing captured so much and it really made me think about writing about this again myself. I am still coming to terms with that feeling of my parents having 'gone': they are still there in so many respects but it's not the same as being with them and sharing all that stuff that had built up with them during my lifetime. I was also struck by how different our writing for these assignments has been and, again, as I said before, it questions all those notions of criteria and validity and assessment approaches in education. It might be interesting to look at and compare and contrast the feedback that we receive. I didn't have time to send off a draft this time so I am a little worried about whether or not I am on the right track.

> Ken drew attention here to our different writing styles, which became the prompt for our initial writing together (see Inquiring into Writing).

OK, good to talk to you. The guinea pigs are good and enjoying the sunshine! Have fun!
Best wishes
Ken

During the autumn of 2004 we both attended a third unit at Bristol, on understanding educational research, and exchanged emails about our respective assignments. In early 2005, with our fourth unit (on narrative interviewing) approaching in mid-February, Ken suggested collaborating on the forthcoming assignment:

On Friday 14 January, 2005, at 07:26, Ken wrote:

Hi Johnathan

> Still struggling with Jonathan's name...

Woke up with an idea so I thought that I would send it to you before I go to work.

We have talked briefly before about our different writing styles and approaches to the EdD units and I seem to remember you saying some while ago that it might be a good idea to collaborate on something around this in the future. Well I am just wondering whether or not the next unit might provide us with an opportunity to do this. I don't really know what Narrative Interviewing is about yet, I have dipped into the readings and have an idea and it occurred to me that we could possibly tap into something exciting and interesting here. Don't worry if you are not sure, not enthusiastic or have something else in mind; I realise that it is early days. I thought that to raise questions and then to explore issues to do with writing styles, personal interests, identity and so on might raise all kinds of lively and challenging material for us to look at. As you know I am interested in all these Deleuzian ideas like the fold and assemblage, nomads, connections, multiplicities and so on and feel that what we could explore, through reciprocating narrative interviews and dialogue could be really exciting. If it worked we could either write an assignment/paper collaboratively or separately depending on what came out and how we felt about it. Let me know what you think.

> The first time that the idea of collaborating is mooted. We are still working with the ideas that Ken outlines here.

Hope you are well
Best wishes
Ken

To which Jonathan responded, at 09:25 that morning:

Hi Ken,
I was going to email you myself this morning...
Thanks for this idea...what a fine one it is! My initial reaction is enthusiastic and interested in exploring the possibility. I have not yet done any of the reading and–less than you, probably!–have not much of a clue about the content of this unit. But I do like the thought of collaborating with you and think that the contrast in styles might be a rich seam to mine and explore (or at least to start off from), and–though they are relatively new concepts to me–the Deleuzian stuff is fascinating. So...yes, let's run with it and talk more at the unit and maybe have a joint tutorial? If either of us begins to feel that it's not we want we can give each other permission to say...But at this stage I am very much up for it.

I have really appreciated and enjoyed your Understanding Educational Research essay *(Ken's assignment for the previous doctoral unit)*. I have read it a couple of times on bus journeys to and from work this week. (The journeys are not very long so I have not been able to read it at one sitting!). I found it clear and thoughtful (as ever) and exploratory. I like the way you guided me through the material (which is complex) and enjoyed, too, the parts of yourself that you referred to–like the story of your mother making cakes as an illustration of the meaning of the fold (Gale, 2007). Lovely image, I thought. Another part–one which I would love to talk about with you–relates to nomadic practices and how you connect this to your experience of teaching people about groups. I teach junior managers about group process and use Tuckman (1965), even though I find it unsatisfactory, which I infer that you do too. What do we do with that? Difficult. (By the way have you come across the work of Wilfred Bion on groups (e.g.Bion, 1961)? Great, though very dense!)

I found the paper as a whole very helpful for me in thinking more about St Pierre's paper (St. Pierre, 1997) and the concepts contained in it, so thanks. I'm not surprised Tim *(Tim Bond–our tutor on that unit)* was positive about it.

Going back to the narrative interviewing unit and the possibility of writing together, shall we keep in touch if we have further thoughts over the next 3 or 4 weeks?

Speak soon and thanks so much for the idea (and the essay),
Jonathan

On Monday 17 January, 2005, at 21:48, Ken wrote:

Hi Johnathan
Thanks so much for your lengthy and positive response to my last message.
I am glad that you think a collaborative piece might be possible and I like the idea of being able to 'give permission' if it doesn't feel right as we proceed. I have a number of colleagues and pals who are involved in various forms of counselling practice and I have learned so much from them over the years. I do like that idea.

> Jonathan's writing about his counselling work was to become significant in our collaboration.

All your suggestions about the possible collaboration seem very sound and I totally concur with the idea of a meeting (perhaps over an early evening beer) followed by (if possible) a joint tutorial with Jane presumably. If your schedule is too tight, bearing in mind your Saturday morning oversight (!) don't worry I am sure that we can rig something up with Jane. I reckon we just need to get our names up on that tutorial board sharpish. I am keen to keep in touch on this as you suggest because I am really into the idea and because I think that as we get into the reading lots more ideas and angles are likely to emerge.

I am teaching on Wednesday nights but I have a really lovely group of MA students doing a module on Discourse Theory with me and I reckon they won't mind if I make a rearrangement for just one night. I know that it will involve driving up and back in a day but I reckon its worth it. I haven't heard of Bion but I would appreciate any references if you think he is good.

My request for support for attendance at the QI[1] conference is going before our Faculty Research and Development committee on the 19th, so I should know fairly soon after that I hope: I will let you know as soon as I hear anything.

---

[1] The 1st (2005) International Congress of Qualitative Inquiry (QI), Urbana-Champaign, USA, organized by Norman Denzin. See The Inhabitants of This Book, pp.25-34

Good to hear from you again: will be in touch!
Best wishes
Ken

Further emails would tell a story of how the collaboration developed. A brief summary of this tale would be that we undertook this joint assignment, and a second (see Inquiring into Writing and Writing the Incalculable respectively). We also each submitted papers to the 2005 International Congress of Qualitative Inquiry (QI), and have been each year since[2].

In the summer of 2005, Ken drafted an individual dissertation proposal and invited Jonathan to comment. In October 2005 Jonathan co-presented a seminar at Bristol on autoethnography. Jane Speedy introduced him to those who attended as "one half of Gale-and-Wyatt". On his walk afterwards, in the rain, down the steepness of Park Street, Jonathan texted Ken to suggest undertaking our dissertation jointly. Ken enthusiastically agreed.

We have not kept our texts to each other over the years, which is a shame: they would have added still more fibres to the felt (Deleuze & Guattari, 2004b).

---

[2] See the following writing space, The Inhabitants of this Book, pp.25-33

WRITING SPACE THREE

THE INHABITANTS OF THIS BOOK

The rain is thick, dense and heavy, a sodden mat covering scurrying souls hurrying to keep themselves dry. Amongst the windswept papers and the contorted umbrellas two men are walking purposefully, their talk animated despite the rain. One interrupts the conversation and breaks enthusiastically into song:

"'Are you going to the party? / Are you going to the Boston Tea Party?'"

This is Ken, a soundtrack always to hand. He sways their umbrella as he rocks to the tune.

Jonathan, the other man, keeping his equanimity despite being intermittently soaked, responds, "What's that you're singing? I recognise the tune."

"Sensational Alex Harvey Band, Boston Tea Party. Great band, fantastic lyrics and theatrical performances: Alex was ahead of the game."

"At last. I'm soaked." He's lost interest in Alex Harvey.

They step inside their destination, a café, the Boston Tea Party. The lighting is low, indie music emanating from the walls; people are milling, relieved to be dry. The two men look around. This is familiar territory; they have spent many good times here talking and writing. They order coffee and find a table near an upstairs window overlooking Park Street, the long hill down from the University to the Bristol docks.

They settle.

Jonathan asks, "Do you remember those Deleuze references to the desert being populous (Deleuze & Guattari, 2004b; Deleuze & Parnet, 2002)? It just occurred to me as you were singing that song on the way in. Many people inhabit our book. Your encyclopaedic knowledge of music made me think about it: your head is populous."

"It's remarkable the different effects that they all have," Ken responds. "Some, like Deleuze, are obviously influential and play a central role in what we are doing, but others out on the margins (like Alex Harvey) have a less obvious but nevertheless significant role. This 'felting'–how we matt people into our writing–is multiplicitous, complex. Exciting. I find it exciting becoming aware of multiplicity and making these connections. What about this verse?", Ken continues,

> "'Fire in the mountains, flames upon the heath
> And the resident spits out the news
> He's biting on wooden teeth
> The children of the colonies
> Got a different tale to tell
> I'm going down to the city
> Tell my folks I'm doing well'

'I'm going down to the city / Tell my folks I'm doing well'. I love those two lines. I think of my parents, of their quiet, almost unquestioning, existence and how warmed and fascinated they would be if they could have a sense of this life that I am having now and the things that I am trying to do."

Jonathan thinks. He notices the father and small boy on the table behind Ken. The boy smears chocolate ice cream onto his face. His father reaches across to take the spoon from him.

Jonathan suggests, "We write about your dad, my dad, our families. We refer to friends, lovers, work colleagues, and clients, some by their 'real' names, others as pseudonyms: Tessa, Joe, Holly, Reuben, Phoebe, Petra, Rachel, Cath. They people our 'real' worlds and we bring them into this writing. We write our responses to them. Our experiences of them enliven, disturb and affect us; they make our writing possible. In the terrain of our nomadic book, our Deleuzian desert, we could think of them as *members of our tribes*. What do you think?"

Ken becomes animated, passionate (which is not unusual). "They give a different, but very profound, sense to the notion of 'inhabitants': our 'habits' emerge from them, we perform ourselves in what we do today in part because of what we have habituated from being with them. I think that our writing together has made me more reflexive about that. I also enjoy working with the way in which these 'inhabitants' blur factual and fictional delineations."

Jonathan looks up, wiping the window's condensation to peer out. The rain continues to fall. "These tribal members, our 'families', permeate our lives and constitute us in ways, through the writing, that increasingly connect us with them. I've written about my dad (Wyatt, 2005a, 2008) but there's still more to write about him."

"I like this line of flight," declares Ken. *Line of flight* is a familiar, Deleuzian phrase to them, a motif. "It provides an escape from the rigours of editing and collating."

"Me too. So we have our tribal members and, if we stay with this metaphor, we have *elders* too."

"Elders? What do you mean?"

"I think of our *elders* as those who have walked our way before, treading the paths that we follow. They have set standards we aspire to, we 'revere' them, to an extent; we cite them regularly. We fold them in. We take their words, their ideas, their concepts, and the images of themselves that they create through these. Our elders would be people like Hélène Cixous, Adriana Cavarero, Laurel Richardson, Ron Pelias, Elizabeth St. Pierre, Bronwyn Davies and Susanne Gannon."

"Foucault too maybe?"

"Hmm, maybe. That's interesting. We're different: you carry Foucault more than me, but he, and, even more so, Deleuze, feels different, not quite our elders. Something else. But bear with me as I think that I have another place for them. Cixous et al. also become our travelling *companions*. We refer to them informally too. We are familiar with them, calling them by their first names in our writing: "Hélène", "Ron", "Betty". We feel we have come to know them. We have seen Richardson, Pelias and St. Pierre at QI[1]."

They pause. These conferences have been important to them both. Ken picks up the cue.

"I am thinking here of Bourdieu's (Bourdieu & Passeron, 1977) ideas to do with cultural capital and how the norms, value and mores, the cultural characteristics that we bring from what he calls our *habitus*, are differentially valued according to the new spaces we enter and try to inhabit. Through our writing we have an emerging cultural capital that enables us to talk of these annual International Congresses of Qualitative Inquiry as 'QI'. We are coming to inhabit that space. It is interesting to see the way in which we have used QI as a backdrop to our writing in the past (see Inquiring Into Writing; Wyatt, 2008). We have written about travelling there, about the short, frightening flight from Chicago and our decision not to repeat it, about the streets and corridors we walk."

---

[1] The annual International Congresses of Qualitative Inquiry that we have attended at the University of Illinois at Urbana-Champaign, USA.

Space figures in this book in important ways. We are 'nomads' travelling across 'landscape', 'terrain', 'space', 'desert' and 'territory'. It is through time that we are placed; we become in certain places. 'Territory' is bound up with nomadic inquiry and the way in which the nomad re/de/territorialises. As we stutter our way, using writing to inquire, we both open up and re/de/territorialise the various spaces that we inhabit.

Jonathan sits back in his chair and drains the remains of his coffee. The father and baby have left, leaving a chaos of plates and half-eaten food.

Jonathan reflects, wistfully, "QI is a place where we have performed and listened, discussed and engaged, have been inspired and enthused by its people and setting. An event, in a Deleuzian sense. The place is surreal, a vast campus located amongst the plains of the mid-West, and it has become an oasis[2], a place in our imaginations that we carry with us in our writings; a place of folklore, perhaps. A place of haecceities."

Ken rejoins, "Yes, it is important; and these inhabitants and the habits we display in these spaces are significant in terms of our becomings. Deleuze has become part of who we are; to talk of haecceities, for example, is now part of our habitus. It is part of our sense."

"OK, OK." Jonathan playfully sighs. "Let's talk about Deleuze. I can see that you're not going to be happy until we do. We've talked about the *members of our tribes,* our *elders,* and our *companions.* It seems to me that we also have *ancestors*: Deleuze, on his own and with Guattari and Parnet. There are others also–you mentioned Foucault and he clearly plays an important ancestral role. We look to Deleuze for our primary ways of knowing. I see you as the 'older brother'. The hairy Esau to the smooth Jacob: you knew Deleuze first, and you brought me to meet him. I haven't stolen your birthright, mind."

"Shall we have some more coffee? This one could run and run."

Ken takes off to the counter, quietly singing to himself:

"'Are you going to the party? / Are you going to the (Deleuze) Tea Party?'"

He returns minutes later with cappuccinos and almond croissants. He is smiling, eager. He leans forward in his chair.

"Your second coffee of the day[3]. You know how to live."

"Funny."

---

[2] See Alterity 3, pp.197-234

[3] Jonathan claims to drink only one coffee a day, which is a lie. It's usually two.

"Do you know, some of my students used to laugh at me if, after about thirty minutes or so, I hadn't mentioned Deleuze. It was an affectionate joke that I didn't get at first. I would say something like, 'And as Deleuze would say ...', or 'In Deleuze we find ...' and there would be chuckles and knowing nudges. I would pick up only on the scuffling disruption. Slowly I came to realise what all this meant and now, with some groups that I know well, I play to the crowd, teasing them by not mentioning his name or by not making a direct reference to a study or a particular concept in his work. I can sense their anticipation, not so much of the Deleuzian pearl to come, but rather of the good humour that will meet its arrival."

He pauses momentarily. Jonathan opens his mouth to say something, but Ken continues. "This became a profoundly important reflective point for me. What was going on here? Why was I quoting this guy so much? The answer is obvious now. With Deleuze, I was doing what Betty calls 'plugging him in' (St. Pierre, 2004). I was taking what I was avidly reading in his work, finding endless connections and excitedly sharing these with my students–and whoever else would listen. I look at my Deleuze books, particularly the ones that I have had for a long time–*A Thousand Plateaus, The Fold, Dialogues II*–and they are battered and worn; their spines are broken, their pages covered with annotations and stuffed with post-its, sheets of hastily scribbled-upon notepaper, postcards and newspaper cuttings. They are alive and it is Deleuze that is alive in them, with me. Betty is right, I have to plug Deleuze in everywhere; he is my PS2, my Xbox, my cell phone, my 21st century prosthetic."

Jonathan raises a hand slightly. When Ken is talking Deleuze, he realises, this has to be done. Ken smiles and nods.

"Since you introduced him to me," Jonathan says. "I have grown with him. I remember buying *A Thousand Plateaus*, and immediately sitting with it on a bench in Oxford–I remember the exact bench–and reading the introduction. I suddenly got why you were so excited by him, and I texted you there and then. And I took *Dialogues 2* to France on holiday: I've written all over my copy, like you. He fuels me; he accompanies me in all my writing these days. Our work with Deleuze is never fixed. It is becoming, as we often say, and we are becoming Deleuzian. Like with your students, what we write, what we read, what we say, what we do, is multiplicitous, interconnected. Our emerging logic is one of sense: we can no longer be rational without also feeling, smelling, seeing, tasting, touching what's around. Haecceities abound."

They have forgotten the rain. The upended, half-folded umbrella is dry. The comings and goings at the surrounding tables pass them by. The almond croissants have long gone.

Ken chips in.

"But what does this say about Deleuze as our ancestor? It feels as if we are paying homage; homage to the man, to the ideas, the words and the books, in reverence. And yet it's not that: we perform ourselves through and with Deleuze and in 'getting' him we promote new and different haecceities, don't you think? We are inquiring into different fields, allowing our nomadic sensibilities to take us into areas of excitement, fun and discovery, where new concepts are always forming, being challenged and taking on new lives. I tend not to name check Deleuze so much with my students anymore; I find increasingly that in what I am doing with them I am encouraging them to become Deleuzian too, which is Deleuzian in itself."

They both sit back in their chairs and laugh quietly, listening to themselves trying to out-Deleuze Deleuze.

"Can we leave Deleuze now?", Jonathan asks.

"If we must."

"Yes, we must. I want to go back to our *companions*. We have had contact with Pelias and, to a lesser extent, Richardson. We have talked with them; we know them and they know us. We have only seen and listened to St Pierre but our embodied experience of her, in lecture rooms, taken with our readings of her, means we feel we know her even if she does not know us. We 'get' her (St. Pierre, 2004). I think of her unflinching theoretical mind and her troubling of the humanist subject; her embracing of Deleuze helped to bring me to writing with and about him. You encountered her at QI2005 and brought back reports of her presentation and conversations with fellow presenters and members of the audience, and how her friends and colleagues called her 'Betty'."

"Yes, I'd read most of her early papers to do with 'transgressive' data, 'circling the text' and Deleuze and education. I'd thought about how clearly she was able to write Deleuzian figures into her work. I'm still influenced by this today. Her session was my first QI experience. I still have the copious notes that I made during her presentation and I've written them into our writing."

Ken pauses and looks out of the window at the brightening day. "Shall we head off to Berkeley Square gardens? I could do with getting out. And you won't cope with another coffee."

They gather their things and wander the short distance up the hill to the fenced patch of green nearby. Ken twirls the closed umbrella as they walk.

"Go on. You were saying," Jonathan prompts.

"Yes. Betty and QI. There was another dimension to this. You mentioned the conversations at the workshops, the informalities and the friendliness that seemed to exist between the presenters and the participants, which I reported to you. I was warmed by the sense of community that this gave me. I wasn't intimidated by the situation and felt able to make contributions to the discussions. For me this was very important and was probably reflected in my excitement when we discussed the workshop later in the day. I'd become a Betty groupie!"

"Yes, you and your mate, Betty."

"But what about you and Hélène?", Ken asks. "She seems to have had an effect upon you."

"I think of her mostly as Cixous, as an elder–distant, unattainable–but she briefly becomes a companion, at the oasis in Alterity 3[4]. At that point, I suddenly need her. In her writing about writing, and about writing as spiritual, she became very important to me after a summer of reading her in 2007. That sense of identification with her meant I felt I could refer to her as Hélène ."

"I could tell. How about Ron Pelias?"

Wandering the gardens they pass the father and child who'd sat near them in the café. The father holds his a boy aloft before placing him on his shoulders. The boy is delighted.

"Ron Pelias," Jonathan says. "To me, he's an elder, like Cixous, in that I feel a distance. His work on performative writing has been important in our work. But he's also a companion to me. He came to the session at QI where I read the first story about my dad (Wyatt, 2005b). As I stood I noticed him squatting on the floor to my right. Afterwards he came up and thanked me. We've had some contact since then, you and me both, haven't we? He feels emotionally close to our book. He's *Ron*. Laurel Richardson, too. Our respect for her is based upon her emancipatory proposal that writing is a method of inquiry, which we've adopted as our own. So she's an elder, but she also feels our friend, our companion, because of the personal support she's given us, primarily, I suppose. Though we never call her Laurel, do we?"

"No…no, I don't think we do. So maybe she is only our elder."

They look at the small boy, who runs after a ball that his father has kicked gently past him. When he reaches it he stoops to pick it up and holds it over his head.

"And then," Jonathan continues, "there are the *spirits* who enter this book's lives: we encounter 'Finger' and 'Spike', who invite themselves

---

[4] pp.221-5

into our dialogue in Therapy[5]. In the souk in Alterity 3 we meet the two women strangers who speak with you. But then all our inhabitants are spirits, in the sense that they are all, to an extent, fabrications."

"I want to go back to Foucault and the influence he has."

The child and father have stopped to sit on a damp bench. Ken and Jonathan walk past. They're circuiting the gardens haphazardly, aimlessly.

"He's an elder, one with whom, as my older brother," Jonathan teases, "you have had more contact."

"He's inspired my–our–thinking about being and action, particularly when we have been reflecting upon the writer and the writing."

The child, perched on the bench, is intrigued by these two slightly bedraggled men and points. Ken says,

"I don't have to think hard to realise that the spirit of Foucault is in so much of what I do and write. I feel that it has had an important influence upon my contribution to the fabric of the book. In many respects my writing has a certain guiding spiritual genealogy smokily wafting around it."

"That's such a Ken-ism."

Ken laughs.

"I mean, the rebellion that through much of my life I have been drawn to mobilise has been charged, first, by the writing of Marx, then by Foucault and now most recently by Deleuze. There have been many others: without effort I think of Sartre and De Beauvoir, Kerouac and Ginsberg and Irigaray and Butler but, if I think of a history, a chronology, then it is these three that seem to signify important stages in my life. I find it fascinating that whilst each gradually over time has displaced the other in terms of my thinking, sentiment still draws me back, from time to time, to their historical predecessor."

"You're still a Marxist then? Or are you a Foucauldian?"

"Neither. Not in the way that I once was. Today, whilst I feel wholly immersed in the interconnected and multiple contradictions and complexities of the Deleuzian becomings, which influence us so much, I remain fascinated by Foucauldian discourse theory in, for example, my situated practices at a large institution like a university. Everywhere around me I see examples of the discursive construction of identities, practices, meanings and knowledge. Institutionally fabricated systems of surveillance seem so thinly veiled; policy technologies with their panoptic gaze appear to determine care of the self and the emergence of docile bodies.

---

[5] pp.179-183, 195-6

"And then I look further back in my personal political history and I see the unequal distribution of wealth still as firmly demarcated as it ever was, when its inequities first fired me as a young undergraduate in the 60's and 70's. I still see all around me the powerful influence of Gramsci and political and cultural hegemonies nurturing conformity and false needs and I still have a sense in which Althusser's concept of interpellation can still be meaningfully applied today.

"These spirits are mercurial; they disappear, then re-appear, they still have the power to surprise us with their relevance and incisiveness when we thought that they no longer applied."

Jonathan puffs out his cheeks and blows hard. Ken is difficult to keep up with sometimes.

"I can see this. Ideas become deeply embedded and continue to influence thought and feeling. They're still relevant."

He sees an empty bench.

"OK to sit? Look," Jonathan says, "these groupings we've got–ancestors, elders, companions, members of our tribes, spirits–I like them, I like the way in which they help me to picture the people in our book and understand how they move around our writing differently, how the terms help to symbolise how we relate to them; but I wouldn't want to them to become rigid, and I know for sure that you wouldn't. Nor would Deleuze. We have to keep their fluidity."

"Absolutely. And is there anyone else?"

"Yes, there's us. You and me, Ken and Jonathan, the 'we' of this book. We travel together. Ken-and-Jonathan. Becoming-Ken-Jonathan. Becoming-Jonathan-Ken. Ken-and-Jonathan-ing, the verb. (And Jonathan-and-Ken-ing, the verb). We are here, in this book. All of these people, and places–events–we've talked about form our machinic assemblage, our body-without-organs."

They look from the bench across the gardens. They see no one else. The father and child have gone.

The two men stand. Time to go.

Ken sings as they wander towards the gate.

"We're going to the party
We're going to the Ken-and-Jonathan party."

"Doesn't scan, dude," comments Jonathan, helpfully.

WRITING SPACE FOUR

"THE WAY YOU DO THE THINGS YOU DO":[1] THE PLACE OF DESIRE IN OUR WRITING PROCESS

In this writing space we engage with the process of our writing together, *how* we do it. We consider: what is this writing that we engage in? How have we written this book? How do we do the things we do?

We know that it is something about our exchanging emails, about the way, mostly, we use attachments, but we still have to ask these questions. Why we do this? What does this mean to us? What are the things we do? Why do we do the things we do? Something in our writing fascinates us; it is productive, it creates desire and makes us sing: The Way You Do the Things You Do.

The Temptations' song is a love song; it is powerfully evocative, its words are words of adoration. You just know when you hear the song that Smokey Robinson wrote those lyrics for someone, a girl who meant so much to him. He places layer upon layer, in chorus after chorus; he is in awe of the girl he writes the song for:

"Well, you could've been anything
That you wanted to and I can tell
The way you do the things you do
(The way you do the things you do,
The way you do the things you do)"

His focus upon the other and the effect that she has is multiple, interconnected; he is absorbed in her, by her, with her, watching, sharing, loving, captured by every moment they share together. He is lost in his experience of her; we gain sense from the tender lyrical passion of the

---

[1] Written by Smokey Robinson (with Rogers) and recorded by The Temptations in 1964 (Robinson & Rogers, 1964).

song that if she were away from him for too long existence would be, for him, unbearable.

> "Well, you could've been anything
> That you wanted to and I can tell
> The way you do the things you do
> (The way you do the things you do)
> You really swept me off my feet"

His absorption in the experience of being with her is complete but it is disabling: 'You really swept me off my feet'. He is off the ground, in the clouds, lost in a world that is detached from everything that is not her. Desire? Desire?

The Way You Do the Things You Do. What do these words mean in relation to our writing? In his affectionate but incisive debates with Foucault late in the latter's life, Deleuze draws out a crucial inflection on the notion of desire. We sense the two men together, close, Gilles aware of the illness wracking the body of his great friend. They talk and argue in ways that they have done as vibrant intellectuals throughout their successful and provocative public lives: their words influence many thinkers in different ways. Deleuze reflects:

> "The last time we saw each other, Michel told me, with much kindness and affection, something like, I cannot bear the word *desire*; even if you use it differently, I cannot keep myself from thinking or living that desire = lack, or that desire is repressed." (Deleuze, 1997, p.189)

Deleuze offers the view that for Foucault desire seems to be a sentiment, one that is so closely associated with pleasure to be almost synonymous with it; if that desire is not fulfilled then life is not complete, it somehow lacks pleasure. Ken remembers seeing an old, grainy, black and white documentary on the poet and broadcaster John Betjeman, not long after his death. There he was, an old man, precariously perched by a fence at the top of a windswept Cornish cliff, his coat wrapped around him, flapping in the wind, a man portraying advanced years in his demeanour. The interviewer, hidden behind the camera, asks him if there is anything that he regrets about his long and successful life and with great candour and simple honesty he replies: "Yes, I would like to have had more sex". This expression by a man at the end of his life epitomises this sentiment, this lack, a suffering perhaps, which Foucault is trying to give voice to in his final discussions with his friend. Betjeman expresses this lack with a certain regret; the sadness of his assertion, whilst tinged with humour, tells a story of loss, yearning and a life that harboured an incompleteness.

In his writing, Deleuze does not promote an exclusively libidinous portrayal of desire. His work with Guattari in *Anti-Oedipus* (Deleuze & Guattari, 2004a) challenges the way in which psychoanalysis defines desire as a lack. Rather, in Deleuze desire is a synthesising life force in which production and creativity come together in the ever-changing processes of becoming. In this productive sense of desire there is always a challenge to the structured and determinate nature of life; nomadic inquiry motivated by desire always leads to a breaking out. Lines of flight encourage escape from the existing order of things; de-territorialisations lead to new becomings. Grosz states this succinctly when she says:

"Desire does not create permanent multiplicities, which would produce what is stable, self-identical, the same. It experiments rather than standardises, producing ever-new alignments, linkages, and connections." (Grosz, 1994, p.199)

Desire both lives within and nurtures the body-without-organs; it is always breaking free from the hierarchical fixed structure of the organised body, opening doors, breaking them down with lines of flight that produce new and vibrant rhizomatic shoots[2]. In writing this book, the positive nature of desire, as exemplified in the writing of Deleuze, has been a driving force. We have characterised both the form and growth of our 'body' of work using a Deleuzian re-working of Artaud's body-without-organs, as we discuss in our first writing space. Engaging in our work seems to be energising and in the spaces that our writing creates, our desire to inquire, to pursue multiple pathways, to make new and exciting connections, has a powerful effect upon 'Becoming-Ken-Jonathan'. The body-without-organs that we both inhabit and cultivate in this book is one of sensation and is one in which desire leaves little room for the disabling effects of lack, regret or suffering. In writing this book we feel that we are both intentionally and unintentionally expressing our desire to write, to become something else through the writing. This 'something else' is not an object of desire; often we do not know what we want to write or what we are going to write: writing has its own phenomenology.

"For me desire implies no lack; neither is it a natural given. It is an *agencement* of heterogeneous elements that function: it is process as

---

[2] Deleuze and Guattari use the "principle of asignifying rupture" to characterise this aspect of becoming in rhizomatic form (Deleuze & Guattari, 2004b, p.10)

opposed to structure or genesis; it is affect as opposed to sentiment; it is '*haec*-eity' " (Deleuze, 1997, p.189)

We will say, both explicitly and implicitly, many times in this writing, that writing becomes us; we are becoming through and in the writing. We have come to know, we are coming to know, that we want to write; in this writing we are performing ourselves to each other in ways that the writing encourages us to explore. So, perhaps somewhat incidentally, this book is about subjectivities: we have written, for example, about what it means to be Two Men Talking[3], exploring our gendered selves, how we feel and know our selves through our ontological and constructed being as 'men'. In doing this it has been our desire to explore our "thousand tiny sexes" (Grosz, 1994) and to try to deconstruct the way in which gender construction often seems to be fixated upon a convenient male/masculine, female/feminine binary. As we reflect upon our 'method', it seems that we are working with a desire to be productive, to think differently and to create concepts that are new. As we live, breathe, create and re-create our body-without-organs we are aware that it is also a 'desiring–machine'.

"Desire is the set of passive syntheses that engineer partial objects, flows and bodies, and that function as units of production ... Desire does not lack anything; it does not lack its object. It is, rather, the subject that is missing in desire, or desire that lacks a fixed subject; there is no fixed subject unless there is repression. Desire and its object are one and the same thing: the machine, as a machine of a machine." (Deleuze & Guattari, 2004a, p.28)

We can imagine explaining ourselves and the work we do in our book through the agency of the Temptations song. Perhaps, at a conference, we will take the podium and sing The Way You Do the Things You Do. (Or perhaps not.)

---

[3] pp.144-164

> Our editing of these introductory spaces has been conducted mainly through the technology of the 'track changes' tool of MS Word. One of us, mostly Jonathan, has suggested edits to the text and commented on them to Ken. Our exchanges have been, at times, passionate. Jonathan, for example, has regularly excised or changed Ken's writing, and Ken has sometimes protested. Conflicts have arisen and been carried in series of comments boxes down the sides of the pages.
>
> The main site of our conflict has been over Ken's use of exclamation marks. The issue at this specific juncture was whether or not the phrase "Or perhaps not", above, should be followed by a full stop or an exclamation mark.
>
> To Ken, exclamation marks are an embodied signal to the reader of his voice; they symbolise how he speaks, and to delete them is to sacrifice authenticity in favour of style. To Jonathan, they tell the reader how to respond: "This is funny: laugh!" Or "I really feel strongly about this: be moved!" He prefers to allow the words space to do their work.

What is important about this image is what we would need to convey in our delivery of the song: not the libidinous desire of the Smokey Robinson original, rather the energised productive desire of our between-the-twos. The emerging phenomenology of our writing is, in large part, driven by the 'what' and the 'how' in which we perform ourselves to each other. Desire is sparked.

We are writing this book, we are performing ourselves; we are also positioned in other worlds, in worlds that place demands upon us, upon our time, upon our literacies and our intelligences and upon our love. Pelias provides an indication of this when he says,

"With connection comes responsibility, a burden dressed in shoulds, an obligation of proof that demonstrates caring isn't a lie. Yet, life conspires with its rules and regulations, with its practical demands of putting food on the table, with its seductions on behalf of lethargy, with its learned inadequacies. Seldom do we give the only thing we have worth giving, an empathic presence. So we story ourselves into approval hiding what we know to be true: We are not what we should be." (Gale et al., 2008)

This writing clearly shows the interactions of the worlds we inhabit and the tensions that can often exist at the *border crossings* (McLaren, 1997), so that if we want to write there are often many things in our way, things that conspire against us and accidents that happen. The "practical demands" and the "seductions" are always there but in writing this book, developing and using our processes, we have begun to break down some of the ethical concerns that are presented in Pelias' writing. If, as we claim, our book resembles a Deleuzian body-without-organs, then our desire to write is embodied. It is about becoming and in that becoming we have a positive and energised sense of ourselves in those becomings: we are what we should be.

A final reflexive note on desire. The following small piece of writing was written by Ken on a scrap of paper as he sat on a rock on Housel Beach[4] in the sunshine one early autumn weekend. He had been swimming in the sea and felt warmed and alive, relishing the energy the late summer sun was sharing with him. Earlier in the day he had been reading some writing that Jonathan had sent him and as he swam, played and jumped off the rocks into the sea with his children, Jonathan's writing was with him, circling, shifting in and out of his consciousness, nudging him and affecting his balance. He was happy but he knew that he wanted to write, to respond to what Jonathan had sent him. This is what he wrote on a small scrap of paper:

> "So, thinking of ways of writing myself into our writing. So many obstacles, real and imagined, present themselves: work, children, marking, cooking and so on. But I always find a way in; this is desire. This is the productive nature of desire, the desire to do, the desire to be, the desire to write. To place myself in the space, ready in that space in which writing takes place. Readying myself for an experience that I am not sure of but know will fulfil me. Sitting down, starting to write; writing becoming me. Me becoming through the writing."

---

[4] Housel Beach, The Lizard, Cornwall, UK

WRITING SPACE FIVE

OUR WRITING PLACES, OUR WRITING SPACES

Our work together in this book enquires, with and through writing, into understanding better the creating of (our) subjectivities; in particular, we explore how this takes place as we write between us. The 'product' of our writing appears as text on pages, as if from nowhere; and yet the words have, of course, been written somewhere, not only onto specific pages and particular screens, but by fingers linked to bodies, our bodies, Ken's and Jonathan's, situated in space and time.

In this (textual) writing space here we seek to trouble the taken-for-granted, the customarily invisible. We make explicit the places and spaces–using 'writing spaces' in this non-textual sense (as well)–where we write, and reflect upon what these places and spaces mean to us. We resist seeing these places and spaces as fixed; we work with them as parts of our assemblage, of our body-without-organs, not to be ignored but not to be viewed as 'out there', static.

Jonathan writes in italics; Ken writes in normal font.

I write here:
On this page, in my black, red ring-bound, hard backed, solid notebook, with lined A4 perforated pages. My writing here shares space with other kinds of writing like notes from meetings and lists of tasks to do. I begin most writing in this book, which I carry with me always. If I write here, I feel loose, round. I feel free, less inhibited than when confronted by my screens. I experience writing here "as a corporeal act" and it leads me to find "memories and knowledge of the writer's body" (Cixous in Sellers, 2004, p.x). I can loop words around the page, write in different colours. I am less concerned to fill space than I am on the screen, where I feel relief when I have written one page, two pages, three. In this notebook I think that I can kid myself that I am not writing. Writing is difficult and painful, and I resist it[1]. Here, I can just write, double-spaced so that I can go back and write in between. My handwriting is neat

---

[1] See Writing Secrets, Writing Desire in Alterity 3, pp.212-217

but inhibited. I do not like it particularly, but seeing it form and reading it is reassuringly familiar. It looks like me. It is "a trace of a dialogue with (myself)" (Kristeva, 2002, p.44).

The blank space? The space I inhabit when I write? Space, the final frontier.

Writing space. Space internal, space external. Transmutation of fluxes disassembling the binary divide. These spaces enter each other and become one and many at the same time. Space: writing space: writing. The space to be described. Space captured in so many ways: assemblage of physicality and mood, materiality and feeling. I shift in the frisson of space and body. Smell; is it the room, is it me? My space. My space? This exists outside and inside of me. This space only has meaning because of my habitation of and within it.

I remember going into my mum's little flat to clear away her things after she died and piece by piece by piece as I picked her things up and packed them away, their meaning dissolved. Moving, dislocating, the material nature of those things in my mother's space, my conception of her space had little significance. Now, nearly seven years since my mother died, those things sit in the same boxes, alone and displaced: I think of my mother now in her space: is her wrapped isolation as final as that of her things, in their tissue paper and brown cardboard coffins?

This space and time. Here now, the cold autumn sunlight tempting me through the glass, the sense of the sea provoking my desire, encouraging me to write and then … to rush to the cliff, to clamber down, down over the rocks and the rough grasses, disturbing stonechats, the sea coming up to meet me, inviting me in, its turbulent encompassing force provoking sensual energies … I race across the beach and into the water, the shock, the shout, the wild splash and in, submerged, gone, another world. But wait; *this* space, I am writing! Each time I do this my mind travels, I began to talk of the window, the view across the rooftops, the trees, the western sky, where I know the weather is coming from. I must stay inside for a moment. What is my writing space? What does it look like?

I write here:
In this café–though not only in this one: there are three that I write in. Away from my desk, away from family, away from work, from television and my beloved wind-up, portable radio. Away from all of these and alone at a table, amongst women with pushchairs, and young men laughing; amongst the talking, the movement, the hiss of milk being steamed, the transporting smell of coffee, the gleam of stainless steel. The café's noise,

its flow of humanity, connects me to writing. I am here and yet not here, immersed in an experience. Haecceity.
    I write here:
    At this desk, in my office in Oxford, in snatched times at the end of the day or during quiet periods where I can justify giving more time to writing. I initially type from my handwritten drafts, amending as I go. I type fast, with every finger and regular mistakes. Then on, further, into the writing, typing new words, walking away every twenty minutes, unable to sustain my commitment. Always ambivalent, both wanting and not wanting to write, never fully immersed, feeling writing's slow, cumulative process (Pelias, 2004).
    I write here:
    In the front room of my house in Abingdon, on my side of the desk I share with Tessa; the living room and its television next door, books to hand on my left on newly erected shelving, together with photographs of family and friends, some blue-tacked to the wall beside. I write onto a small laptop that contains and constrains, the rectangular screen disciplining my text. Behind me, through the window, there is a small garden, a hedge, a fence. When I write here it is mostly dark outside, so I draw the thin blue curtains against the suburban world of 1930s semis that I inhabit. Tessa's books and art materials fill the rest of the room–I have a corner, a quarter, of this space–our space overlapping; I breathe in her energy and creativity, enjoy in her clutter her presence here. Sometimes I long for a room of my own where–in fantasy–I have space to spread out, to make mine; but I think I would, instead, atrophy, stifled in my own thin, stale air, suffocated without the presence of her breath.

Books! This tiny room is full of books. What do I say about this? Here is a diary entry dated 17th August 2007:

"Here I am in my office waiting for my printer to churn out secret writings, rough scripts; words that might become the stimulus for another bout of love and loss. Head on chin, a day's growth of whiskers rough in my hands; if I could see myself now I know I would look grey, tousled, a tad bleary, just past sixty! As I run my eyes over the bottom left shelf of my library (a grand descriptor!) I am suddenly struck by the titles that I am reading there: from left to right: *The Affluent Worker* by Goldthorpe and Lockwood, *Folk Devils and Moral Panics* by Stanley Cohen, *Hustlers Beats and Others* by Ned Polsky, *The Theory of Social and Economic Organisations* by Max Weber, *The German Ideology* by Mark and Engels, *The Sociological Tradition* by Nisbet, *Social Origins of Dictatorship and Democracy* by Barrington Moore, *Structure and Function in Primitive Society* by Radcliffe-Brown, *The New Working Class* by Serge Mallet, *The*

Social Construction of Reality by Berger and Luckmann ... and so it goes on. Just that one shelf, no ... that one half shelf!!! ... tells such a story. What a small part of my life but a part that has created movement and change, a small step perhaps, out, away, in a different direction. Those books that I have read, those books that I know, that I have absorbed, whose contents I have understood, interpreted and shared with hundreds of students. Memories of teaching sociology, all those years ago, now such a small but significant fragment of my life. Funny! Now I would challenge those writings but with a certain fondness, I know."

I wonder, will I open them up again or will they sit there as a testament to my past, as an emblem, a stepping stone, a distant trigger for my memory perhaps? Today in carrying out some research for this writing I picked the most unlikely of books from my shelf, Judith Bell's *Doing Your Research Project*: a book that in so many ways is anathema to me; formulaic, expository, informative, rigid, and oh so boring. And yet, today it did me a little job: tiny, so insignificant, and relevant only, perhaps to the cryptologist who is interested in my work when I become a famous writer, philosopher or something! But there, nevertheless, a minor footnote in the most minor of histories! Aha!

So there are many books here, they tumble over and upon me like the houses in a picture of an old Elizabethan street. Some remain untouched, tidy and alone, collecting dust, like the sociology textbooks from my past. In many ways they are representatives from an arboreal, hierarchical past; in unsuccessfully attempting to establish the *logos* of formal, structured, established thought they have become redundant. They now exist in a sedentary striated space (Deleuze & Guattari, 2004b). Others shift and move, jump out from their places on the shelves and find themselves residing with new companions, sometimes in freshly configured rows and at others times in precariously balanced piles all over the floors and the tables. In this *nomos*, this smooth space (ibid.), lines of flight and escape occur, new relations are made in pulsing, vibrant and amorphous nomadic inquiries. Books and journals spew out their contexts, pages bulge with scribbled sheets of folded A4 and bright yellow 'post-its', covers are creased and tidy typescripts are littered with multi-coloured spidery annotations. Deleuze, Foucault, Auster, Butler, Irigaray, Kerouac, hooks, Pelias, Cixous are rarely allowed to rest in sombre, conservatively and carefully classified rows, they shift around, sometimes book-marking each other in vulgar erotic poses, their spines stretching with the grasping tension of their passionate interlocking embrace.

Those books, they are like lovers, they exist in relation to me; all of them display different levels of intimacy, connection and sensuality. There are intensities here, connections and multiplicities; their topographies, their words, their writings are many and various. Some are transient and impermanent and I easily forget them; they have drifted into my life but I do not struggle to keep them there. Others, by vivid contrast, I cannot be without and if I have not shared reading and writing, thinking and feeling with them for a few days, I search around, in and amongst the rows, disturbing the unruly piles, until we meet and, again, instantly embrace. So, *A Thousand Plateaus* is never far from me. Sometimes I read passages that I have read a hundred times before, indulging in the poetry of the writing and finding pleasures in the unusual tropes, feeling taunted and teased by the figures that come dancing out of the pages and, on other occasions, often quite absent-mindedly, I will lift it from its resting place, take it to a chair with a beer or a coffee, open the pages at random and find myself being taken to new heights of intimacy, enjoying pleasures that I hadn't dreamed of. Many of those sensual encounters have found themselves reappearing in these pages, in direct quotations or more often as the machinic energy behind the writing that is here.

All these books, these lovers, could be characterised as study books, text-books, reference books; they are the books that I have directly associated with my writing, my teaching and my research. Outside the permanently open door of this room, known variously as 'Daddy's Office', 'Ken's Study', or 'The Office', is a long hallway piled high on either side with more books, books of a different kind, novels, many children's books, maps, books of poetry, cookery books, annuals and photograph albums. Silently, these books peer into the office, they lean over and the ones nearest to the door often find their way in and sometimes are allowed to stay. So, after many years of longing, cliently waiting and largely being ignored in the hustle and bustle of the busy hallway, Kerouac has now found his way back in and the many garishly covered cheap American pulp editions now reside comfortably on these shelves. In recent years Auster, Kundera, Marquez, Borges and De Lillo have made similarly successful journeys: like old friends, they have shown their resilience, demonstrating that we have shared places in each other's hearts. Now their words influence mine. I find them seeping into my work. I sometimes invite them in like old friends but at other times they arrive uninvited, surprising me with their wit and candour. As I allow myself to identify myself as a person who writes, as I am happy to acknowledge that this writing becomes me, their presence in my living becomes more and more welcome.

I write here:
Inside me, within, through, me; inside, where there is Ken-ing[2] too; I
write here, together with a Ken within, writing that sometimes seems to be
not mine, or even ours, but to flow–hesitantly, stammering–through me.
I write here:
In between Ken and me, in a space that I picture being somewhere
geographically between us, over Salisbury Plain perhaps, a virtual
sorting office where Ken-and-Jonathan-ing takes place; where our
writings cross, and where their traces, their offspring, maybe sit together
and talk, sipping tea, considering each other, and spawn other writings of
which Ken and I have, and will have, no knowledge.

As I sit here now, the walls smile back at me. Here, as I look up for
inspiration, as I grapple with and for words, as I feel myself into my
writing. Posters with the faces of Jimi Hendrix, Faithless, Andy Warhol,
PJ Harvey, the Stones, Ike and Tina Turner and New Order provide
comfort and sometimes it is their music that I enjoy when my fingers are
all tapped out and the reservoir of words has gone dry.

And there are spaces that I inhabit as I journey into my computer:
Word>Ken>EdD>Assignments>Book>Our Writing Spaces. This journey
takes place in a space. Usually I am eager to enter this space and feel
excited as I activate the stops on the journey; sometimes I stop by in other
spaces, places where I have expended great energy, spaces where I have
sometimes loved, laughed or cried: 'Petra', 'Two Men Talking',
'Therapy', all evoke great feeling and often they prepare me for the stay in
the new space that I am so eager to open up. As I think and feel this
writing space I am aware of my reading into this experience, the way in
which I am performing myself, taking me on my journey, always aware of
Jonathan there, the person who is going to read these words that I write in
response to his writing. Our disembodied selves inhabit and territorialise
these 'cyberspaces', formed as a part of a 'consensual reality' (Gibson,
1984); meaning, knowledge and identity are negotiated and established
there, if only for brief fragments of time. This seems helpful in one way
but it does not talk of what we carry on our journey or of what we take to
our spaces and how what we take to the spaces influences those spaces
themselves.

The spaces are interior and exterior. So there, for me, in the warm
autumn sunlight of Housel Beach[3], space was created. It was a space of
haecceity and vast assemblage that was cartographic, climactic, emotional

---

[2] See Two Men Talking, pp.164
[3] See p.43

and driven by the productive desire to write. Writing to this book, to
Jonathan, with him and for me: the powerful phenomenological energies
of this writing in those moments were violating the tranquil but forceful
energy of the beach, opening up new 'fields of play' (Richardson, 1997a)
in that brief rushed moment of having to write something down on a
creased scrap of paper. But of course it was not simply me taking those
energies there. It could not have been any where. It was the beach. It was
the beach on a beautiful iridescent sunny afternoon, the crashing waves,
the sheer clarity of Cornish light, of salt crystals forming on my sun-
drying body and my children dancing in the surf. As St. Pierre asks:
"What is the meaning of our attachment to certain places; why do we
return to them over and over again?" (St. Pierre, 2000, p.259) . I sense
liminality here. It is as if the comforts of familiar space provide the basis
for moving forward, of entering new spaces but each time carrying
something of our self forward in a new direction. Braidotti says:

> "Identity is retrospective; representing it entails that we can draw accurate
> maps, indeed, but only of where we have already been and consequently no
> longer are." (Braidotti, 1994, p.35)

My mind understands this but my body resists. I know that I am hailed
by the call and I know that my response to this call identifies me. I know
that the discourses of morality, family and institutional managerialism all
seek to define me but in this writing I am revelling in the delights of
transgression and of possibly creating something new in and of my self.
Bachelard captures a sense of this liminality when he says:

> "And here the threshold is a hospitable threshold, one that does not
> intimidate us by its majesty. The two images: the calm nest and the old
> home, weave the sturdy web of intimacy on the dream loom. And the
> images are all simple ones ... to make so gentle a comparison between
> house and nest, one must have lost the house that stood for happiness. So
> there is always an *alas* in this song of tenderness. If we return to the old
> home as to a nest, it is because memories are dreams, because the home of
> other days has become a great image of lost intimacy." (1994, p.100)

The poetics of space that Bachelard evokes seem to provide a place for
the affection, comfort and familiarity of known spaces that combines with
the agentic volatility of adventure, movement and change. So whilst, in
part, I am happy to agree with Braidotti's (1994) claim about the
retrospective nature of identity, I am also very excited by the opportunities
that are offered to transgress these identifications and to cut new

trajectories that open up, through incision and excision, new relations of self and action in these spaces of comfort and adventure.

Folding and unfolding. Interior, exterior. Endogamy, exogamy. Lines of flight striating the smooth spaces, vectors cutting across established strata, nomadic violations providing the excitement of new and vivid territorialisation: we are in this place, this space, it is so exciting. See who is here! See what we can do! Reading! Writing! Talking! Nothing is fixed, these becomings are so compelling. As I write I feel transported, up and away from these cold, dark awakenings, these early mornings of not enough sleep, of thoughts of the day to come and of practicalities that weigh like wet sand in a sodden bag. This transgressive writing violates, like the red weal of a fresh scar burning into the comfort of soft flesh, it cuts and makes a mark but slowly, gradually through time, it becomes the body, its absorption into the flesh, its becoming-flesh, is simply but wholly the transmutation of fluxes that is the body-without-organs. As I write this I am fascinated by Braidotti's claim that:

> Nomadism, therefore, is not fluidity without borders but rather an acute awareness of the nonfixity of boundaries. It is the intense desire to go on trespassing, transgressing. (Braidotti, 1994, p.36)

BETWEEN-THE-TWOS

WRITING SPACE SIX

INQUIRING INTO WRITING
(FEBRUARY-MAY 2005)[1]

This was our first collaborative writing, a testing out of form, method, content and relationship.

Prologue: Morning, May 3rd 2005, Heathrow Airport, London

We wait in the departure lounge ready to board our plane to Chicago. (Don't you think that purgatory–a liminal space? an inter/view?–must resemble an airport lounge? A mass of people in transit, trapped until given direction to leave. So much movement, enforced lingering, uncertainty.)

As we wait, we begin to relax. Anxiety–about leaving home, tasks unfinished and what might delay our respective journeys from Oxford and Plymouth–has been with each of us. Checking in was straightforward; seeing our luggage disappear was disconcerting. No turning back.

Now, we feel anticipation. We begin to talk about the conference in Illinois[2] where we are each presenting papers. We exchange conversation describing our hopes for the next few days. And we realise we have the opportunity to discuss, for the first time since completing it, our shared writing project: our interview.

We clear the table of cups and other debris, take out a copy of our manuscript and begin to read.

---

[1] A version of this writing space was originally published in the journal *Qualitative Inquiry* (Gale and Wyatt 2006)
[2] 1st International Congress of Qualitative Inquiry, May 5-7, 2005, University of Illinois at Urbana-Champaign

Introduction

We enjoy discussing and sharing work; and notice the contrast between how each writes. Ken's writing is more consistent with traditional academic writing while Jonathan's transgressive 'I' is prominent. If these writings were landscape, Ken's would be a rich, verdant forest reached only via a long, satisfying trek over mountains, Jonathan's a beach in the Costa del Sol with easy access via Ryanair.

We conducted an interactive interview (Ellis and Berger, 2003) via email–"asynchronous…semi-private…computer-mediated communication" (Mann and Stewart, 2003, pp81-82; see also Fontana and Frey, 2003, for an overview of developments in on-line interviewing)– between February and April 2005. The focus was the *meaning* of how we write; and it became an inquiry into writing as a process. The disparity in our styles is less stark in this project, we feel.

> In this first piece, we make play of it being an 'interview'. It felt important, a way of justifying our working together in this way. We make little of this in later writing but it remains to us a useful and intriguing way of conceptualising what we later began to name our 'between the twos'.

We frame this as a *postmodern* interview (Gubrium and Holstcin, 2004): our intention is to be collaborative (Ellis and Berger, 2003), to capture understandings (Atkinson and Coffey, 2003); to create selves rather than reveal them (Atkinson and Silverman, 1997).

What follows are the chronologically-ordered attachments that we exchanged. The process is appropriately incomplete (see Bond and Mifsud, 2005; Rhodes, 2000); it has opened up further possibilities and more doubt (contrary to Jarvinen's (2000) view that successful interviews have a narrative trajectory "from self-delusion to self-realisation", p387).

The first pieces we wrote 'blind', hence the parallel format, after which we respond to each other. We end with separate reflections on the process. The whole is our Inter View (Kvale, 1996; Hillman, 1984).

The interview

Writing stories (Jonathan)

Killing a Snail (Ken)

I have been thinking about how the way that I write is tied up with my self esteem and self image–for instance as a teacher, as someone who works in an academic community, as a counsellor, and as a man. As part of this train of thought I have been revisiting some stories:

In the early 80s I was an English undergraduate at York. In my second year I did a course on the 20th century novel and my tutor was Hermione Lee (who's since become quite a pop-don). I'd had a crisis earlier in the year and I'd spoken with my tutor about taking a year out or changing degree. What was frustrating me was the expectation to offer reasoned and erudite critique, to speak in the abstract, to generalise. There was no room to give a personal response, to say "this poem moved me, made me think about how I frame my life".

My tutor suggested that I didn't change degrees or take time out yet but he'd arrange for Hermione Lee to teach me on my next course. I would like her, he said.

I did. She was fantastic–lively, stimulating, invigorating–and I enjoyed her course. But one tutorial she gave me back an essay. I was on my own (my tutorial partner must have been sick) and she tore into it, not so much about its content but about its style. I don't remember the words she used but the overall message was that it was naïve and clumsy and that I needed to take the way I wrote more seriously.

I was mortified. And at least, this time, it was *my* writing. In the first year, I had written an essay about

Today, in the garden, I killed a snail. As soon as I did it I vowed in my life never intentionally to kill another creature. But I have just woken up in the middle of the night, thinking about the snail. I only broke its shell but breaking that shell ended its life.

What is the significance of that snail and its shell? For the snail its shell was not simply its protection from being killed, or simply its home: it *was* the snail: breaking the shell equalled killing the snail.

What has that got to do with writing? In my sleepy reverie I have connected writing with the shell. This is not meant to be a simple figure of speech which allows me to think that cracking the shell of (my) writing will somehow crack some hidden code and lead me to a profound understanding of self. But there are some parallels. Writing is not simply a shell or a code which protects us or allows us to be identified in certain superficial ways; our writing *is* us, or to paraphrase Richardson (1997), writing becomes us, we inquire after ourselves through our writing. So, finding out about our writing is also finding out about ourselves. Every snail shell is idiosyncratically unique, allowing us to identify every snail. The snail's shell is becoming, it grows with, the snail; there is no separation.

So my writing is not there simply to identify me, nor to protect me nor to give me my home–it is me, its fluid, energetic, emerging shades, it is me becoming. It <u>is</u> identifying me, it <u>is</u> protecting me, it <u>is</u> my home but can only be characterised in these ways

Beowolf for a different tutor. I had gone to the library and had found a good book about the text.

And copied great chunks out of it.

The tutor had made fulsome comments about my essay, particularly about its style.

Hermione Lee turned out to be only brief respite. I subsequently made some unwise choices (two terms of Dante) but stayed doing English, didn't take a year out and actually began to enagage; but the damage was done and I ended up with a third. I didn't read a novel for years.

I did a masters degree while a teacher in the late 80s and my tutor said he liked my writing but never gave me very good grades. When I asked him about this he implied that my writing was too informal. Even doing my masters in counselling at the end of the 90s I wrote my first essay and got a high grade, but the comment was that the essay was good, "albeit idiosyncratic". What I'd done was to frame an academic piece around a short story, breaking up the story to do the commentary.

Remembering these episodes has reminded me of how long it's taken me to find a voice; writing how I do now feels precious and hard won.

through the constant fluid movement of becoming. So between the two, me and my writing, exists a multiplicity of connections, a state of fluidity, an ever-changing nexus of identifications, infinitesimally small but hugely significant moments that give something to my sense, my feeling of knowing, of self. I am going to write about this, write about my writing, about me–sharing this with Jonathan and sharing this with myself.

This thinking has emerged or has been influenced by our interest in our different styles of writing. Of course our writing is different but for us our writing is *noticeably* different, given some of the contextual or habitual frameworks within which a lot of writing exists, particularly so-called 'academic writing'. So here is the stimulus for this writing. A joint inquiry into writing and the self, through the eyes of self and other.

Being possessed (Jonathan)

You and I spoke over the telephone yesterday, and we discussed the surprise that we had been experiencing–I in composing this and you in reflecting upon my first piece–how the process we are involved in is taking on its own shape. This has reminded me of White's description of the role of the 'outsider witness'. He directs 'reflecting team' members to consider not their judgment of someone's stories but what in those stories

captures their attention? What images do the stories evoke? What
reverberates? (White, 2000).

I can remember 'killing' snails. On damp summers' evenings I
unwittingly feel the crunch–and then the moisture–under bare feet. I feel
disgust but no more. I don't think that I shall be able to be so unthinking
again. Perhaps I shall carry a torch. Or wear shoes.

You say that you had to get up in the night to write. Late last year I
attended a conference for staff developers in higher education. On the
final morning I was due to present a paper about my work at Oxford with
postdoctoral researchers ("postdocs"). The evening before was the
traditional conference disco. That night I couldn't sleep.

The evening's events–sitting, eating, drinking and dancing with
colleagues–had 'filled' me. And they were pushing me, nagging at me.
The morning's workshop was only hours away and I was looking forward
to that. The two seemed connected: the nagging about the evening and the
forthcoming workshop. As I lay awake I knew that the only likelihood of
getting some sleep lay in raising myself and writing with what I was
experiencing.

Here is what emerged. I do not lay great claim to it. You probably had
to be there:

A very short story: Conference Disco Blues

Is it the one-more glass of red wine that leads me to feel such loss as I
dance to the familiar, evocative songs? Is it me or is there sadness when
one ends and we wait for the band to strike up the next?

The intensity of these moments hurts, aches, wrings me; makes
redundant the soul-less language of the day; speaks only of the
exquisiteness of life.

And then they are gone, like breath on glass.

I never quite get dancing, never feel as if I am in it entirely. My feet
don't move where I want. Arms whirl hopefully. I look longingly at
people I can't ever be like nor shall ever know, ever touch. There are
passing seconds when I'm inside the music, like I belong, and then they're
gone.

And that final time of decision, when the band finishes playing and
fails to return for an encore after half-hearted pleading; when those who
remain seem connected. My two companions are in thrall. I sit, but at a
distance from them, put my feet up as if to demonstrate nonchalance (I
belong and have no reason to envy). Watch the laughter as huddles gather.
Drink imaginary wine from my empty glass. And depart.

I walk out of the hall, leaving the beauty behind, and head for the lift. I begin to think again of the workshop on working with postdocs that I shall lead tomorrow morning, thoughts of which have intruded–not unpleasantly–all evening.

I wonder about connections.

Postdocs and dancing, for instance.

Writing is more than what we do. It's what we are, whom we are becoming. The experience of writing "Blues" was more than simply typing what was in my head. It was a process of enquiring into what I was experiencing, and it became what I was experiencing. Like the snail's shell, the writing was me.

And I–like you–had to do it. It impelled me.

Covers (Ken)

In "Writing Stories" you talked about the effects of past experiences. I gained a sense of your needing to go back to these, both as a way of explanation and as a way of revealing these events, exposing them, bringing them into the open. I am thinking that perhaps they had been somehow covered by time, by your own concerns about the ways in which you had seen these events as shaping your life. I began to think again about the snail and the way in which the shell is a part of the creature, that the covering is part of the creature, just as the creature is part of the shell. So if writing can be seen as a method of inquiry, in what sense is it an inquiry into what is, or has been, covered? I am thinking of uncovering, recovering, and discovering; which of these are we talking about here? If we are uncovering are we simply revealing what is hidden in the present, simply pulling away the covers to show what is there? If we are recovering are we saving something, retrieving it or bringing it to life in the present? If we are discovering are we finding something that has been hidden, intentionally or unintentionally, through our excavations and our archaeologies?

I am going to show you something that was written by my friend/colleague/roommate at work, Emma, in response to a conversation that she and I had about gaining our voice through the process of writing. This is not the whole piece but it is the part that seems most relevant:

> "I have used my colleague's writings in my own work. In them I found an anomaly which he and I discussed (and I found it because I recognise aspects of me in the same paradox). He fights ("no I don't–I am just trying to find a way to reconcile", said my mate … "but isn't reconciliation called

for when a tension or argument or conflict arises?", riposted I) with academic conventions: the conditioned compulsion to effect an intellectual distance (the objective) from immersion and the emotional, the ripples of self (Ely et al., 2001) that play over a subject (the subjective). He wants to find his voice, to risk his voice being heard, but often presents another's/others' instead–as do I. As I pause to reflect I still feel the sadness that I felt at that moment, at the loss of identity, voice, connection and deepened understandings of selves through our research stories, that positivist notions of rigour and epistemology hijacked and imprisoned. Yet, always present was a 'self', albeit not named or owned; maybe it was too intimate, and for many quite alien, to do other than ignore."

It feels to me that Emma is after something similar to what you talk about in your first piece; a removal of covers to reveal something that is 'truly' there. You said something powerful, significant and evocative: "Remembering these episodes has reminded me of how long it's taken me to find a voice; writing how I do now feels precious and hard won". It feels that something has been released or, perhaps, realised. As I am writing this I am wondering in what sense this means that something has been made real for you through the writing that you are now engaged in. I am wondering how to do this for myself. Emma suggests that maybe in my case the 'covering' is to do with me having reconstructed myself and my writing in ways in which I perceive the academy wants me to be. She sees this as my way of achieving what a respectable academic is supposed to do. I have made myself up. I am one of the lunatics trying to take over the asylum and I am afraid that I am going to get caught. I am an impostor: who am I to be doing this job? The character and influence of my working class background has never been far away from me. Despite often appearing confident, outgoing and extravagant I always feel that an insecurity about my background has infected me and had an influence upon the way I am.

As an only child and a member of a large extended family I was always conscious of differences. Although I managed to fail my 11+ along with all my cousins and many of my friends, I eventually managed to have a university education and take on the professional identity of teacher. I still feel a part of my wider family but I also feel somehow distinct from it and different. "Still teaching then Ken?" is a question that I usually hear at the few family functions, usually funerals, that I now attend. It's as if they are all still expecting me to get a 'proper job' which involves a bit of muscle and getting my hands dirty, so that they can welcome me back to the fold. I am beginning to think that my awareness of benign prejudices of this kind has affected the way in which I write; it ensures that I still have a sense of the place that I have come from which in turn influences the way that I head forwards. So is it that when I am writing I am trying to prove myself, to identify myself as the 'academic' who knows the rules of the language game (Wittgenstein, 2001) and who is able to play the game as proficiently and eloquently as the rest?

The line of inquiry that you have taken to investigate your writing style seems to be influenced, in part at least, by your professional counselling skills. You have the ability to excavate, to probe, to dig down, to try to find something that is, or has been, covered in some way. My friend Emma is also a counsellor and it is interesting that in the piece that I have quoted above she appears to be doing something similar in her thoughts about me. I have always had some kind of ambivalence about approaches of this kind. I *do* think of myself often in terms of things like my working class background, my status in the family as an only child. I *do* think of my mother's humility and love and my father's outer strength and inner softness and how these things have influenced me. However, I find myself being startled like a rabbit in the headlights when, in conversations of this kind, someone talks about the way in which these things can have an influence. I begin to reflect with excited, almost vain, curiosity: "I wonder what this will reveal. I wonder what this will tell me about myself."

I keep going back to that lovely phrase that you used in your earlier piece of writing and which I have already quoted (about how long it's taken to find your voice). Whatever has influenced my writing in the past I have to say that I am enjoying writing like this now, that it has opened me up. I want to write now. I am always trying to find time to do it, whereas before it felt much more of a chore. Writing like this is less of a struggle and more rewarding. Now that I am enjoying using this voice so much I hope that, like Billy Bibbitt in One Flew Over the Cuckoo's Nest (Kesey, 1962), I don't go back to stammering.

> We referred to 'stuttering' in Writing Space One, and here we talk about 'stammering'. Though they have different meanings in their psycholinguistic usage, Deleuze seems to use them interchangeably. We return to 'stammering' and 'stuttering' later in our writing, finding them a helpful metaphor to help articulate less, as here, how we individually struggle to say/write something, and more, in Deleuzian terms, as the struggles of language itself. See, for example, Alterity 2.

In support of stammering (Jonathan)

I smile, and feel sad, when you describe your family's quizzing about your chosen profession. There's the poignancy of a phrase you use: the functions where this happens are "usually funerals".

I also notice the thoughts that the stories of your life trigger for me. Do you always experience your family's comments as "benign" prejudice? Are there moments when you catch yourself wishing they wouldn't make that are-you-still-teaching inquiry? Maybe these questions are more about me and how difficult I find it to explain the work I do

Your takes on my stories get me thinking. I am left considering whether or not I experienced writing those stories as a "removal of covers". I'll try to explain:

The evening before last, at the end of the first warm spring day of the year, I stepped out of the back door to lock the garage. I was in my socks. As I turned to go back to the house I saw a small frog. I must have stepped over it without noticing. I realised the horror I would have experienced had I trodden on a frog. Your story of the snail came to mind. Last year, say, I would have been shocked but there was something else this time; something to do with an awareness of fragility, preciousness, responsibility. Now that I carry your writing with me there was fresh significance to realising that I had nearly killed a frog.

So I have thought about those "writing stories"–re. Hermione Lee et al.–at times over the years but undertaking this project with you means seeing them anew. It is not a removal of covers. I am viewing them from a different perspective. As narrative therapists would say, I am re-authoring them.

There is something else about Covers. You talk about having developed your style of writing to fit with being a "respectable academic". You say you have "made yourself up", that you are "always afraid that you are going to get caught". An image of your having to put yourself into a uniform in order to be acceptable–to mask yourself with make-up–comes to mind. You speak of enjoying the new voice that you have found but express the hope that you don't go back to stammering. It suggests vulnerability to me. My emotional response is to feel anxious. And protective.

It's stammering that has captured me. You gave me a chapter from Deleuze to read when we last met. Our conversation in this project is about writing style and Deleuze writes: "A style is managing to stammer in one's own language" (Deleuze and Parnet, 2002, p.4), which is, for him "constructing a line of flight" (ibid, p.4).

Style is like charm to him, and both are life-giving (ibid). So I am left wondering about whether it is possible to rehabilitate stammering. Whether, in fact, it is vital–in its truest sense–for the process of writing to involve stammering in order for us to be fluent, for us to find our direction. Charm is an interesting word to use; it often connotes pretence or phoniness, but it needn't. It can be authentic. Our charm need not be slick; the charm is in the stammering.

More than at any time that I can remember I feel as if I have stammered my way through this. I have to fight for words, writing without knowing what text is going to come out onto the screen, frequently going back and deleting, starting again. Even now I am not sure where I am going; I am struggling to hold onto my trust in the process of writing. If we were conducting this interview face to face I think that I would begin to speak, then pause, then try again and tell you that I wasn't sure what I needed to say. My throat would be sore; I would be losing my voice.

This is hurting me, this inability to write. My 'style' feels halting, difficult, stilted. I am in a fog, trudging through mud. My style is me: clumsy today, constructing my "line of flight" with leaden fingers and a heavy heart.

My brother Simon stammers. Less now than when we were growing up. He is the pastor of a church and when he preaches he never stammers, nor when he sings. He is a pianist and he has always sounded effortless.

He tells the story that when he was at boarding school, newly arrived aged thirteen, he was walking back to his boarding house from the sweet shop. The institution was an ancient independent school that saw itself as developing future leaders for the nation. (Most alumni end up as stockbrokers.) Authority was valued; teachers, if not revered, were certainly treated with respect.

Pupils and staff alike were in awe of the headmaster: a huge, barrel-chested, ageing warrior of a man: Oliver Van Oss, "Ovo". When he spoke at Chapel Ovo's *basso profundo* needed no amplification.

Simon needed to walk past the Headmaster's Residence to get back to his house. Thin, pale, fair haired, oversized school blazer, sleeves extending beyond his fingers, he was dreamily working his way through a packet of fruit gums (against school rules: indoors only). Ovo was weeding his garden, bent over the beds a short distance away. Deciding that a gardening headmaster might like some refreshment (and that generosity might disarm)), Simon called out:

"Mr Van Oss…Sir… w-w-w-w-w….."

Ovo levered himself into standing position and turned, as an oil tanker might, to face the source of the reedy voice. Simon peered upwards and tried again:

"Sir, w-w-w-w-….w-w-w-w-… w-w-w-would you like a fruit gum?"

Apparently, Ovo simply smiled, thanked him and said no, and Simon, unperturbed, continued his journey back to house. The scene was observed by some older boys and has become apocryphal: "a new boy once offered the Head–Ovo–a fruit gum and got away with it. Can you imagine?"

I love that scene, my brother stammering to Ovo. It makes me smile, brings him close.

Eloquence, confidence and certainty, seem, by contrast, to distance, to close down.

A story and a response (Ken)

A critical incident: day two of the latest doctoral unit (the day you weren't there), the whole thing buzzing, I'm really enjoying it. You know what I do, I get into the material, I want to contribute, ask questions, inquire, offer suggestions, disagree and so on. It's last hour of the session, I make a point about performance narrative and the engagement of the audience/interpreters in the 'performance' through a reference to Augusto Boal and Forum Theatre and his idea of the 'spect-actor', the active participant, as contrasted with the 'spectator', the passive observer (Boal, 1979). I think that it is relevant.

The moment I finish I catch the eye of one of the group. I glance at her, I don't know why, and I see her raised eyebrows in a brief look toward the person sitting next to her and I read it as: "Clever bastard, there he goes again". I catch those raised eyebrows and for a split second we share the briefest moment of eye contact.

Well you know all that stuff: did I _read_her gesture? I don't think that it was directed at me but to the person sitting next to her, or did I, have I, _read into_ it?

Here is a possibility:

I am insecure in the academy, so what do I do? I read and absorb all this stuff, theories, theorists, and then I use it: with my friends, with my students, with my doctoral student colleagues and in my writing. It informs my writing style. Like Emma said, I am using these other voices to say me. I am using their language to express me. I am insecure so I will use this language to identify myself.

I am trying to use what Deleuze calls, the "logic of sense" (Deleuze, 1990) as a way of trying to make me transparent. I hadn't thought of it in this way but by writing this I am trying. That simple expression today has evoked so much in me. I am relieved to have this connection with you: to be able to write it down. Bare text? Confessional narrative? Performance? I don't know! I haven't analysed myself like this before, I enjoy it, for itself, the cut and thrust, it feeds me. I enjoy the challenge that these inquiries set up but I am not at all sure where they are taking me. The ride is exciting: my knuckles are white.

Here is a coda:

A moment like a flying splinter of glass. The tiniest split second of eye contact preceded by the raising of eyebrows in a look towards a colleague. I had caught a flash, a flying spark, frozen in an instant. My angle of repose had helped this to crystallize within the briefest moment of space and time, where intense feelings, meaning and knowing all seemed to come together. Out of all the fragments and shards flying around in the heat of the conversational melee that incisive piece of shrapnel tore into me. The impact of the wounding was instantaneous, its effects prolonged. I said no more, I retreated within myself. I withdrew. In that moment I had made myself vulnerable. I had used that language. I had displayed an erudition. I had transgressed.

Some thoughts on "In support of stammering":

I felt a strong message coming through from you to me. The way you finished stirred me and got me thinking again. You painted such a lovely picture of your brother, deep in his reverie, happy and dreaming. Reading the simple language that you used to describe him evoked such warmth and good humour; I warmed to the image of him that you created. My Dad used to tell me of a soldier he knew during the war who had a stammer and a beautiful singing voice that never faltered. His mates would defend him if anyone 'took the piss' out of his impediment; they all liked him. At a conference at Plymouth last week a presenter used a form of highly articulate language, steeped in erudite academic references and delivered in a style that was learned, confident and full of assertion. The stifled yawns, the restless shufflings and the studied reading of the conference brochure of those in attendance all suggested to me that they didn't like him or what he was trying to do. There were no questions afterwards, no heated discussion; just a relieved procession out of the small room.

You say that you "stammered your way through" the last piece you sent to me, to paraphrase Deleuze, stammering in your own language. In many respects the passage where you talk about this is the most 'charming' part of what you have written to me. I don't really gain a sense of your struggle but I do know what you mean; and that emerging sense of finding a self through the process. I said at the end of "Covers", "writing like this is less of a struggle and more rewarding. Now that I am enjoying using this voice so much I hope that … I don't go back to stammering!" My struggle at the moment seems to be with the ways in which, differently, we are thinking, feeling and talking about stammering. On the one hand we have that lovely image of your brother; we smile and are drawn to his charm. On the other, I have a powerful memory of Billy Bibbitt, unable to deal with the realities of having to return to the world of institutionalised formality and repressed self.

I have in my head at least two notions of stammering. They seem to be incommensurate and ambiguous but I feel happy about that.

Reflections (Ken and Jonathan)

Each of us now stands back from our writing in this space. Our reflections remain part of the "co-constructing of our narrative" (Ellis and Berger, 2003, p171).

> When we originally wrote and published this chapter we framed these reflections in the third person ("Ken said x", "Jonathan put it like y"), facing outwards to address our audience. Here we have positioned ourselves in the second person, facing each other, since this is what we have become used to doing. We notice the heightened intimacy that this suggests.

Jonathan's reflections

I have been asking myself two sets of questions about our project, the first about how I have experienced it; the second concerns the nature of the process we have been involved in. I explore these questions together.

You have sent me A Story and a Response and I acknowledged it via email but have not responded to it fully. This takes me directly into one of the aspects of this project that I have experienced as surprisingly difficult: how challenging I have found it to do justice to what you have written to me.

I read your piece again last night. I was moved, engaged, affected by it–but this doesn't capture fully what I felt.

The picture of your putting himself on the line at the doctoral unit is vivid. My experience of you at these events is that I enjoy the way you engage with material so openly, and value how much you have read. I had not registered how much of a risk it is to speak, and therefore how much courage you demonstrate.

There is the risk you take too in the writing; you make yourself vulnerable again.

Mann and Stewart (2003) write about the issue of how to develop rapport when interviewing on-line. You and I know each other and have a face-to-face relationship, so we have established and maintain rapport through that contact; but the on-line aspect of our project has had an impact. Mann and Stewart talk about on-line interview participants ensuring that (as with any interview) trust is developed; they say that openness is key. They emphasise employing good interactive skills– reassurance, listening, and verbal expertise. I wonder whether this is where I've struggled. I can do these face to face, where how I respond verbally is backed up by non-verbal signals (Mills, 2001), but not via email.

As I wrote in Being Possessed, Michael White's description of the role of the outsider witness within *definitional ceremony*[3] (White, 1995 and 2000; see Myerhoff, 1982) seems closest to how we have worked on this project. We have responded to each other with images and stories, "practices of acknowledgement" rather than "practices of applause" (White, 2000, p.9). However, in definitional ceremony, the outsider witness is present and therefore the narrator can see how s/he responds, hear the tone of voice, notice the look on their faces. In the first interview stage of the process (White, 1995) the narrator is talking to an interviewer, who does not carry out the outsider witness role but is there only to support the person. For us, the two roles have been conflated both because we are carrying this out on-line and because we are co-researching. We have been both interviewer and outsider witness.

There is a second issue that straddles both sets of questions that I began with. I have been interested in what we haven't talked about or have only glanced at. I referred to my writing style being related to my identity: as a teacher, as a man, as a counsellor. We (I) have not explored these. However, we have alluded to our class differences. You have referred to your working class roots; I have told the story of my brother's public school. What I didn't say is that I followed my brother there.

---

[3] A term coined by Myerhoff and adapted by White within the context of narrative therapy practice to describe a structured process whereby people reflect upon their lives in the company of others ("outsider witnesses").

Where would writing further about the influence of class take us? What would it mean to us? I wasn't conscious of avoiding this, but it is an area of "unevenness" (Gunbaratnam, 2003) between us.

> 'Class' remains an area that we have not yet explored.

White (2000) notes the cathartic possibilities of interviewing and Speedy (2004) the therapeutic potential of co-research. Myerhoff (1982) draws attention to the opportunity that 'performance' offers for attaining self-definition; Jarvinen (2000) suggests that autobiographical processes can be life-creating. So a question that I am left with is: in what ways has our process been cathartic, therapeutic, self-defining or life-creating?

I had not registered before how much the process of writing, and the way in which I write, meant to me. Making that explicit to you has been significant.

You have taken me into areas that I did not expect–for example, the thinking about stammering and the various possibilities of what that means, and the metaphor of the snail. How profound that image is: the snail and the shell, the shell is the snail, the writing is the self.

We have a "negotiated accomplishment" (Fontana and Frey, 2000, p663). It has become something more than the words we exchanged. Our writing has had a life of its own; it is the "inter" (Hillman, 1984, p8) of our interview that matters. As Deleuze, wrote about his work with Guattari:

> "(W)hat was important for us was less our working together than this strange fact of working between the two of us. We stopped being 'author'."
> (Deleuze and Parnet, 2002, p17)

A different take on this element of our work leads me to Bakhtin's idea of the dialogic, as opposed to monologic, force (Bakhtin, 1981): narrators and readers being constituted by their discursive consciousness, different voices sharing–and sometimes competing–over different ways of speaking. Our collaboration contributes to a discourse of resistance (Foucault, 2002) against the prevailing formalism and abstract objectivism of systems of language that are grounded upon neutrality, single meaning and logic. You have invited me into your world. I have images of your house, garden, office, colleague, family; and I also have glimpses of you, what matters, how you frame the world, how you think and feel. These images–and your willingness to show your vulnerability in your writing– open up possibilities for me, new spaces of communication.

Ken's Reflections

Rogers et al. (1999) talk of "languages of the unsayable" and this has relevance in relation to what you observe in your reflections about what we haven't talked about, the negative spaces. You refer to the "unexplored" areas of identity. I think of age and gender and the great differences in our life experiences.

I am fascinated by what has been said and why. I have found myself writing in a way that has surprised me. I have felt something being released. I have found that through writing collaboratively I am expressing myself in different, unexpected ways. This feels like the muddy waters Speedy (2004) refers to between so-called research and so-called therapy. It is a blurring of genres that seems to "allow the unsayable to speak" (Budick and Eiser, 1987, p.xii). Perhaps, more significantly, through these processes of 're-authoring' and co-respondence, we have, as White suggests, "provide(d) conditions under which it becomes possible for people to step into the near future of the landscapes of action of their lives" (White, 2002, section 4, point 7). Working within these "zones of proximal development" (Vygotsky, 1962) seems to have provided a scaffolding which has encouraged the writing and constructions of the self to grow.

Laurel Richardson describes how producing her poem 'Louisa May' led to her "suppressed 'poet'" and the "overactive 'sociologist'" discovering each other, integrating (Richardson, 1997a, p.152). You and I have developed this, perhaps: whilst her *intra*-actions allowed for integration, our written *inter*-actions also have taken us into shared territory; into communion, as Richardson might say (Richardson, 2001, p.37).

You talk in your reflections of the way in which we appear, though not consciously, to have adapted White's description of the roles of the 'narrator', the 'interviewer' and the 'outsider witness'. You talks of a conflation and I feel comfortable with this. I love working with ideas, things that appear different and fresh: the opportunity to take chances and try something new for me offers exciting research possibilities but also a kind of therapeutic potential. Your role in this has been so significant and I doubt whether I would have used these "languages of the unsayable" (sic.). I have come to trust you. You not only write yourself, but also write to me, about me. Your writing has allowed me to begin to say the unsayable and to write in ways that have surprised me. In response to you I have begun to find a different voice.

And I mean this in not only the therapeutic but also the political sense. I think again of stammering: our writing together, as you say, has its own dynamic, *signifiers*–like 'stammering'–leading us in an endless play as our reflexive engagements place meanings *sous rature* (Derrida, 1978). We begin to nurture an alertness, immanently enriching our positions within each moment of communication; a kind of empowerment I think. Writing together has political energy.

Epilogue: May 3rd, 2005, eleven hours later, approaching Urbana-Champaign, Illinois

The plane on our brief connecting flight is narrow and insubstantial, every encounter with turbulence an argument it feels likely to lose. The journey has given us hours to continue our dialogue. Now we sit in silence, eyes closed, willing this tin cylinder to remain aloft.

Ken's paper at the conference will discuss the impact of policy upon teachers; Jonathan's, the experience of loss. We have discussed how we might have written differently had we produced them now. Maybe both our voices would have been more vulnerable.

Next year, perhaps, we will present a paper here together.

And take the train from Chicago.

> We did present a paper together the next year, and have done so each year since. We still haven't made the train journey, but haven't endured the flight again either. We drive.

WRITING SPACE SEVEN

WRITING THE INCALCULABLE[1]

In this between-the-two we continue to follow our inquiry into writing, developing it in the following two directions:

In Inquiring into Writing we tentatively saw our project extending Laurel Richardson's (1997a) conception of writing as an internal process of integration; our interactive writing process, we suggested, took us into collective terrain. Here, we seek to disturb the internal/interactive, inner/outer binary: we investigate the dynamics not only between and within Ken and Jonathan as whole 'subjects', but also those *between* our respective multiple, transient selves. We want to trouble the notion of autonomous subjectivity. We explore through nomadic inquiry (St Pierre, 1997; Braidotti, 1994) how writing is not only affected by the contact between us as 'individuals' and not only through reflection upon our 'selves', but also by the way in which our 'selves' are in relation to 'other'.

Secondly, and related, we explore writing and reading–every time we read we write (Bauman, 1991; Gonick and Hladki, 2005)–as *performance*. As we write for each other, and as we read each other's work, we are involved in constructing our inconstant selves (Crapanzano, 1992; Gonick and Hladki, 2005), our "historically and locally specific" subjectivities (Richardson and St Pierre, 2005, p.961). We become attuned to there being no essential Ken or Jonathan, only our agency within a social and cultural milieu (Denzin, 2003). However fragmented, we are also acutely conscious of the energy that these 'performances' give us, even when the process is difficult. Our acts of writing are an "affirmation and exploration of subjectivity, however problematic, endangered or uncertain it may be" (Davis, 2004, p.132).

---

[1] A version of this writing space was first published in the journal *Qualitative Inquiry* (Gale and Wyatt, 2007)

Stigma: 1 October 2005 (Jonathan)

I have to write this story. To you. For others to read too. I hope that it will help me.

I say "I have to write this story". There is me (subject) and "this story" (object). And I will write it to you, for you. But I do not know what I will write. At this moment I am conscious of *multiplicities* (Deleuze and Guattari, 2004b): this could go anywhere. I think I have a picture. Of myself, my counselling client[2] and what happened last Wednesday. But maybe the story will write me.

I have questions: until I write it–until I *perform* this story–does that mean that it didn't happen? In the sense that there are myriad versions, not just one story, this must be so. My clinical notes were sketchy but they have already performed one story of what took place. I have other stories, as yet unarticulated. At home I spoke about what a shit day I had had. I could not say more. It would not have been ethical, for a start. But I'm not sure that I wanted to; I needed to keep it, keep the her-and-me inside me, within.

> This is the first point at which we consider explicitly the ethical issues involved in our collaborative writing. The ethics of writing about others – and of how we are with each other – becomes a matter of discussion, contention and challenge at later points in our between-the-twos. See Therapy and Alterity 3.

Ethics. I have regular supervision but I will not see my supervisor until next week. Does protecting a client's confidentiality mean that the client-in-my-mind, the me-in-my-mind and the client/me-relationship-in-my-mind (to misappropriate Armstrong, 2004), does keeping these to myself mean they stay shadowy? I think so. I feel so; in my body, I feel so. So I am writing this now in order that these might take form.

To make me feel better.

And which self am I going to perform here? At this moment do I have a choice which self to show you? Or will the writing take charge?

Here's the story (I say, as if I have prepared it earlier which, by the time you read this, will be partially true):

---

[2] Jonathan is employed by the UK's National Health Service one day a week as a counsellor of adults in a medical centre.

My final client. It has been a long, long day. I'd booked additional appointments, both first thing this morning and during my break, so I am tired. She is the eighth person I've seen. I thought I was fine–I've been home and slept for half an hour–but I'm not.

Janice is in her early sixties, a small, neat, educated, articulate, white woman, a mother and grandmother. She's come to see me because of her relationship with her daughter in law, Louise. (Janice has three children and this is the partner of her son, Adam, the eldest.) The relationship with Louise is causing her agony.

Adam, Louise and three small children live abroad, a long-haul flight away, and they are staying with Janice and her husband for a month. I first saw Janice at the beginning of August, before the family arrived for their visit. She wanted help to prepare herself. They return home in two weeks' time. Today is our fifth session, next week our last.

As always, she brings me Louise, the daughter-in-law in her mind. Louise's behaviour is, if I believe the stories Janice has told me, outrageous. To give you examples: staying in Janice's house she spends long spells on the telephone without consulting Janice. She invites her friends to stay (without consulting Janice). She tells Janice that she and Adam are going up to London overnight and that Janice is looking after the children. In these stories Janice experiences Louise as being rude, as treating her as the unpaid help. More destructive for Janice is that Louise can also behave deviously and manipulatively. She will lie over the pettiest things, she will patronise Janice's intelligence, she will–and this is devastating to Janice–treat Adam shabbily.

The greatest source of pain to Janice is that she sees no way out. She loves her son and adores her grandchildren, but contact with her daughter-in-law (even over the telephone) leaves her clawing the scree above depression's abyss. Janice's experience of how Louise treats her has powerful echoes of how she was treated as a child and she feels unable to protect herself, much as she did then.

It is coming towards the end of the session. She breaks down saying that this situation with her family can't continue; she can't cope. She faces Sophie's choice: her son (and grandchildren) or her inner, vulnerable self. She can't protect herself while she continues to have contact with her daughter-in-law; she has lost two of the last six years to depression, each time sparked by this relationship.

(As you read it will be as if I am relating it to you without interruption. But I have frequently had to leave writing this.

In order to get some distance from it.

In order to leave 'her' and her-and-me.

Maybe even to get away from the telling of it to you. Away from the you-and-me-ness of this writing.)

She is distraught. I wonder how this will end, how I can end. I have watched her gradually edge towards despair. I have felt unable to help. So, now, with barely five minutes left, and allowing my frustration to take charge, I give her advice disguised as a gently confronting question:

"What does Adam know of how you feel? You seem to be carrying all of this on your own, but it seems to me that he shares some responsibility here."

I know the answer. She knows I know but she tells me anyway: he is aware of only some of this. She protects him; she does not want him to have to take sides.

Anger with me is layered into her despair.

It is time. I say that we have to draw to a close. We have one more session. Shall I see you then, I ask? I thought we had two, replies Janice. No, just the one. Well, will you be able to help me?

I'm sitting forward, towards the edge of my chair, about to stand. I don't know what to say. I know that I can't help, not in the way she means. I can't change her situation and I haven't been able to help alter how she experiences it. Nor will I be able to next week.

I say, quietly, looking directly at her:

"I don't know how to answer that. I shall be here to support you, to help you think about what is going on."

"And we have to finish next week?"

"Yes."

"Do you see people privately?"

"I wouldn't be able to see you. I'm not allowed to. If I've seen you here I can't then see you privately."

"Why's that? What about me, the client? That seems stupid. If you're helping someone."

"I would risk being accused of feathering my own nest."

"That makes me so angry. I can't believe the way they make up these stupid rules. Does that mean never? You can never see someone after you've seen them here? What if I contacted you in a few weeks' time?"

"No, I still won't be able to."

"Well, it's just ridiculous."

And it's now over ten minutes past the end and I feel that I have lost my way. I am no longer containing her. She stands and so do I and we walk towards the door. I ask "So, am I seeing you next week?". "Yes please", she replies.

I sit and write a few notes and, well, you know the rest.

All writing, Cixous (2005) suggests, aims to "flee the fatal nail...that threatens to immobilise" (xii). It is an endeavour "to find a form to accommodate the mess" (Beckett, in Driver, 1961). I am seeking to find where the words and sentences will lead me, to see if they will take me towards "revelation" (Cixous, 2005, p.xii). I am cultivating the stigma.

I feel that I have performed a self to you that is despondent, puzzled, guilty, maybe ashamed. I am not the counsellor (today) I thought I was. I should have handled it differently. I know this. But none of this is irreparable, I tell myself. Her despair is not of my making. I know this. But I do not believe it.

I have written in order to work at the stigma, the wound, and to move on from it. To make sense of it, to not let it 'nail' me; or maybe to let it do so but not allow it to lead to a kind of death (Cixous, 2005). By writing it and, specifically, by writing it to/for you I am looking for the "promise of the text" (xiv) in its broadening of the struggle (Coles, 1989); offering you the text as a searching for space where something different might occur (St Pierre, 2004). The giving of it to you, when I click 'send' on the email, I am looking forward to that; not because I will find rescue but because this writing will lead us somewhere.

Somewhere we do not yet know.

Somewhere *incalculable* (Cixous, 2005, p.xii).

> Jonathan began "Stigma" on 1 October 2005 (a Saturday) and sent it to Ken on the morning of Monday 3 October. That afternoon Ken acknowledged it. Went to work, slept, went to work. Lived our lives. Thinking. Ken writing, Jonathan waiting. Ken sent his response – "It" – later the next day, Tuesday 4th. "It" follows this box. At other points in our dialogue there are longer silences; weeks, sometimes, with Jonathan especially. Here, on the page, there are no intervals except spaces between our texts. Historical time. Narrative time. (Freeman, 1998). At another point, in other writing, we will explore the spaces on the page. Our silences.

It? 4th October 2005 (Ken)

Writing in response to Stigma has set me off in all kinds of directions, lines of flight cutting through traditional structures of explanation and representation. The hesitations that inhabit the opening paragraphs are disrupting established ways of looking and doing; already by being 'you' on the page you are disrupting the pre-conceptions, opening up new ways of being: these are becomings. I don't want to look for points, only lines (Deleuze, 1993). Jonathan as counsellor, as writer, as Ken's friend and many other things are brought sharply into focus as you que(e)ry established ways of thinking and talking about your self and what you do. Your first sentence leaks structure. 'I have to write this story', seems to be you wanting to/having to do this for yourself; it feels like a mission, a quest, a compulsion. The next two sentences offer a new stratum, a public one, including me and perhaps others. And then, the last sentence moves from the private/public axis to the world of help, of therapy; the performance of the writing will, in some way, you hope, help you. I don't know how much of this you intended, or how much I have read into what you have written in those first four sentences, but so much of what is here seems to intersect and disturb the traditional, overtly expressed intentionalities of writing.

In the next paragraph you are up front with that subject/object dichotomy. You want/have to write this story because it happened, because it troubled you, because it is there, but, as you acknowledge, the telling of this story 'could go anywhere'. You have been subjected to (Foucault might say, disciplined) by this story; as an 'event' it has affected you, it has made you want to tell the family you had a "shit day", it has made you want to write (to me) about it: it has energised you. But what you say at the beginning of the third paragraph is exciting: "I have questions: until I write it–until I *perform* (your italics) this story–does that mean that it didn't happen?" In one sense we have to say, "Come on Jonathan, of course, *it* happened!" but in another sense we have to say that *it* has an absence of presence, *it* has slipped into the multiplicity of signifiers, that alluring attempt to trap *it*, on the one hand, but delight in articulating and metamorphosing *it*, on the other.

I want to explore here two things. First, Heidegger (1962) and *dasein*, of being-in-the-world, where our existence is not something lasting but something that is recognisable in this moment in the now with certain things 'ready-to-hand'. As we surge up in the world we have these 'encounters' with it and consciousness somehow 'tells' us about it. This is looking at it through a phenomenological lens. Second, Deleuze and becoming, of assemblage of haecceity, of "5 o'clock is this animal" (Deleuze and Guattari, 2004b, p.263) and later with Virginia Woolf, perhaps with direct reference to you and Janice: 'Taking a walk is haecceity; never again will Mrs. Dalloway say to herself, 'I am this, I am that, he is this, he is that … Haecceity, fog, glare.' (ibid) Your writing already acknowledges that you are with this, illustrated by your abstraction that 'there are myriad versions' but it is almost as if you are still hanging on to a grasp of the *reality* of the exchange between you and Janice. 'My clinical notes were sketchy ... I needed to keep it, to keep her, keep the her-and-me inside me, within'. Atkinson (1990) talks about ethnographers 'writing down' their field notes, in the moment, at the point of contact, so to speak, and then 'writing up' these notes in a form to pass on to others. I don't think that he attends to the potentialities of fabrication or performance; it feels to me that you do, you have said so, but something–something visceral, honest, spiritual–seems to want to capture that moment, that *'it'*. If *it* wasn't *there* you would be less concerned about Janice, about what to do next[3].

It seems that in your paragraph starting "Ethics", *it* continues to dog you. It has forms, first as the 'shadowy' entities 'within' you and then as the forms that will be created (or revealed) as you write. Bringing these forms into the public domain and giving them another form is attractive: your writing in this paragraph suggests that this will be a kind of therapy; you seem to hope so. If you don't tell someone, or write about *it*, you seem to suggest that some kind of repression will take place: the "me-in-my-mind", the "client/me-relationship-in-my-mind" will be bottled up, the genie will never escape the confines of the lamp. I am not sure if I have 'read' you and your writing in a way that you would read it or if I have read something that you didn't intend to convey. I am sure, however, about what you say in different places through the first page of your writing: maybe "the story will write me" (Para. 2) "until I *perform* this story" (Para. 3) "will the writing take charge?" (Para. 6).

So, it feels to me that this writing of yours (all writing) is a performance, an event which I feel I have taken part in and, in part, constituted. I have talked with you here about *it*; it feels to me that what needed to be talked about was where *it* was situated. I am not sure which 'self' you feel that you have performed here. I feel that I have a 'self', a Jonathan, which has performed here but of course that 'self', that 'Jonathan', is part of my performance as the reader of your writing. Despite what you might have intended I have 'seen' the performance in my way. You have written it for me: you might write it differently for others and at another time for yourself; whatever you have done and continue to do, it will be part of a becoming. The dissecting lines that each telling and re-telling sets up will serve to re-configure preconceptions, established interpretations and practices. I think, for example, that though your experiences will not necessarily encourage you to resist hegemonies of counselling practice or to explicitly offer counter discourses you will,

---

[3] We return to, and say more about, haecceity on pages 91-93

nevertheless, practise differently in the future. The line of flight that this case has taken you on seems to have revealed (rhizomatic) complexities that will have folded in thoughts and feelings and encouraged different ones to unfold.

As a footnote to this, I read Stigma last night and made some notes about it. In a way that writing was another performance, in addition to this one, so I am going to send it off in the post to you. Another layer, perhaps.

No it today: 10th October 2005 (Jonathan)

There is no *it* today.
No impulse to write about an *it*.
There is only a compulsion to write.

I need to qualify that: there is a compulsion to write *to you*. It's true what you say: the writing would be different if it were not for you, for us, for this shared enterprise. My writing is not only part of your performance when you read it but also as I write now; you contribute to my performance at this moment, on an overcast autumn Saturday with the scent of cut ivy on my hands.

If you were not going to read this I would not write. It is the Ken-in-my-mind that I am writing for now.

(At this point in the text I began to tell you about my final session with Janice, how she was and how I was; and how I talked about her with my supervisor beforehand. I wrote a few lines but realised that I was merely filling space on the screen. I am surprised. I thought that I was interested. I began to write in her voice, imagining the story of the session from her point view.

So now there is the absence of her presence and the absence of that text's presence. Though I have deleted the text from the (virtual) page I know that she was there and still is.

I used her last week and have thrown her away today as if she no longer serves my purpose. It worried me last week that it might be unethical to write about her and today I worry that it is unethical for me not to write about her.)

Writing is physical. It's physical of course in the feeling of fingers on keyboard and eyes on screen. (Cixous says that she always writes with pen and ink–"the text needs the paper" (Cixous, 2005, p198)). It is physical too in where it comes from. Janice was in my head earlier today but as I wrote she seemed to go no further. She was only in my head. I did not *feel* her. Last week I felt her inside me, in my stomach, in my chest, in my lungs and throat. Writing as vomit; writing as sputum (see Lee, 2005).

Writing is physical. Text on paper. You sent me your hand written annotations on Stigma. Single words, sentences, phrases, question marks, underlinings, arrows and a long message at the end. All in ink. Your marks on my typescript. Marks that top and tail, enough to provide a frame all around the first page and which leave my text less crowded (less loved?) as the pages progress. I realise how little I know your handwriting. Your handwriting is you, differently to the typed, Arial 11 *"It"*. More raw, immediate; less crafted. More intimate. In the annotations you seek to capture the moment, to use words as witnesses to the instant (Cixous, 2005). You say:

> "Tomorrow, my writing will be more reasoned, more structured, more thought through perhaps."

Tomorrow you will retreat, I infer.

And, in that paragraph at the end, on the back of the paper, you hint at the resonances for you in Janice's story, resonances left out of *It*. The annotations are private. You allow yourself more vulnerability there, it seems.

Here, now, in typing this I have made your hand written comments public. The personal outed by type. I nudge you towards a wider audience. I want to detain your words, for others as well as ourselves, but in so doing am I transgressing a privacy code hidden in hand written annotations?

This piece is (not) entitled: Tomorrow you will retreat, I infer: 13th October 2005 (Ken)

I was going to give whatever this turns out to be the title Tomorrow You Will Retreat, I Infer; it resonated with me, it caught me off guard and I feel really good that you have had that effect on me. I am sat at these keys, at my desk, at my window, facing the still, pallid greyness of autumn sunshine. This is some of the physicality of my writing to you. It doesn't touch the acrid, visceral intensity of the physical I felt in Stigma. I knew when I read your piece that you had to write: it was with you, tormenting, you were looking for some release, some help, some explanation. When you write about feeling Janice inside you, you make literal the feelings that were seeping out of you and into your writing, staining the page, allowing the effects to make their mark.

I am aware of something Deleuze said about Guattari:

"Always the same Felix, yet one whose proper name denoted something
which was happening, not a subject." (Deleuze and Parnet, 2002, p.16)

I am aware of the becomings that our writings are. I am aware of the
performances and the silences. In a strong physical sense I felt you writing
this weekend. I was aware that you were rehearsing something that would
become your performance. Later, I pored over the electronic page and,
sitting in the garden, read the print-out, each time different effects
(per)forming me, moulding my feelings and responses to you in
unplanned and idiosyncratic ways. I am aware of the silences that will be
returned to you; silences created by my focus upon one thing you say and
not another, silences because of my 'retreats' into 'inner' worlds. I am
aware of the things that might be left out: I want to touch it all. Each
exchange seems to have its own liminality, a welling space of ideas,
feelings and touch, seemingly ready to erupt in any direction, according to
where fissures might be or where potential flows might offer passages to
interpretation or discovery. Stigma was so full of Janice, of your concerns
about her as a 'case' and I felt a little troubled after I had sent 'It' off to
you that I had not responded in relation to her. I allowed her to be absent
from my writing, I was sucked into the you that was writing about her.
And today in No It Today you touch that feeling of mine by the powerful
emotions that you express when you say:

> "I used her last week and have thrown her away today as if she no longer
> serves my purpose. It worried me last week that it might be unethical to
> write about her and today I worry that it is unethical for me not to write
> about her." [4]

This seems grounded upon the stratum of your counselling practice, a
part of you, a 'you' perhaps. I read you in the passage above feeling sad,
guilty, but ultimately having to let go because the line of flight has cut
across that stratum. The feeling that you evoke in me is close to feelings
when an intimate relationship has ended and I am moving from intimacy
with one person to another. There is no turning back here. The first
relationship does not end but it will never be the same again, the talk
about it will be from another a place, from a new distance. Becoming.
So, I am going to retreat am I!?
It is not bodies of approval and expectation of academic rigour that are
threatening this writing. It is, as before, giving a voice to the unsayable

---

[4] Jonathan's ethical position as a counsellor later becomes a matter of heated
discussion—see Therapy, pp.171-179

that is hard. You say, "The annotations are private. You allow yourself more vulnerability there, it seems." I am happy that you have "outed" my hand-written annotations because it is making me struggle with what I am writing here, making me think hard, confronting me.

I am not sure where this is taking me. I am not in retreat but I am finding it difficult to move. I have a sense of a self that is troubling. I suppose that it is a sense of a self that might be touched by the words of a friend, a mentor, a counsellor. It is a sense of self that appears to be deep, hidden, private, scary. The rhizomatic interconnections that are constitutive of and are positioning me, specifically in relation to my writing to you, seem to be infected by this troubling sense of self. You talked about the physicality of writing towards the end of your last piece and the infection that I feel here seems to be a dis-ease.

So. No retreat; instead, a hesitant and worried step in this messy and multiplying zone of indeterminacy. At this stage I can only think of making this step through the use of a poem. Ostensibly and passionately it is about my son, Reuben, but also I hope it evokes something of what I am struggling to begin to talk about here. I hope that this connects.

Conundrum of Self

The passion of Father,
of talking, head close,
in deep intimate
gestures.
Sweeping aside
all graft of everyday,
immersing in the deep pool
of his game,
his question,
his quick loving glance.

The swirling undercurrent
that rips and pulls you away from this;
that sand swirling tow
that brings you the reality of swell,
taking you from the
bright iridescence
of sharing his childhood,
that playful knowing of now,
that deep immediate

grasp of love
(inspecting a cockle shell,
extended, overhanging;
the pool full of shrimps,
wet knees, belly down
peering into the deep crevice
to see the edible crab –
"There Dad, there it is!")

But there in the distance,
like a spectre
is that figure
whose sapping energy draws me,
an artist creating form,
dashing aside all other
perceptions
I am cast,
like a sculpture?
like a pebble in the sea?
Your force
creates this turbulence,
this massive tide,
this ripping of stability,
tearing at the fabrics,
shredded and so easily dissolved –
Your blood, your passion,
your life juices permeate
everything.

I am immersed,
in this pool of love
bathing in happy sunlit preoccupations -
my son,
my blood too, involves me
determines that intense,
happy examination
of a washed up
fishing net.

But you are there,
bobbing me like a cork.

I have no resistance,
powerless in these swells,
dashed on these
barnacled rocks,
unable to gain a hold,
a footing,
washing me up,
down,
across these surfaces;
my knees bleed
in the water, like a flood.
It is immaterial as I search
for a grip on reality,
tossed in this current
I want to hold,
to feel warmth,
security,
replenishment.
To be away from cold rocks,
mysterious eddies
and tortuous currents;
I turn from those
damp, mean, windy,
cloudy finalities,
those ends with
no sunshine,
no hot rocks toasting my feet.
I want to talk with him
and not feel the current.
I want to share his place
with no thought or concern
for pasts or futures,
to share his now,
to feel it as mine.

A tortuous current: 23rd October 2005 (Jonathan)

You sent me This Piece Is (Not) Entitled: Tomorrow You Will Retreat, I Infer (to be referred to, from hereon in, as TPNETYWRI, which is so much snappier don't you think?) one Thursday.

That afternoon, and in a hurry, I printed TPN (for short) at work and read it for the first time whilst waiting for a bus and again later that evening at home. I struggled to engage. TPN went with me to London next day (Friday), on the bus to Marble Arch, for a walk across Hyde Park to Imperial College and up to the top floor of the Electrical Engineering building.

I've said that I was not engaged. On the Thursday I had read TPN physically but emotionally I had kept it at bay. I did not have the space. On the Friday, too, I had this sense of TPN being 'outside' me. The paper (stapled at the top left hand corner) in my bag until the bus journey home, its meaning and impact carried on my shoulder as I walked past the early morning roller skaters and joggers by the Serpentine. Your writing was not yet inside me. Reading (and not reading) is physical.

I have felt compelled to write the previous two pieces of our this between-the-two. This time the laptop remained unopened for days. I was not able to get near it, not even into the room where I write.

I don't know why I have kept it, kept its associations and resonances–kept you–at such a distance. Why still, even now as I am writing in response to it, I have to look at your writing to remind myself. TPN is still outside, a stranger to me.

Your poem. You and Reuben. You and the problems you are experiencing in your relationship. I am on the beach, feeling the intensity of your love for Reuben, can see his face close to yours, excited by discovery, warmed by your company, your interest in him. And I feel you catch yourself, maybe suddenly aware of your pain (or maybe it's simply always there) as you remember the troubles in your life, troubles that seem to threaten this joy you have with your son.

I am finding this difficult. It's like once before, in the previous writing space, when I felt I was 'stammering'. Writing can sometimes be an outpouring, almost uncontrollable, a "gesture of longing compelled to give voice" (Lee, 2005, p.935). At others, as now, it is more like trying to deal with a blockage in my lungs or in my gut. It requires surgery but my attempt to excise it is clumsy, primitive. I am digging around, trying to locate the clot. But I feel I am f(l)ailing. Words are not coming to mind. I do not know the words so I cannot know the feelings. "I'm on the verge of giving up: I can't, I can't" (Cixous, 2004, p.121).

Or perhaps it is simply emptiness. There is no blockage, only my thin voice echoing across a barren landscape. Nothing. I become in touch with terror. I look inside, expecting to find hope, and find only void. "To be lost and ponder words is pure heaven" (Lee, 2005, p.938)? Not for me, not today.

Writing is spiritual.

At this moment I feel as if I cannot go where you are leading. You have taken us into territory that we have only talked around, in snaps of conversation, in emails here and there. I feel I am resisting. You have taken us over an edge and my writing self is struggling to follow, unwilling to leap after you. What can I say? What can possibly be an adequate response to you?

"Tomorrow you will retreat", I said.

But you didn't.

Instead, it's me. I'm retreating.

But I can't leave it like this. What would that say to you? In this dialogue you have taken a risk and, as it stands, I am not up to responding. If I left it like this where would it leave us?

All I can do is trust the writing, follow where it leads…

I had a dream some days ago:

I am in a dull, bleak urban setting. It's late at night and there are few people around. Empty office blocks, closed shops, a deserted garage forecourt. I walk past and between them. I'm wary, unfamiliar with this place, but when I look around I am surprised; it seems quiet, safe. There are no observable dangers.

I'm making my way somewhere, home maybe, and as I walk along the pavement I am suddenly aware that the night has become impenetrable, opaque. I can't make out even my hands stretched in front of me as I walk, feeling my way forward. I sense rather than hear someone walking towards me and I feel I should be afraid but as they pass me I brush against them and I realise that it is a woman pushing a child in a buggy. She pays me no attention and is not perturbed, despite the hour and the darkness, and walks on. To my surprise I remain feeling safe.

I pass side streets and parked cars. The blackness lifts. I'm still trying to find my way somewhere. I feel purposeful. I cut through a car park to my left, around sleeping houses and workplaces. There's a play area with fallen trees to climb over, chains to hold onto, ropes to clamber up. It stretches up the side of a hill, at the top of which are houses and streetlights. Activity. Life. There are other people in the play area, sitting, standing, talking. I ignore them and begin to tackle the obstacles, gradually gaining height. My optimism strengthens.

Telling you this dream, working with this dream data (St Pierre, 1997), leads me not towards any glib search for its 'meaning' but towards connections, towards the multiplicities into which "its own are inserted and metamorphosed" (Deleuze and Guattari, 2004b, p.4).

Towards your poem, to the beach, to you crouched and engaged with Reuben. To the power of the "spectre", and how profoundly it disturbs you, its violence ("ripping", "tearing", "dashing", "shredded", "my knees bleed"). To your longing to be free of it. Back to the ominous darkness present in the scene you describe.

Towards Janice, whose joy in her relationships with her son and grandchildren, whose sense of herself as a whole person, is threatened by the destructive power of her experience of her daughter-in-law. The abyss I mentioned in Stigma into which she feels she is soon to fall has no trees at its base to climb over, chains to hold onto, or ropes to clamber up.

The dream takes me to Joe, over whose small sleeping form I cried, many years ago now, after a day in which Tessa and I had argued, as we often did, over how to handle him. I had felt wrenched between two people I loved.

The dream leads me back to writing: how all we can do is press ahead, through the darkness, in the belief that we will discover (Cixous, 2004). And it does seem very dark, sometimes, doesn't it?

Connections, multiplicities and difference: 10th November 2005 (Ken)

Our writing about selves does not come easily. We seem to have led each other into apparently multi-dimensional mazes of becoming whose structures and strata have become incised, making for further complexity and connectivity. We began with our selves: Ken and Jonathan. The constitutive signs of these identifiers soon crumbled as we came to write and to 'know' each other. Our multiple selves became apparent and manifest. At first 'Jonathan the counsellor' or 'Ken the father' seemed to offer tangible signifiers, transcending time and place, giving comfort to troubled souls and offering continuity and a unified sense of self. As we began to write these sedimented forms, characterised in terms of gender, class and age, became disturbed, sending up clouds that drew us in to further inquiry. We became aware that 'selves' perform and in so doing create new forms of self. This enticing complexity suggested to us a nomadic, rhizomatic mode of inquiry already pursued by others (St.Pierre, 1997, 2000; Tamboukou and Ball, 2002).

Even as I write this I am becoming aware of my self talking through the use of an embracing 'we'. I am not sure that you see things in this way. However, what this writing seems to have facilitated is a willingness, for both of us, to write, to acknowledge Richardson's (2000) inducement to write as a method of inquiry; and to accept and to enjoy the often uncertain, incommensurate and ambiguous nature of this form of inquiry. Writing in this way has enabled me to experience sharing Lyotard's "incredulity toward metanarratives" (1984, p.xxiv). I had always understood the rhetoric of this phrase and its power to challenge modernist forms of thinking but this writing has enabled me, for the first time, to gain from the disbelief that I had learned from and always shared with Lyotard. You have expressed a concern here about leaving 'Janice': "I used her last week and have thrown her away today as if she no longer serves my purpose." It is as if you feel you have acted in an unethical way, as if Janice is only a pawn in our game. I do not share this feeling. Our shared concern for Janice should not require us to essentialise her in some Kantian noumenal form. The "field of play" (Richardson, 1997) that our writing of Janice opens up allows us to see her not in a singular way as some kind of immutable presence but rather as a multiplicity connected to other beings and forms. I find myself connecting my thoughts about 'her' to other ways of thinking. As Rajchman says, "the abstract doesn't explain; it must itself be explained by re-insertion into a multiplicity." (2000, p.53). My thinking about Janice does not exist within a logic of transcendence but within a "logic of sense" (Deleuze, 2004). I make sense of her by connecting with her, plugging her into the multiplicities that I have access to; that I am connected to. In this profoundly ontological way we will make different sense of 'Janice'. This is what is so exciting yet so tantalising about this writing; we write to fill the spaces between us and yet sense that we never will. It is the play that we make of the words, the seriousness with which we play with these words that makes 'Janice' so important.

The terrain is both uncertain and always challenging. A Deleuzian conceptualisation might suggest dual reference to an extensive world of structure and form, on the one hand, and a more complex and intangible world of intensity on the other. However, the potential for the writing to create new spaces and new liminalities through recognising its performative character and potential renders such dualist forms of thought redundant.

Historically, it can be seen that knowledge and meaning has become established in layer upon layer of fossilised custom, tradition and habit. These strata possess the authority of time and durability and nurture a slavish adherence to their normalising fictions. Allegiances form, through the effects of hegemonies and patterns of socialisation, regimented solidities of thinking and action that resist reflexivity, questioning and the spontaneity of risk. These resistances offer frameworks of assurance and support to conservative ideological forms and customary practices, and diminish the incommensurate lines of flight of the curious nomad. It is within the spaces opened up by these that our writing takes place and by writing in this way it seems as if new spaces are also being created. I feel that we share the urgency expressed by Braidotti to

"elaborate alternative accounts, to learn to think differently about the subject, to invent new frameworks, new images, new modes of thought." (1994, p.1)

(It has felt as if the preceding passage was squeezed out of me. I found myself not being able to write. It seems as if the mindfulness of the exercise constrained the feelings; telling rather than showing became increasingly difficult. I again feel an empathy with Richardson when she talks of her struggle between her "overactive 'sociologist'" and "suppressed 'poet'" (1997, p.152) I am both fascinated and concerned as I find myself and my writing drifting back to the 'academic' self that troubled me when I first began working with you. That performance I found difficult but I am feeling eased, almost elated by allowing myself to engage in a different performance; one that brings that self into focus, one that sees that it acts as a representation which can be brought into the territory we are now beginning both to create and to share.)

I am becoming aware that an intensifying reflexivity is helping me to work with connections and multiplicities. Deleuze and Guattari persuade us that

"(t)he territorial assemblage is inseparable from lines or coefficients of deterritorialisation, passages, and relays toward other assemblages." (2004b, p.367)

I feel drawn by the enticing spaces that seem to exist in this world. As we write I feel we are making sense, making these connections and yet each piece of writing also has a disabling effect, making our world a little less familiar, a little more strange. Derrida says that, "Without the possibility of differance, the desire of presence ... would not find its breathing space" (1976, p.143).

WRITING SPACE EIGHT

ALTERITY 1:
JANUARY–MAY 2006

The following exchange continues from Writing the Incalculable, exploring further what we mean by 'self' and 'other', 'me' and 'you', us. Subjectivity.

Ourselves and others (10 January 2006, Ken)

Writing to you–unsure of beginnings, thinking of becomings.
Notions of self are deeply wound up in notions of other.

Thinking of performance and how this seems to provide a clue to the nature of the relationship between the two. The self performs the self to or because of the other: in this respect the self identifies itself in relation to the other. This suggests that the self is not simply relational to but subject to[1] the other. Alterity provides a constitutive sense of self; the self has meaning in relation to the other. Becoming is therefore also highly relational but also and necessarily multiple, connective, (un)conscious and (un)intentional: our sense(s) of self is/are embedded in these complex rhizomatic (sub) terrains.

How have I come to think about this? I am writing this to you because I want to push our writing forward, but I also am aware of the need to do this through the actual experience of writing to you. This writing could so easily be written in one of my notebooks or diaries but I want to change the way I do this.

---

[1] Foucault (2002) describes discourses as *technologies of self* where the self is not only the subject *of* the discourse but also is subject *to* the discourse. In this sense the discourse disciplines the self, in that it is a means (technology) of identifying the self in particular ways, e.g.: Laura Mulvey (1975) sees the male gaze as identifying and therefore constructing women, say through media representations, in specific forms. In short, the discourse, through its disciplinary nature, transforms subject into object.

I wrote an email to you before Christmas briefly trying to explain my lack of work on our writing because of the problems that I was having in my relationship at home. I suppose what I want to put in here is that me in relation to you; how I am beginning to see it anyway is opening up a terrain (of complicity? of intimacy? of honesty?) that will begin to reconfigure the way I will talk to you and will therefore affect the way we talk and the way you will talk to me. I have been reading Deleuze over Christmas and also some Levinas and I am beginning to think hard now about other and alterity. In one sense, what I am beginning to say to you is unique to us; at the very least, a representation of my sense of our relationship as it begins to emerge through these writings. So I begin to give you more bits and pieces of my life at home in ways that I do not give to others. In the context of what becomes us this begins to reconstitute you as Other, which itself is constitutive of the alterity that we are part of as we write. I am aware of course that I am performing me to you. I am also aware that you are receiving me, accepting me, reading me and of course understanding me, constituting me through the way in which you read into the performance, how you interpret the performance and also how you read between its lines. This is so crucial. It is so much of what we cited in Inquiring into Writing but have not yet developed. And now I feel it is time: I want to write more of Deleuze, to extend the quotation from him that meant so much when we first started writing:

> "We were only two, but what was important for us was less our working together than this strange fact of working between the two of us. We stopped being 'author'. And these 'between-the-twos' referred back to other people, who were different on one side from on the other. The desert expanded, but in so doing became more populous." (Deleuze & Parnet, 2002, p.15)

So, obviously, I am thinking here of our 'between-the-two' but also of how it is inextricably linked to others in our lives. So for me at the moment so much seems to be shot through by what is happening in my relationships with other important people on my life; significant others, perhaps. How I write to you, and even if I am able to write to you, is influenced, is infected by, what I am experiencing in these relationships. In this populous desert others are also relevant and influential and their significance varies.

I think I am saying quite simply that I can only write and communicate with you (Other) in ways that are deeply affected by these other relational parts of my life. I have experienced the breakup of a relationship where although I can continue to experience my partner as Other, as we tear apart, as the fabric of our relationship shreds and rips under the growing pressures and tensions between us, we move further and further apart. Less and less able, less willing, perhaps, to understand each other, alterity still exists but moves from unity to disintegration: affect is still there but seems to work in very different ways.

So much of me that comes to you and becomes us is deeply infected by these things. What will these affects be? There have been occasions in the past when I have been unable to write. There are times, like now, where I am driven to write. There is a need, on the one hand, to 'get it out' (the diary function that I referred to earlier, perhaps) but also there is a need to communicate with you (Other) to begin to build up this sense of understanding between us, to fulfil this desire to write. I feel that I am beginning to open up, to acknowledge the intense and highly complex plurality that surrounds and constitutes our writing. Our "unsurmountable life" (Deleuze, 2002, p.12) is made up of surging, welling forces that carry us forcefully in many directions.

I am aware that in my writing in the past I have been pulled toward the academic, the formal and the erudite and, whilst I do not want to abandon that, I am aware that I now need to allow these other forces and energies to express themselves through this 'outlet' we call writing. I am definitely writing to you here, Jonathan. I am not entirely sure what this means but I know it is to do with being able; with becoming, through the processes, the nomadic inquiries that we have undertaken so far, to begin to write in ways that I have not done before. This is how I am beginning to understand our alterity. It feels as if there is a freeing going on (the word permission came and went then); it is also to do with the very fortunate accident that appears to have taken place by bumping into you!

Who said accident?! What could it be? Fate? Serendipity? Compatibility? Space? Time? I think that I will leave it there for a while because I am not sure what all those questions are about or where they might lead us.

Myself and another (Wednesday January 18th 2006, Jonathan)

I want to pick up on your thinking about yourself and others within our writing, and the place of writing itself in this. I need to write. It's a good feeling.

Since Monday this week I've known that I've needed to write. I've deliberately contained the 'content' of what I need to write about because

I have imagined that talking about it would have led to the drive to write dissipating.

I know that it's you I am writing for. Other potential readers seem genuinely distant. I don't even know whether there will be any others.

I am aware that, also, I am writing in response to Ourselves and Others. I've felt it hanging. I've been aware of it asking me questions, demanding something of me.

Monday, this week. (As I begin to write I feel the tears that I have held back since then beginning to emerge. I'm at the surgery, as I am each Wednesday, seeing clients referred by the doctors. I mustn't cry here. In 25 minutes I shall be seeing someone else, someone new, a client I haven't met before. 25 minutes to begin to tell you this story and then gather myself.)

Monday this week, lunchtime. Oxford is dull and damp. I'm walking towards the train station.

I'm meeting Rachel off the 12.39 train from Wolverhampton.

Rachel and I went out together, twice, once when she was 15 and I was 17 and again three years later. Both times the 'going out' didn't last long: four months and perhaps a year respectively. I remember the intensity of feelings that surrounded these times in my life: the longing, the delight, the pain; how awkward the relationship felt, like it didn't quite fit.

We have recently been in touch again after more than twenty years. I initiated this renewal of contact in December. (The prompt was my coming regularly to Bristol again, where her family lives and where I sometimes used to stay when she and I were together.) The last time I saw her we were both at the beginning of the relationships that we are both still in. Twenty one years maybe, though we had some contact until about eighteen years ago–occasional telephone conversations, Christmas cards– but nothing since then. Until a few weeks ago I didn't know where she lived, how she was, whether she was even still alive.

At Christmas she emailed me some photos. There was one that was of her teenage daughter and a friend. When I first looked at it I thought that the daughter was Rachel and that the friend was her daughter–that it was a picture of Rachel and her daughter together. And there was another picture of her daughter playing a guitar in a band. I thought that that was Rachel too. They look so alike and I believed that Rachel must have simply 'preserved' particularly well.

I reach the station and stand at the barriers. I have had to walk briskly to get to the station in time. There are many people flowing from the platforms. I try to picture her, imagining how she will look, remembering the many times that she and I met each other off trains. And then she's there, emerging from behind a row of students.

She walks towards me and I open my arms and we embrace. She says, "You haven't changed a bit" and I echo, "And nor have you."

You haven't changed. Nor have you.

I am not writing this because we had a great time together on Monday and that I realise I still want to be with her. I'm not writing because I'm full of regrets, or because I don't love Tessa and hanker after Rachel. None of these is the case. We did have fun on Monday: we went for lunch and we talked about the lives we now had, about our families, and about some of what we had each done over the intervening years. After lunch, in the rain, we walked around an Oxford college and, more relaxed now and aware that I had to go back to work and Rachel had a train to catch, we talked about our own relationship, incidents that we remembered, episodes that made us laugh, how and why we broke up.

It was good, but not too good. On the face of it our meeting after all this time was uncomplicated.

No, this is it: she said to me that I hadn't changed and I replied that nor had she. But Ken, you see, and I know that you could have told me this and I know that I knew this, she had changed and so have I. She isn't the girl, the young woman I have in my memory. She isn't the young woman that I had wishfully and wistfully read into the pictures that she sent me. No, she is in her forties and I cannot bear it. Cannot bear knowing it, being faced with the unarguable physical reality of her aging.

She was lovely and she is lovely. Truly. But even after watching my father die, even after beginning to come to terms with the prospect of losing Tessa's mother soon, after having had my forty-fifth birthday, after my mother turning seventy-five, even after years of counselling training, working with clients' grief, and being in my own therapy–even after all these–I have not believed, truly registered, the reality of mortality. My mortality. Rachel will never be the young woman, the stunning young woman, I once knew. And seeing her, and knowing that, I am devastated. I cannot bear it, Ken. We can never go back. I can never go back.

I feel in a hurry to write this and send it to you. I've tried to set aside worries about the 'art' of writing it. (I haven't been that successful at this– I've remained interested in its form.) I have not intended to pay attention to theory, but just now I left the surgery–it's still Wednesday 18th January, about 4pm–and went into Abingdon[2] to get a coffee and read. I took Hélène Cixous with me. I read this:

---

[2] The town where Jonathan both lives and practises as a counsellor.

"It's very nearly the end. It's very nearly life.
Extend the hand, write, and it's all over with the end." (Cixous, 2005 p.97)

Writing about Rachel to you has, in a way, set me free. When I walked to the café, having been writing to you, I was conscious of enjoying the sounds of the town, seeing the children in buggies, the kids on bikes returning from school; I was conscious of life and loving being alive. By writing, by extending a hand to you, by 'giving' my sense of loss to you, it begins to feel bearable.

I am thinking about how what I have written is unique to us: my/our becoming in this writing of mine here, now, to you as Other, now. The me/you-ness of this writing is inseparable from its content. And our me/you-ness is not static. I would not have written in this way to you a year ago, and it is the 'becoming-you' at this moment, following our meeting together last week, following our recent writing, following our history together, to whom I am sending this.

> Jonathan's writing in 'Myself and Another', above, picks up only obliquely on Ken's preceding writing (Ourselves and Others). Jonathan leaves alone, for example, the pain about his relationship that Ken so poignantly refers to. Over time we have become more aware of the choices that we make and how these choices always have an impact. There is always loss. (See Where Are We Now?, pp.265-289.)

Multiplicity, Connectivity–Relationships?
(February 2006, Ken)

Writing in response to your last piece has crept up on me. In the past I have found myself needing to write back very quickly. What you wrote seems to have opened up a space of creativity, openness and of great liminality. I am going to try to respond in ways that connect with what you have written but which also begin to multiply some of the concerns and ideas that I wrote about in Ourselves and Others.

It seems funny to find the way in which 'relationships' have slowly crept into our writing. They have become an important part of our subject matter and they are manifest on many levels. I remember saying to you that I thought that I wanted to write, was ready to write, about relationships a long time ago. Since then so many things have happened and perhaps I have used these happenings to allow myself to retreat from this subject. I wasn't ready. I wasn't sure what to say. Your last piece seems to be leading me back into this and it is good.

I am going to write first at what might seem to be a tangent to our writing. You said in Myself and Another,

> I know that it's you I am writing for. Other potential readers seem genuinely distant. I don't even know whether there will be any others.

(There is a silence here; not because of what I was writing about but because of the intrusion of other realities: life! I have read our recent writings again and I am going to try to pick up the pieces of our conversation after a break of nearly two weeks.)

I feel that there is so much to write about which connects us to other events, other people and our lives outside the microcosm of our writing. I am drawn again to Deleuze and Guattari's notion of *haecceity* (Deleuze & Guattari, 2004b).

Haecceity is based upon the coming together of elements into some kind of assemblage. It does not preserve knowledge in any congealed sense; rather it frees the individual from absorption into fixed categories. It is a temporary and transitory resultant in a moment of becoming, a point on a trajectory. It is a moment of heteronomy, not of autonomy, in which a sense or a knowing of other and difference come together in a captive but elusive and mercurial moment in space and time through the 'logic of sense'.

> "Climate, wind, season, hour are not of another nature than the things that populate them, follow them, sleep and awaken within them … Five 'o' clock is this animal!" (Deleuze & Guattari, 2004b, p.263)

I think of moments of communication with friends or colleagues which go beyond words and which seem to embody unity of thought, feeling and emotion. In this sense, haecceity is not about discovery or learning in any conventional sense; it is more about opening up, about acknowledging difference and, of course, about the celebration involved in making the familiar strange. There is a kind of individuation here but it is not of the self; it is more momentary, where in that crystal moment of time and space something is felt, briefly held and the drifting of the space or the moment into the next dimension or point on the trajectory is something that is celebrated rather than a moment for nostalgia or mourning. The crystalline qualities that are evoked by this haecceity are prismatic, refractive, of multi-layered intricacy and offer infinite possibilities of mood, interpretation and meaning. Richardson provides an excellent critique of the research method of triangulation as a method of 'testing', which not only provides a clear illustration of haecceity but also encourages us to envision our theories and our practices, not in some flat two dimensional way but instead through

> "...the central imaginary (of) the crystal, which combines symmetry and substance with an infinite variety of shapes, substances, transmutations, multidimensionalities, and angles of approach. Crystals grow, change, alter, but are not amorphous. Crystals are prisms that reflect externalities and refract within themselves, creating different colours, patterns, and arrays, casting off in different directions. What we see depends upon our angle of repose. Not triangulation, crystallisation." (Richardson, 2000b, p.934)

As I've suggested, this is not a moment for nostalgia, rather one in which the moment itself, through its unfolding, perhaps, offers a future trajectory of optimism and growth. St. Pierre provides an illustration of this in her description of her own research interest in identities, when she says that

> "(k)eeping subjectivity in play, mobile, a line of flight with no referent and no destination is my desire and my ethical charge … subjectivity is a mobile assemblage that arranges and rearranges itself outside all totalising paranoia." (St. Pierre, 1997, p.413)

So much of the writing in your last piece reminds me of this. I think about you walking down the road in Abingdon after you had written the first part of your piece to me: you said that you felt alive; you noticed the street noises, "the children in buggies". It's as if the intensity of the event, the experience of writing about Rachel, what you referred to as a freeing of yourself through the writing, creates a new and different sense of self. It seems to be one which is oozing with sensuality, hope and optimism, even though you represented its subject matter in somewhat sad and forlorn ways. You seem to have happiness despite the rain; by writing (to me) there is a further sense of "keeping subjectivity in play". You open yourself out; you do not close yourself down beneath the weight of those thoughts that seemed to evoke your sadness.

Through writing to me in such a poignant way about the thoughts that were prompted by meeting Rachel and about the sadness you felt in relation to the presence of mortality that came from this writing, you seemed to create a new sense of self. You seemed to be freeing yourself from the rigours and constraints of "totalising paranoia" and not allowing your use of language to become essentialised. So this language does not congeal, and neither do the thoughts you have about Rachel, about aging and about mortality. Your thinking and feeling are not producing you in some transcendental or noumenal way; rather, through the writing, these become events. They are events which affect you and lift you and open you out to the street scene that you encounter on your walk. You see the "kids on their bikes", you hear "the sounds of the town", you feel "set free". Your subjectivity is in play. You say that "By writing, by extending a hand to you, by 'giving' my sense of loss to you, it begins to feel bearable." It seems to me that being 'bearable' at that moment was a great feeling after all the sadness that you had felt immediately prior to writing.

So reflecting upon this, it seems to me that the writing, the opening up of this 'self', is a way of engendering connectivity and acknowledging multiplicity. The haecceity expressed in your description of your walk to the café after writing about Rachel and mortality is a vivid, life-affirming event, shimmering with crystalline sensuality and potential. It cannot be captured. We should not attempt to capture it. Its elusive and mercurial absence is its magnet. Through folding in this deep and sorrowful awareness of the fragility of life into our dialogue you have unwittingly engendered an aesthetic moment, where your senses are open and where a new and vivid sense of self comes into play: if only for a moment. Within the haecceity becomes an unfolding. It re-positions you, re-aligning your sense of self and also it has pushed me.

Reading your writing here has made me think and feel about how I shall write to you. Before I started writing this I was struggling with how I should respond to you. I didn't know how to or what to write. It has only been through the writing that I have begun to be in the writing. Being with your writing through my own writing has been a struggle but I feel, as I write now, that I am coming through another side, another sense of self, perhaps, keeping *my* subjectivity in play. It is not that I feel any more able to deal with, say, the grief we might feel about aging, but I do feel a strong sense of the value of writing, of allowing the writing to become us, of encouraging that freeing up that you talked about. This seems to place things differently, to create new orientations and, perhaps, in positive ways, to make familiar feelings, or thoughts, by the displacement that takes place through our shared writing, strange. So it is not about the relationships themselves, or the sadness we might feel about their ending, or about the inevitability of our mortality; to focus upon these alone would be, in some ways, to objectify or to essentialise them. By writing in these ways we are moving things, placing these thoughts and feelings in new relational spaces and feeling freed by the potential of that.

It feels that the processes of our writing, and the twists and turns that it takes, inevitably draw in new subjects in the form of people, relationships and topics that interest us. It is this that brings me to thinking about our writing to and from each other and about others who will read it. It seems to be important at the moment that it is you and I who are writing to each other. It is this process that seems to be affording us creative potential. It is important to continue to acknowledge that; we seem to be building a means by which these flows enable us to keep our subjectivities in play. You said: "I know that it's you I am writing for. Other potential readers seem genuinely distant. I don't even know whether there will be any others". It is the same for me. This is interesting because it is not for me a pre-conceived exclusivity. What seems to have emerged through our between-the-twos is a kind of enabling, an easing into new fields and terrains that have seen the becoming of new plays of difference, each with their own liminal force. I am simply not aware of anyone else when I write these 'pieces' to you. If I place myself outside the intensity of this terrain of consciousness then I become aware and know that others will read them, but that is secondary. In my consciousness it is you that I am writing for and this frames what I write as I am writing. I am aware, however, of the potential for change that is there, simply through the processes of becoming that our writing seems to embody. I am very curious!

Intersects, rhizomes and haecceity
(15-19 March 2006, Jonathan)

I have struggled lately. I have found it difficult to know not just where to begin in relation to our recent exchanges, but how to begin.

> We return to writing as struggle on many occasions, particularly Jonathan. We are aware of what Lyotard (1984) might refer to as the *agonistics* of our process as we search our selves and each other.

There has been the major life event of Tessa's mum dying, which you know about, and its fall-out: support for Tessa's dad in his grief, Tessa's grief, the rest of us mourning in different ways. Joe was unable to handle an exam a few days afterwards and walked out having not written a word.

And there have been routine aspects of day-to-day living–Holly's[3] school performance, Joe learning to drive, the usual going to work thing.

> The phrase in the previous paragraph "which you know about" intimates that we have other ways of knowing, that there are other, more private, performances, between us. They are out of the reader's earshot. The reader can infer that these hidden layers exist, but this makes their presence (absence) explicit.

I presented a seminar to colleagues at work last week and it figured large for weeks beforehand. I felt full of it. I dreamt about it. I was looking forward to it but it felt like there was so much at stake. This was the first time that I was formally to talk about our research and probably the most difficult aspect was that it meant that I needed to be clear, for myself, about its rationale. Maybe I still doubt it. Sometimes it doesn't feel like real research.

As well, I have been distracted by the sheer variety of foci to our (and my) work: there has been so much (good) going on but I feel in new territory: I'm used to focusing upon one thing at a time, doggedly pressing on until it's done, then on to the next[4]. This is stretching me but it's good too.

I find myself wanting to take a different line of flight, to use your most recent writing to me as another cliff from which to launch myself. Aware of this I find myself doing something new (for me) here: instead of starting with story, I want to begin with an exploration of an aspect of the literature, to fix my gaze upon theory. Maybe this is about becoming more familiar with the 'Academic Ken' part of me. You seem so comfortable with thinking and articulating theoretically: I am trying on this Ken's clothes for size.

I feel hesitant. I might get it wrong or show myself to be not up to it.

I experienced reading your last piece as affirming. Your take on my walk into town after writing gave me new insight into that experience. Haecceity is such an elusive concept but your writing about it helped me get near it. That's what I want to write more about here. The writing to you now, Wednesday again, in my room at the surgery during an hour freed by a cancellation, having just eaten my lunch, with a client due in a

---

[3] Joe is Jonathan's son (17 at the time of writing), and Holly is Jonathan's daughter (14)

[4] At this time we were involved in preparing papers for presentation at QI, we were finalising a joint paper for the EdD, and we were each working on individual writing projects.

few minutes, with a disgusting herbal tea to hand (no real coffee here). Feeling physically good, the pleasant effects of a game of football yesterday evening still in my limbs; yoga this morning loosened them. I work in a room that is used as the baby clinic. There are diagrams in front of me about how to breast feed, about the stages of a child's development, and about how to minimise the risks of cot death[5]. Now, this instant. Haecceity.

I have been re-reading St Pierre (2004). She talks about the revolutionary impact that her reading of Deleuze had upon her understanding of subjectivity. She says that reading about haecceity resonated with her. She had no trouble getting hold of the Deleuzian assemblage:

"This Deleuzian assemblage made sense to me. *I got it*, or, rather, I plugged it (however one makes sense of *it*) into my own musings about subjectivity and it worked." (St. Pierre, 2004, p.289, emphasis in the original)

She doesn't claim to understand. Later, she goes on to take up Deleuze's idea that "it's a mistake to believe in the existence of things, persons or subjects" (ibid., p.290). She asks "how does one think/live outside 'I'?" (p.290). What are the ethical and relational implications? Instead of the autonomous, a priori individual, what if we thought about individuations as constantly in flow, new assemblages being constituted but never fully so? I take both her and Deleuze to mean that it is the event–the assemblage–that matters, with the ethical responsibility being to "not be unworthy of what happens to us" (Deleuze, 1990, p.149). The humanist, phenomenological subject is a fiction but there has to be enough subjectivity to get by. There is a tension: we can't function without any concept of an autonomous subject. We have to "reform each dawn" (Deleuze & Guattari, 2004b, p.178).

Where am I going with this? I want to compare Deleuze's (and St. Pierre's) way of conceptualising subjectivity with a psychoanalytic idea that I was reminded of by a book on psychotherapy and spirituality (Field, 2005) that I finished reviewing a couple of weeks ago.

There's a chapter by Klein (Klein, 2005)–Josephine, not Melanie–that explores the proposition that we have an underdeveloped language for describing what happens *between* people. I've read her before and find her sharp and challenging. We are acculturated, she says, to thinking of you and me: I'm Jonathan, you're Ken. We are less clear how to talk about

---

[5] See also A counselling story: Petra, pp.205-208

how we affect each other. There is no membrane between our minds akin to the skin. There's Ken and there's Jonathan; when we meet we share certain things that are 'us' and 'ours': we overlap. She uses the metaphor of the Venn diagram:

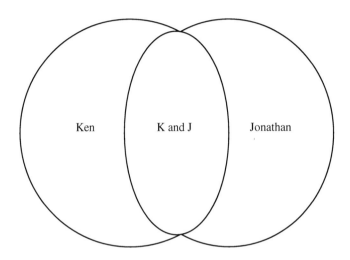

(The diagram is meant to show two full circles overlapping but my drawing skills in Word are not up to it. There's a slight bulge in the middle as you can see.)

There is a crescent shape showing what is now Ken and not me, and a corresponding area that is Jonathan and not Ken, and an overlapping area that is 'K and J' in a narrow sense–what we have in common. The whole diagram is, in a broad sense, us too–what "we command between us" (Klein, 2005, p.162). She coins the term *intersect* for the process that we both recognise when we say 'we', which, I infer, could mean both in the narrow and broad senses, depending. (Our 'we-ness', of course, takes place in a broader, nuanced context not represented by the diagram–where we live, where we work, the context of our writing together, and more, all of which are part of 'us'.)

On the face of it this seems obvious if we only think about it as operating at a conscious level. However, drawing on other psychoanalytic theory, she explores the unconscious intersects. She talks, for instance, about *projective identification* (Klein, 1984; Ogden, 1986, etc.; see Bion, 1961). This is the phenomenon where we 'make' other people feel things for us. If I have a part of me that is too powerful, or too disturbing, for me to acknowledge to myself, I split it off and project it into you–and you experience it for me. For example, I am sometimes aware with counselling clients of myself feeling, say, fatigue and I know that it isn't 'my' tiredness. At my best and when not overwhelmed by it I think about such an experience as being an unconscious communication from the client. In this example of feeling tiredness it's as if the client is pushing me away–shutting me down–so I find myself wondering what they are 'telling' me: is it their aggression they are communicating to me (metaphorically knocking me over the head) or their emotional disengagement, perhaps, or both–or something else? An example that comes to mind is when you wrote in Writing the Incalculable, in response to my writing, No It Today:

> "In a strong physical sense I felt you writing this weekend. I was aware of the silence and was aware that you were rehearsing something that would become part of a performance for you and then some different kind of performance as I opened the attachment." (p.76)

I remember thinking about this at the time. One way of reading the experience is that my labouring over 'No It Today' was something that I needed to let you know about and I unconsciously communicated to you. You felt my experience of writing. Projective identification?

Klein discusses Jungian thinking about the collective unconscious and religious experience as being examples of intersects; in the latter case she terms them *ineffable* intersects. I have a self, part of which is not me and of which I am unconscious, which in religious experience makes itself known to me. "It is (Jonathan) in an intersect that also holds something Other" (p.164).

She also refers to Martin Buber (1937) and a number of others including Donald Winnicott. Winnicott was a child psychoanalyst who proposed that there was no such thing as a baby, only a mother-baby entity. He was not a Jungian, nor was he interested in the religious/spiritual dimension, but he wrote about the "intermediate area of experiencing, to which inner reality and external life both contribute". (Winnicott, 1958, p.230) Here's Ogden, following Winnicott, writing in this case about the psychoanalytic relationship:

> "I believe that, in an analytic context, there is no such thing as an analysand apart from the relationship with the analyst, and no such thing as an analyst apart from the relationship with the analysand...(There is the) experience of being simultaneously within and outside of the

intersubjectivity of the analyst-analysand, which I will refer to as 'the analytic third'." (Ogden, 1994, p.4)

The analytic third, in other words, is an intersect.

In the psychoanalytic world Winnicott opened up the possibility of having conversations about experiences and phenomena that are neither quite Jonathan (nor Ken) nor quite not-Jonathan (or not-Ken), but are between Ken and Jonathan. They don't belong entirely to you or me (Klein, 2005, p.175).

The following questions excite me:

Could projective identification be thought of in Deleuzian terms, as rhizomatic in the sense that feelings and anxieties that I might experience can be seen, at times, not to belong to me but to be 'ours'? They are between us.

What are the similarities and differences between the psychoanalytic idea of intersects and the Deleuzian concept of haecceity? Both acknowledge that there is something 'in between', but haecceity is more than about the betweens of people. It is the moment, the event, the dog, the road, the 5-o-clock is this animal. It seems to me to go further than notion of intersects does. But, in her chapter, Klein refers to Buber's musings on understanding how we connect not just with other human beings but to nature. In looking at a tree:

"...that living wholeness and unity of the tree, which denies itself to the sharpest glance of the mere investigator...discloses itself to the one who says Thou. (Buber, 1937, p.158)

And again with reference to the tree:

"Our habits of thought make it difficult for us to see that here, awakened by our attitude, something lights up and approaches us from the source of being...and...we have to do justice to the reality which discloses itself to us." (ibid.)

So, here, maybe intersect and haecceity are not so far apart, though 'source of being' sounds essentialist. (I am not trying to make the concepts the same; in fact their differences are more interesting.)

I am excited that in our work together we have not just been talking about these ideas but are in there, researching and experiencing them. It gives our work life.

Writing to Jonathan in reply to 'Intersects, rhizomes and haecceity'–31st March 2006 (Ken)

How much is being 'driven' to do something to do with wanting to 'drive'? I know where I am going when I ask that question. I know that the balance between that which is trying to determine or influence me and that which I am choosing to do for myself is fine and intensely variable. To complicate this, I am aware of being 'driven' by my desire to be driven. I actually want to do this and I enjoy the state of 'being driven'. What is this preamble about? I am being driven to write to you and I have pondered what that means many times and over the next two, three, whatever, years, I see myself asking this question over and over again. Each time the answer will probably posit new questions for me to try to answer but that is OK.

To enter into the discussion that you opened up in your last piece, I wonder how much your 'projective identification' is driving me to write. I have needed to sit down to write to you this morning. I am driven by the need to write but I am also driven by the immediate circumstances of my life. It is as if I need to write to you to put a little distance between me and the unhappiness that I feel in certain aspects of my life. Writing to you like this is like writing in a cocoon (a snail's shell perhaps); it builds up my life like the snail builds up its shell. The body of the snail metamorphoses with and is one with its shell: the writing is me I am the writing[6]. Increasingly, of course, we are the writing and that is something that maybe I will get to write about here: I am thinking about your use of the Josephine Klein diagram and the overlapping intersection that is our writing life, our life writing. Why am I writing? Part of it is simply to be in the process of writing to inquire, or writing just to be; the intensity of writing to you draws me in, or, perhaps, 'drives' me, I am driven to write, but I want to be driven to write. It is not a force I resist or reject. These metaphors, 'driving', 'drawn', are powerful, and indicative of Deleuzian folding and unfolding: I am feeling these forces, these energies; they are playing on me but I am happy to be in their flow. I think of surfing and the great energy spent in getting to that wonderful point in the wave that lifts you and takes you plunging through its boiling power. It carries you; you are so much a part of its energy and yet so susceptible to it, almost (but only almost) powerless within it.

I began that paragraph wondering about projective identification and how much we are influencing each other to write. I have had your last

---

[6] See Inquiring Into Writing, pp.50-66

piece with me in my bag since I received it last week. I have picked it up three or four times and each time have read it through. It is now covered in notes and comments; my annotations have begun my conversation with you. I have been thinking mostly about projective identification because although I have a sense of what it means, I don't know Josephine Klein's work (or Melanie Klein's, Bion's and others') and am not familiar with the arguments and issues that surround the concept. I have enjoyed your take on it and I have grasped what it means in relation to our writing. I thought about the phrase of hers that you mention–what "we command between us"–and thought about the force of that word 'command' in relation to my feelings of being 'driven', of being 'drawn' into the writing. I smiled when you apologised about your drawing skills in Word because, on the one hand, I know I would have the same problems if I tried to do such a drawing but, on the other, the drawing, inadvertently perhaps, actually represents something that I think we are looking for here. The 'bulge' that you apologise for is evocative, suggesting a bursting of ideas and feelings, indicative of a pressure, perhaps, to connect, to multiply, to fold things in and to see what unfolds as a consequence. I feel driven into that 'intersect', I feel myself using my energies in such a way that the bulge grows around me and into me. I have a sense that this becomes me.

What does this mean? I have become uneasy with the conscious/unconscious binary that appears in your writing about Klein's work, and a part of me does not want to nurture that distinction. I am aware of and sensitive to the folds and flows between the so called 'conscious' and 'unconscious' parts of me. I am aware of the 'conscious' and 'unconscious' energies that I send to you and that you send to me but I am aware that they do not fall into those simple categories; nothing seems to me simply 'conscious' or 'unconscious'. (Even as I write this I am aware of a feeling lurking in me; is it sub-conscious? un-conscious? becoming-conscious? conscious?) There is a sense of 'bringing out' here. What is this? Emotions? Feelings? Truths? Values? Meanings? I am not sure but I feel positive about this not knowing, because it feels a part of the spaces that we are opening up in our writing.

These spaces are like lacunae, where fractures seem to exist, where conventional thoughts or perhaps convenient dualisms become challenged and no longer seem appropriate and where new ideas, fusions and disintegrations occur and are so much a part of our life force. I have a quotation from Luce Irigaray which, I think, goes some way toward capturing the kind of fluidity of thought and exchange that attracts me to what we are doing here:

"(They) are contradictory words, somewhat mad from the standpoint of reason, inaudible, for whoever listens with ready-made grids, with a fully elaborated code in hand. For in what she says too, at least when she dares, woman is constantly touching herself. She steps ever so slightly aside from herself with a murmur, an exclamation, a whisper, a sentence left unfinished…When she returns it is to set off again from elsewhere…One would have to listen with another ear, as if hearing an 'other meaning' always in the process of weaving itself, of embracing itself with words; but also of getting rid of words in order not to become fixed, congealed in them." (Irigaray, 1985, p.29)

I keep skirting around projective identification. I feel that I am opening up my own hermeneutic circles around it, having feelings about what the phrase conceptualises but I am unable entirely to commit to one fixed view of what it is, or of what I think it is. So I will try again! You know that I often express my concerns to you about our shared work; I sometimes worry that I am not contributing enough or that the editing work that you do, what you call the 'obsessional stuff', goes unappreciated. Well sometimes I get this feeling that I am writing back to you too quickly, that perhaps I should be more reasoned and more circumspect, less visceral and spontaneous. Now where does that feeling come from? We both talk about looking forward to receiving each other's work; we have used the words 'excited' and 'urgency' to describe the anticipation of what the next thrilling instalment is all about. And yet I have this feeling. Is this an example of your projective identification, telling me to slow down, encouraging me to mull over your writing more carefully and thoughtfully? Would you like or do you have an anticipation of a more reasoned response? Is there a sense in which you are 'projecting' something on to me here? I have this feeling. 'I have', not 'you have given me'. I talk of my feeling and not of what you have projected on to me. We are in this space where our sensitivities are nurturing so much liminality, so much growth, such a wild proliferation of contradiction, complexity and positive energy.

I am reading Sadie Plant's book *Writing on Drugs*, and late last night I read a passage which has just come to me: I mean that as I have written this, it has just come to me. She starts with an unreferenced quote from Deleuze and Guattari, which I should think is from *A Thousand Plateaus*:

"(T)he system is not a transcendent entity as the "self" is commonly supposed to be', but rather a 'network of pathways' which is 'not bounded with consciousness but extends to include the pathways of all unconscious mentation–both autonomic and repressed, neural and hormonal'. It is 'not bounded by the skin, but includes all external pathways along which information can travel'. These external pathways are traversed by pheromones, the chemical transmitters that are thought to underwrite the chemistry of sexual attraction and the syndrome that allows the menstrual cycles of women living in close contact to synchronise ... The 'contact high', for example, which seems to allow people who have not taken drugs to pick up something of their effects from people who have taken them, suggests that the chemical messengers at work within individuals might also pass between them." (Plant, 1999, p.197)

I haven't worked with this material yet, I am including it because of the synchronicity that I sense in relation to some of the content. I am still working with your introduction to projective identification and rather than try to 'understand' it immediately, I have felt comfortable about playing with it, seeing how it fits in with us and how it coincides in some kind of way to what Sadie Plant is talking about in her book (reading this has also sent me back into *A Thousand Plateaus* again!). I feel a tolerance of the ambiguities that seem to exist around this area. I don't feel certain about any of this and I find that exciting!

WRITING SPACE NINE

ALTERITY 2:
FATHERS, OTHERS (MAY 2006–JULY 2007)[1]

This exchange focusing upon the 'other' begins from and returns to a consideration of our being fathers and sons. It takes us further into thinking about writing and how writing becomes us. In this piece we are aware that we are also working with form and style, and that our representations of self and of other, and the performances between the two of us, seem to stutter. We referred to 'stammering', citing Deleuze, in our first and sixth writing spaces writing space, and to how Deleuze interchanges the word 'stammering' with 'stuttering':

> "It is no longer the individual who stutters in his speech, it is the writer who *stutters in the language system (langue)*: he causes language as such to stutter. We are faced here with an affective and intensive language (langage) and not with an affection of the speaker." (Deleuze, 1994, p.23)

And so, with Deleuze, here, in this space, using this "affective and intensive language", we have engaged in "a poetic undertaking" (ibid). Richardson (2003) has alerted us that "(a) deep and totally unnoticed trope used by social researchers is the reporting of interview material in prose" where, she suggests, "(t)he technical mechanisms of explanation are quarantined from the human processes of interpretation" and where "(t)he actual linguistic practices in which the researcher/writer is engaged are hidden …" (p.188). The use of these experimental forms and styles resonates with a brief discussion that Ken shared with Laurel Richardson at QI2007[2] when, in response to Ken's reluctance to call some of his writing 'poems', she encouraged him to think that, if he was unsure of the form he was using, it might be better to think of what he had written as

---

[1] With Joe Wyatt
[2] 3rd International Congress of Qualitative Inquiry, University of Illinois at Urbana-Champaign, May 2007

poetic representations (see Richardson, 2003; Richardson, 1997b; Richardson, 1992).

Chronologically, the beginning of this writing space follows from Alterity 1, which ended with Ken's consideration of *projective identification* in light of Deleuzian thinking. Jonathan, here, starts somewhere else, which, as the reader will see, initially troubles Ken. The conversation in this space was interrupted for a long time by other writing tasks, and stuttered for some nine months. While writing Alterity 2 we also worked on other spaces.

Fathers and sons again (5 May 2006, Jonathan)

Sometimes I think that I must hate writing. If I didn't, why would I find it so difficult to start?

I am beginning this in a hotel room in Urbana at QI2006[3]. We have been talking over the past day or so about some of my anxieties associated with our writing and, even though these are real enough, I feel as if I have not been able to articulate something. I have not been hiding this from you: I have not been clear about what it is. However, I think that I might be getting closer. I am frustrated because I have not written.

This is not to say that I have written nothing. I have written. But it is work-related writing that I can hide behind. It is not writing me. It is not writing us. I think that I easily underestimate how writing has the capacity, the potential, to convey vulnerability, which can be therapeutic but which carries risk. I think that I must have been wanting to protect myself.

So.

I have some writing which I have not yet 'outed'. I have been thinking again recently about my father and have wanted to continue my dialogue with him by writing about him. I haven't yet done so but I have written, as a father rather than a son, about and with Joe (now 18, though we started when he was 16). For a year we agreed to write, occasionally, about each other. It was a struggle. In the same way that I have written above about finding difficulty with writing you and me, I found myself resisting writing Joe. And (as you'll see) he experienced this similarly–but he attributed clear reasons for this.

It is a line of flight–of escape, perhaps–away from where we were (projective identification). But I felt the desire to offer you something of

---

[3] Second International Congress of Qualitative Inquiry, University of Illinois at Urbana-Champaign, May 2006

my subjectivities that I have not offered you before. I guess it is also a way of responding to your poem about Reuben[4] in our earlier writing, where you are with him on the beach in Writing the Incalculable[5].

Joe and I wrote all of our pieces 'blind'. We only showed each other our writings at the end of the year.

My text is in italics.

10 September 2004

The look on his face. I shall never forget it. Calling it happy would not do justice: he smiled as though something was about to burst out of his mouth. Eyes wide. He was some distance from us and cars drove past quickly and noisily, so he did not attempt to speak to us. And his walk: rolling from side to side, fast, I was worried he might fall. Waving his pieces of paper. He's a big boy–tall, strong–and falling would involve a considerable thump.

It was one of those moments that will stay with me. As he reached us,

"Fucking, bloody fucking bloody fucking hell. Look at this. Fucking A*, fucking A, fucking A, fucking no more fucking Maths. Ever. C. A fucking bloody C."

And this week he started college, and I can't stop asking about it. I want to know who his teachers are, what happened, where he was when, who's in his groups, what the lessons were about. I told him yesterday that I want him to put me in his bag and take me with him.

27th September 2004 7:21 pm

Writer's block is a terrible experience that one is only able to fully comprehend once one has experienced it oneself. You can observe hapless, mentally drained writers going through this heart-rending, morale-sucking poverty of the imagination and perhaps feel sorry for them. You may wish to help them by bringing them cups of coffee (not recommended by the way: it just makes them more agitated and more prone to schizophrenic changes in mood). However, in the end you're left thinking, "What's the problem? It's not exactly hard, is it?"

Well let me tell you: I have been in the aforementioned position and take no pleasure in giving you a hearty "Fuck you!" slap in the face. That's how angry I am. And I don't suppose having Anthrax's *Spreading*

---

[4] Ken's son
[5] See pp.77-79

The Disease blasting away from a speaker several inches away from my left ankle helps either.

So to get to the point, I have finally decided to get my arse into gear and begin this bizarre diary scheme my dad cooked up a while ago, more out of desire for a change from schoolwork than anything else. And I have writer's block. And it's horrible.

Of course, I haven't got writer's block anymore otherwise I wouldn't be writing this would I? I have now thought up a cure for writer's block, one that could make me millions and millions from washed out writers all across the globe! It is very simple: If you have writer's block, then simply write about having writer's block. C'est facile, non?

And so, my writer's block cured, I move on to the task at hand. That task being writing something about my beloved paterfamilias and this crazy scheme of his that he no doubt believes will bring us closer as father and son, and will take around an hour of my life away from me each week. I am determined to make this work, however, as it provides a change from analytical essays on obscure, melancholy poems written decades ago by people I've never heard of. I also want this to be the first writing project I have ever had which gets past ten pages in length, and when it does there will be an entire entry celebrating this fact and going on about all my past, short lived projects in great detail. Oh the wonder, the anticipation! And that entry will also have about as much to do with father dear as this one (i.e. fuck all. Blame the writer's block).

And so I will end this by stating my frustration at being branded a "Goth" merely for predominantly dressing in black and wearing a spiky necklace and long leather jacket. Can you not see, dear pater, that I have moved on from wanting to be a Satanist?

Of course when I had the idea of becoming a Goth I had in my head an image of me that is almost identical to the way I dress now (except I don't have any facial piercings), but after six months on internet messageboards listening to tiresome elitists attacking little Rasmus fans who went around proclaiming:

"i Iz WeArIn BlAk An SpIkEs An LiSsEnIn tO MaRiLyN MaNsOn WiTcH mAiKs Me A gOff, InNiT?"

I have learnt the error of my ways. According to these elitists, "real" Goths listen to nothing but The Cure, Type O Negative and Bauhaus style bands. And since I can only stand The Cure out of that list I have rejected the idea of being a Goth. I am a Metalhead, Dad, why can you not get it right? You managed to stop saying "cool" all the time as though I always used that goddamn word–despite having not uttered it for four years–so why can't you stop telling people I'm a Goth? I do not listen to Bauhaus, I do not wear make up or black nail varnish (okay, there was one occasion, but that was an isolated incident!) and I'm not depressed and I do NOT slit my fucking wrists. Ergo I am not a Goth.

6 October 2004

He sent me an email. Badgers jumping up and down going "Footie, footie, footie, footie." It was a scream. I was touched. He hates football.

7 October 2004

Yesterday was college parents evening. There was a load of blah, blah, blah and then conversations with a couple of his tutors. First one: "Oh, you're Joe's parents. Well, no homeworks, I'm afraid." Home. Back to GCSE nagging. Tessa did most of it, but I was just as frustrated with him. But it was funny too.

27 October 2004

Tomorrow we're going to see a film together. Alien vs Predator. I was thinking yesterday, as T and I were downstairs and he was up in his room again, how little time I spend just with him. Last week Holly and I went to my mum's together on our own. We listened to her music in the car, talked about the things that she had brought to do–like the cards from the Fat Nation programme about healthy lifestyles–and were taken out to lunch by Grandma. T and I go to the leisure centre, out for coffee, into Oxford, out to see friends, just as the two of us.

The last time Joe and I spent time together was on a sailing dinghy in France, back in August, when I spent much of the time shouting at him to "pull the sheet in" and, puzzled look on his face, he kept tugging at the already taut rope in his hand. It wasn't a great event; I was stressed and Joe just went quiet. (The first time we did it, a few days before, had been fun. There was just something different about the stressy day: different dinghy, different wind, different 'set'.)

Before that we went to "Shaun of the Dead" earlier in the summer. Oh, and we played squash a couple of weeks ago. After the thirteenth time of having to ask for the ball back from the irritated experts on the next door court we decided to call it a day.

So blood-thirsty boys' films it is. And I'm looking forward to it. I won't have to 'teach' him, or be the one who thinks he knows. We can just sit, eat chocolate and drink coke. And I can hide behind the seat, trying hard not to embarrass him too much.

Afterwards he'll ask me what I thought and I'll say "well, OK. Not great, but quite fun" in my usual condescending "it wasn't highbrow enough" kind of way. And Joe will tolerate this and say he thought it was great. Crap, but great.

22nd October 2004 21:39 pm

Screw weekly entries! This will be monthly and monthly only. The only reason I'm doing this right now is to ease the boredom of having no homework to catch up with and no new CDs to listen to. It was a mistake and a dumb idea for me to expect anything more from my dilapidated sense of motivation.

And that was by no means the only dumb idea I've had recently; take today for example. Since becoming an ardent heavy metal fan about a year ago I have culminated a large collection of CDs by a variety of bands and around three months ago realised I had never in my life been to a live performance, and that I had merely six months in which to catch up with my mother (who had attended her first gig at sixteen).

Since then I have committed myself to go to eight separate performances and have failed to attend a single one, and when quizzing my dear ol' Dad about his first gig, it turned out that his first live experience (Meat Loaf, when he was 18) would be doing a UK performance soon. Now, my spur-of-the-moment decisions are rarely my best ones and I immediately asked if he'd like to go, with me tagging along. I had neglected to consider that, it being Meat Loaf and all, I'd very likely be the only one attending and the fact that attending my first EVER live performance (always the most momentous day in a metal fan's life) with my forty three year old, stylishly-retarded and musically-tasteless father would do a hell of a lot to my street cred. That is, in a negative way. Bugger.

Fortunately the performance was three hours drive away in Cardiff on a Friday night and would finish eight hours before my nine-hour shift at Tescos so my pride was to be preserved for at least a few more months.

31 December 2004

Why so long since I last wrote? It's not as if things haven't happened nor as if I haven't felt things about him. My excuse has been that I've been preoccupied with work, with Tessa going into hospital, with writing for my doctorate, but I'm sure that it's not as straightforward as that.

I've begun to doubt this project that we've started. It feels harder than I thought it would, committing myself to thinking–and sharing–how I experience Joe. It's much easier not having to think.

New Year's Eve. We're off to a party. Will I have a go at him for over-eating? Probably.

1st janury 20051 37 pm

lofve muydad. He didn't get too fucking nagry botu me gewting hammerrrred tonight. He defenfed me against mum as well, whagdt a good man. Plkdus pkds plsu *plus* I jsjds just foundred out hwo shard is to type while yosu got alociohol doing sa marathonraca race throught yoer fucking artreeeees

EDIT (5th January 2005)

This was left with original punctuation and spelling for the sake of authenticity.

16 January 2005

He and I argued this morning. I walk in to his room–I knocked first–and he's in bed. It's 11am on Sunday. There's a mountain of clothes (clean, I assume) on the floor; he has exams tomorrow. He owes Tessa and me money, which he said he would get yesterday but didn't, so I ask him, since I am travelling into Oxford, if I can have his card and withdraw it for him. No, his PIN code has been blocked. So why didn't you tell me? Because that wasn't the reason why I didn't get you the money. I just forgot. (Keeps playing game on his mobile.) Raises his voice. So do I. End of row.

17 January 2005 10:35 pm

So, monthly entries, huh? Screw that. Quarterly: That's the way to go for me! It seems as though I am destined to write nothing but nasty, evil things about dear old pappy in these entries but then again, he's asking for it really. Fresh from my admiration of daddy-dearest for not kicking up too much of a fuss about getting pissed on New Year's Eve I have decided to revert back to the unpleasantries. Dad: When your son has just come back from a day consisting of five exams back to back due to timetable clashes, it is advisable *not* to ask him how his day went.

Seriously, it brings memories that he's just managed to forget flooding back into his brain so DO NOT under ANY circumstances ask him how the exams went. It's a very bad idea; there's some very rare, useful son-to-father advice, use it wisely.

Ending on a positive note: I'm set to go to a gig in less than a month's time, which means that I got to a gig before my 17th birthday and therefore my mum ISN'T gonna beat me. HAH!

Contact (June 2005)

As we say good night
He and I slap hands

Brief, sharp,
A crack
I wring my hand in mock pain and we laugh

Some nights the contact is soft
Not a shake, though, not holding as such,
No, no

The last time I remember holding him he was half the size
And weeping

Joe talking to me a few days before he goes away, alone, aged 17, to his first rock festival (June 2005)

Piss off, Dad, you're soft you are

What time does the train go on Friday?
11.30. OK.

From?
Oh, the station.

Yes, I've got my ticket.
And I catch the shuttle bus when I get to Derby, don't I?

The rucksack's fine. Thanks.

How does the sleeping bag roll up?

Don't be soft, Dad, I'll be fine.
I don't mind going on my own.

I thought I'd just eat from the stands and burger bars and stuff

Yes, I'll take my phone
And that belt for my money.
And I won't take it off

Can you lock a tent?
Oh. Right.

See you.
Have a good time in Bristol.

Piss off. Don't be soft.
I hate you too.

17th June 2005 9:30 pm

Let's have us one last minute entry shall we? Four months since my last entry and not so much as a peep from me. Well, now Dad wants us to show each other each other's work and I'm dreading seeing what he's written about me because of the high likelihood that it'll be some sentimental twaddle (no offence Dad, you know I love you really).

I have the three pages that make up his contribution to this diary project sitting in front of me like three sheets of pulped and dried guilt that I haven't put a spectacular amount of effort in, and that I haven't said an immensely large amount of nice things about him in my past entries. However, I haven't read through anything but the first three lines of it, because that'll ruin the effect. I have Joe Strummer yelling, "WHITE RIOT, I WANNA RIOT!" in my ear, I'm typing away at my computer, and I'm in my writing mindset so I know I can churn this stuff out.

Of course there is one significant event that has happened recently, in which the ultra-concerned parent that rests inside Dad has had a chance to shine:

"Are you sure you want to go on your own?"

"It's three days, in some campsite, filled with strange people"

"I'll be worried about you, it's your first festival and everything, a new experience"

"Try to catch the train on time, and if anything goes wrong throughout the entire weekend you know you can just call me"

…And words to that effect. You get the idea. I should have seen it coming after all, this is the first time I've ever gone to a music festival, let alone one full of nasty rock types like those that'll undoubtedly appear at the Download Festival (some bastardised, enlarged lovechild of the Donnington Rock and Monsters of Rock festivals). Turns out the concern he and Mum had for me turned out useful though: I would not have survived without the stuff they sent with me, even though Dad's old camping rucksack really did my back in as a result. Gah.

Parents who seem overprotective and clingy at the time can turn out to be pretty damned useful after all, it seems. I've just got to make sure Dad never finds that out, he'll never let me live it down.

Right, I think I've run out of things to say on this particular subject so I'm goin to finish this with a poem. I'll say that this is in honour of Dad, but of course the real underlying reason is so I can fill space:

Dear Ol' Dad

For all the rows,
For all the arguments,

Every time I add another wrinkle to your brow,
Every time I'd said what I hadn't meant,

For all the pain,
For all the backaches,

You've just gotta know one thing,
It's something to which,
I don't like having myself to bring,

Like Yoda I am talking,
Off topic I am walking,
Circumlocution is a terrible thing,
When used badly, with bad timing,
You could say the same about the forced rhyming,

But you know I love you,
Don't you?

My God does this poem suck,
I'm using this as an excuse to say, "FUCK"

You're my Dad,
It's my job to say that.

***

"Make the language system stutter … if the system seems to be in
perpetual disequilibrium, if the system bifurcates–and has terms each one
of which transverses a zone of continuous variation–language itself will
begin to vibrate and to stutter." (Deleuze, 1994, p.24)

***

A Response, Sunday morning: 13th May 2006 (Ken)

My first reaction to the last piece was the strangest reaction that I have
had to anything that you have written to me during our co-respondence.
Wait for it! Amongst other emotions the dominant feeling that I had was
one of disappointment.
Disappointment?!
What is that all about?
I read your piece yesterday morning almost as soon as I got up. I had
checked the inbox late the night before as I was switching off the
computer and saw your message there waiting for me but I decided to wait
for the morning to read the contents. So I was looking forward to reading
what was there. I have been itching to be writing again; attending the
conference[6] has set me going. I am fired up with ideas and feeling very
motivated. Overburdened with the mundane chores of marking, meetings
and administration that mounted up whilst I was away in the States, I have
been feeling a growing sense of frustration as the days have gone by and
the opportunity to write has not opened up.

---

[6] QI2006

I read your piece, put it down and went back and read the last piece that I sent to you some time ago[7]. I couldn't see the connection. What had this writing to do with the fissures that I thought I had opened up in that piece of writing? That was 24 hours or more ago. Since then your writing (and Joe's) and my initial reaction to it has been on my mind; not in the forefront but lurking there, re-emerging, asking me questions, making its presence felt. Gradually those thoughts subsided within the context of a troubled day. My day felt heavy and leaden, directionless and sad and ended with me sitting in the chair morosely and unenthusiastically reading about magical realism and what that has to do with my writing.

This morning was different. I awoke, totally fresh; the sun pouring in the window. Clear thoughts about our writing process were washing around in my head. Phoebe[8] made me a cup of tea and you know how it is; no matter what the essential quality of the tea is, it tasted so lovely because she had made it for me.

Here I am now sitting in my sarong, in front of the computer, in the sunshine, urgently wanting to get this down.

I see your last piece in a wonderful and really valuable light. I am so pleased to have this writing to think about and respond to; I see so much in your writing with Joe that talks to our concerns about subjectivities and by sending this to me I know that you have opened up a rich vein of thinking and feeling which will sustain us for a good while in our writing.

In my thinking I visited my disappointment and I laughed at myself:

I wanted you to write to me.

I wanted you to address the things that I wrote to you about.

I wanted you to respect my writing and give voice to the issues that concerned me and which I had expressed to you.

Instead you sent me something quite different which appeared to have no connection with what I had said to you.

Sitting in bed drinking Phoebe's cup of tea I experienced a simple moment of haecceity. The tea, the sunshine, your writing, the birds singing, a feeling of freshness in my spirit and the emergence of a clear idea about our writing all fused in a moment of energised passion. Normally, on a Sunday morning like this I would be opening the sports pages, sorting out the children's breakfast, maybe clearing up the detritus of last night's fun. Instead I am here, shutting off the noises of the children's television and the pressure of thinking that I should do something.

---

[7] The final writing of Alterity 1, Ken's Writing to Jonathan in Reply to Intersects, Rhizomes and Haecceity, pp.100-103

[8] Ken's daughter, aged 8 at the time of writing

Yesterday I was looking for linearity, wanting a direct response to my writing, instead I received some thing that tangentialised, moved off in another direction and I recognised, in a flash, a line of flight that simply created another direction, another folding, another connection: something that added complexity in the rhizome. In that flash I have re-conceptualised your last piece of writing to me. I see that what you have sent me about your relationship with Joe is so rich in things to respond to. It has provided another 'layer' or another dimension to our writing; something which I guessed was there but had not fully articulated. I have put my disappointment to bed but I will not let it sleep because it is also part of my subjectivity in relation to you; it has to do with expectations and also the way in which I had naively expected the process of writing to take its course.

> "In Deleuze, 'logic' acquires a new sense. It is called upon to do new things suited to the "image of thought" he tries to work out: a logic of 'multiplicity', a logic of sense." (Rajchman, 2000, p.50)

What you have done by sending me this piece is to open up another rhizomatic shoot for further nomadic trails to be taken. I know now that we will go back to that strand that I have left you with in my last piece. We will think again about 'projective identification' and the take that I offered you on it; I will encourage you to think about what I said there and you will offer me further musings on the notion and tell me more about what Klein has to say about it. I am beginning to enjoy living with these "asignifying ruptures" (Deleuze & Guattari, 2004b, p.10)

I am feeling good this morning.

I am feeling good because of what this moment has revealed both in me and for me.

I am feeling good because I am spurred to writing.

I am writing myself again as I write to you.

This is good.

All the while I am thinking and feeling our writing; I am wanting to 'get on' with it, partly because I feel that I need to co-respond with you, that this is what we do, but also because I want to do it for myself.

I am feeling pressed to write.

As I reflect upon your writing with Joe it suggests to me the 'planes of immanence' (Deleuze & Guattari, 1994) which hold many concepts as events, and many dimensions of thought and feeling. This is, perhaps, what Derrida referred to as *differance* (Derrida, 1978), something which cannot be held within the confines of binary constructions and their limited dualistic constrictions.

"Concepts are concrete assemblages, like the configurations of a machine, but the plane is the abstract machine of which these assemblages are the working parts. Concepts are events, but the plane is the horizon of events, the reservoir or reserve of purely conceptual events: not the relative horizon that functions as a limit, which changes with an observer, which makes the event as concept independent of a visible state of affairs in which it is brought about." (Deleuze & Guattari, 1994, p.36)

It seems to me that we are working with and within these planes, these indivisible milieux (Deleuze & Guattari, 1994), using writing as a method of inquiry, making concepts through our narrative inquiries. So the concepts we create in our writing are 'events' in themselves, which, through the means of expression that we use, our performances, perhaps, help to create other events.

"The only regions of the plane are concepts themselves, but the plane is all that holds them together. The plane has no other regions than the tribes populating and moving around on it. It is the plane that secures conceptual linkages with ever increasing connections, and it is concepts that secure the populating of the plane on an always renewed and variable curve." (Deleuze & Guattari, 1994, p.36-7)

There seems to be so much fluidity here and it seems as if we are only just beginning to be aware of this, to begin to tap into in its liquid potential. The plane of immanence that we are both a part of and which we are constituting by and through our writing is, again as Deleuze and Guattari would say, an "image of thought", (ibid, p.37). It is not there to tie us down, to configure us in any way but to 'image' the processes of our contemplating, our reflecting, our communicating. I cannot get away from this writing. All the time that circumstances have been preventing me from being able to write I have had the writing with me, I have been ready to perform it.

This is interesting too because it has only been this morning that the performance has appeared in the way that it has done. I have been concept forming; there have been many conceptual events if you like; there are many scraps of paper in my notebooks which have attempted to capture this. These all exist within this plane of immanence and it is the fluidity of this that connects me to you and your writing. I am now wondering about these fragments, which are themselves 'images of thought'; they are constitutive, they exist in this plane (and perhaps others) and I am wondering how to convey them to you. Within the Deleuzian 'logic of sense' they will appear as fluid and indistinct ideas; they will have a sense of being formed, they will have form, they will appear on the page but I am concerned; I don't want them to congeal and become enshrined in this medium.

Performance. This is why performance is so important; performance seems to embody senses of becoming, of having folded something new into the mix, of having being, albeit mercurial and elusive: I feel here a powerful sense of how haecceity works for us and is so present in what we do in our work.

> "Thought as such stutters because it must think, yet cannot think in a major language nor in the silences between words; yet stuttering at least produces something, generating an arrangement of asignifying signs in its performance. Concepts only live in creation and performance." (Goodchild, 1996, p.53)

As we stutter in and with the exciting vagaries of our *minor languages* (Deleuze & Guattari, 1986), viewing things from oblique and marginal angles, it feels to me that the performance has uniqueness, it exists in its place, in its time, but also that its qualities endure on a plane of immanence: the *differance* of performance seems to give it its endurance, its hope, its life. We *become* through the performance; it is a striving, a searching for quality, excitement, fulfilment and pleasure on the part of all of those who engage in it. So, on the plane of immanence there are performances, concepts are created, they have life and then dissipate and perhaps reform in different, new and exciting ways.

I began this piece two weeks ago by talking about disappointment; somehow, I couldn't connect with your response to my previous piece. Now I am ready to write back to you about what you talked to me about. I found more of you in your exchanges with Joe. I found differences in you as I read what you wrote to and with him; in a way these were things that I expected in some ways to find in the setting of your father and son relations. Joe and you perform each other through these exchanges and it is fascinating to read your writings as you both write independently and yet are so obviously so wrapped up in each other.

I was at Bristol with you when Joe went off to Donnington. I hardly knew you then, I remember laughing when you read me the text that he had sent to you not long after he arrived, which just went "Aaaaaah!!!!" In the context of these exchanges that means something very different now and I realise that whilst you laughed with me at the time, there was a great deal more going on inside you than you were able to disclose at that point. At that point you performed yourself (a self?) for me. You appeared strong, able to share a laugh about the mad time that your son was having and, as I read these exchanges now, I can see that you performed your self (a self) effectively and well, covering the obvious apprehension and concern that you obviously felt about the whole thing.

It seems that we are always in the process of performing ourselves. As fathers, we are not 'growing up' into some pre-conceived notion of fatherhood or self, we are performing ourselves, our thoughts, feelings and actions constituting events which come and go. It feels to me that this coming and going has an eventual quality: within this plane of immanence, the folding and unfolding of experiences that the exchanges between you and Joe tell me about help me find out about you. When you say "I was touched" or, at another point, "I told him yesterday that I want him to put me in his bag and take me with him", it is like you saying "This is me", "This is who I am". It feels like part of a drama unfolding as your performance presents aspects of a self that I am ready for and prepared to 'see'[9]. It is as if the event of experience as exemplified in your words becomes the grounds for my experience of you: to paraphrase Deleuze, becoming-Ken-and-Jonathan.

In this becoming, subjectivities always appear to have transience, along or within this plane of immanence. There is you, you with Joe sharing your events of experience, there is you writing to me about you and Joe and these events, and there is me with my images of thought (Deleuze, 1986), 'having' my experiences of you in relation to the events that I read about. What we seem to be discovering in these writings of self, these processes of inquiry, are these 'between-the-twos' (Deleuze & Parnet, 2002, p.17) that are transversal, that encourage further nomadic inquiry into and across the myriad multiplicities and connections that make up 'becoming Ken and Jonathan'. This is clearly rhizomatic: the arborescent and foundational nature of so much writing into subjectivity is not of this form, wanting to congeal, to fix and provide established knowledge of how we are and seem to be.

> "(Authors) … cause language to flee, they make it run along a witch's course, they place it endlessly in a state of equilibrium, they cause it to bifurcate and try to vary in each one of its terms, according to ceaseless modulation." (Deleuze, 1994, p.25)

And now later as I sit and think about this writing before sending it off to you I am struck by the fascinating complexity of it all, of what we are 'in', of what we appear to be trying to do. I have been aware in writing this piece to you that we are also inquiring into the narratives that we have

---

[9] This reminds me of the ending of my poem, Conundrum of Self, that we included in Writing the Incalculable (p.77-79)

written (to each other?). This narrative inquiry is about our inquiry into subjectivities but it is also about the narratives that we are using to write about these subjectivities. So many levels are unfolding which then, of course, fold in upon themselves, because also, of course, some of the writing here, like some of the writing of you and Joe, has the quality of a "performative utterance" (Austin, 1962; Lyotard, 1984). In this latter sense there almost seems to be a kind of existential or phenomenological dimension to what is written; I think that it is Merleau-Ponty (1962) who has talked about art and poetry as forms of self expression, somehow preceding language.

That is something to look at for the future!

Becoming in the rhizome? 30 June 2006 (Jonathan)

I have been reading our earlier writings and feeling good about what we are doing, happy to keep exploring in the way that we are on the basis that it will come together (and/or diverge?) appropriately as we work. But I also feel at a moment of crisis. A little lost. Lacking in confidence. This is a good–if anxious–feeling, though. It is born of wanting to work at the edges, to push at the/our boundaries.

We have talked recently about shape and at this moment I feel that I want to get a sense of the shape that we are creating, the forms that we are working with, as we write. This has left me feeling as if I am in the rich, verdant forest that we mentioned at the beginning of Inquiring into Writing. I have been on a path that we have jointly made and I am at a junction where a number of other paths shoot off. These are also paths that we have created. They are different to when we first traversed them because I am seeing them now, from this position, with different experience. I feel that all are appealing in different ways and I want to tread them anew. (There are others that we could take that I am not yet aware of. Silent, untrodden, paths; paths on which I/we might end up.)

So I have been writing about my father again (see Wyatt, 2005; 2006). I want to explore with you my uncertainty about whether this new writing is 'ours' or 'mine'. This uncertainty concerns keeping or not keeping space between us, individuality versus togetherness, me and you versus us. I ask myself whether all my writing now is about us, even if you are never to see it (which, of course, you will because I want to share it with you). You say in A Response: "I cannot get away from this writing" (p.120). I agree, and I also cannot get away from *us*. All my writing now has your presence or the absence of your presence.

"Language is subject to a double process of choices to be made and sequences to be established: disjunctions or selection of similars: connection or sequel of combinables." (Deleuze, 1994, p.26)

I'm at very early days here, Ken: at the moment this is a series of fragments. My intention (one intention) is to explore the experience of when the intensity of loss, and the sadness that accompanies this, diminishes. There's a lot that needs further development and filling out.

No Longer Loss[10]

"We lay on our backs and wondered what God had wrought when He made the world so sad." (Kerouac, 1976, p.57)

I type.
I usually type.
But this is different. With this I have been, until now, writing by hand. I have stayed away from what has recently felt like the harshness and constraint of the screen. I have held onto the tentativeness, the immediacy of my handwritten, double-spaced script. I have felt possessive of the A4 black, red-ring-bindered notebook. I have carried it with me these past few weeks. In my bag, to work, on planes, to tables, in cafés.
My fear now is that as I type this up something will be lost.
A connection.
A newly re-found connection.
With him.

Last year he was here.
Even as the plane circled the vast, flat plains and patchwork fields.
Walking the long, straight streets, past thick kerb-side grass and wooden houses.
He was here.
I knew he would be.
In oak-panelled rooms, along corridors of grey, austere white men,
Passing tan leather chairs occupied by sleeping students,
As people clustered, engaged in animated conversation,
In the smell of coffee and fast food,
In the welcoming warmth of spring sunshine–
After the long, dreary English winter it had been enough to make me sing–

---

[10] A later version of this writing became Wyatt (2008)

He was here.

And then, as I composed myself that Friday morning to tell stories about him

In this room, by this chair, at that door

He was here.

In me.

In my body.

Alive.

This year, I am here, walking the same streets, past the same cafés and restaurants,

Revisiting relationships,

Reminding me of his presence then

And assaulting me with his absence now

These remind me of him:

Trimming the hedge. (Me, now, stood on a wall; him, then, balanced unsteadily on a ladder.)

Mowing the lawn. (How, sans stick, he would hop, skip and jump after the speeding mower. Sometimes it would get away and crash into a tree.)

Clipping the long grass on the bank, sat on the ground, right leg folded under him, left leg stretched out in front.

His soft, black, leather briefcase. Emptied at the table on his return from work, to produce newspapers and, on Fridays, apple pie. A gift from Mrs Newell, the cook. Mrs Newell's apple pie. My son now has the briefcase, stuffed with mementoes from schooldays.

Hymn singing. At Christmas. Visiting Worcester cathedral, and hearing the choir, I think I hear his strong tenor voice.

Sunshine.

James Bond.

Swimming in the sea.

Always that. Always swimming.

Always swimming.

(Is that all? Only these? Surely there were more once.

They are slipping away.

Sometimes, it is as if he had never been here.)

No longer loss.

Absence.

He and his older sister are on an expedition aboard a large, gray, rubber dinghy. The stone harbour wall curves around them, stretching from the shore behind and looping to enclose the fishing boats moored in the harbour it creates. The two children—he ten, she fourteen—are happy. It's summer, early on in the annual family holiday to the same Dorset seaside town. The weeks stretch ahead forever.

If it is high tide, in the mornings, before the others rise he and his father will take the long walk down the steps from the house, towels slung around their necks, to the prom and thence to the beach. (At low tide the journey to the water is too far.) He will walk on his father's left so as to avoid impeding his stick. They will not encounter many people so his father's self-consciousness will be lessened.

They will swim together for a time, then his father will swim out further while the son returns to the beach and waits, watching his father submerge and emerge, a six foot three inch, dark-haired, green-trunked whale.

His sister calls to their father and big brother aboard the second dinghy. "Ice creams! Come on! We'll go and get them if you like!" She rows over to them and their father reaches over to pass the youngest—'Titch'—the coins. Titch turns up his palm and clutches them, but not tightly enough. Somehow—his fist is maybe not yet big enough—they slip out into the water and are gone.

The holiday mood is broken. His father growls his disappointment and irritation. The son is mortified.

There will be ice creams that afternoon, and a rapprochement, but not for a little while.

He calls out. I have tried to sleep but can't, knowing that the call will come. A small voice, quiet, sad, indicating discomfort.

I'm by his bed.

"I'm sorry to wake you," he says. He is on his back, which is uncomfortable for him.

"That's fine, Dad. Hold on a moment."

I lift up the duvet and take the rubber strip—laid across the bed underneath him to assist turning him—in one hand and manoeuvre my other underneath him.

"OK. Ready?"

And pull firmly so that he turns onto his left-hand side in one movement.

When I first did this shift on my own, as our mother recovered from an operation, this rolling of him would take me half a dozen attempts. I would sweat with anxiety at my responsibility for him. I still am anxious, frightened by not knowing what he wants and by the prospect of failing.

My brother and I joke that, even when it comes to nursing our father overnight, it matters which of us does it better. Our sister does it better than both of us so we don't include her in the competition.

I traverse to the foot of the bed and settle his right leg into place on his left, a cushion between them to soften bone on bone.

"How's that?", I ask and kiss him lightly.

Alone in the bed next door I listen, trying to settle, half sleeping, half alert to the next call. When I leave him in the morning it will be with a measure of relief.

It is the evening meal. I announce:

"Tomorrow I am going to get my ear pierced."

Silence.

He places his cutlery on his plate and looks at me:

"If you go ahead and do that, then don't bother coming home." And resumes eating.

It is the best thing he could have said.

I feel the elation of rebellion.

At last.

I am 23.

This is how it might be:

I walk into the garage, past the carefully parked car, into the order and neatness at the far end. The darkness is illuminated by a naked bulb, which casts light onto the square tin boxes of nails and screws, each box labelled according to size and type, and the wood-handled tools hung on the breeze block wall. 'Any Questions' plays on the transistor radio.

He sits on a mat on the floor, in front of the clumsy chest of drawers, drawing sandpaper across a spark plug, the lawn mower beside him. His right leg folded almost underneath him, his left leg outstretched. This is how he sits. Always on the floor, always with his legs like this.

"Hello, Titch." He switches off the radio.

"Hi, Dad."

"And what I can I do for you?" (Is this how he talked? Would he have said it like this? Why can't I remember?)

I hesitate, then implore:

"Come back. Stay. Talk to me. Explain. Don't leave. Help me. I don't know. Any of these would do."

Dad blows on the spark plug. "There, that should do it." Begins to re-fit the spark plug. Looks up and, with warmth, says

"Don't be silly. You know I can't do that."

Loss still has presence. Absence seems bleak. And writing an attempt to traverse its barren landscape. Loss is conscious of what has been present, resonant and redolent of the lost. With absence there is forgetting.

The dictionary: Absence–from the Latin, 'to be away'–the fact of somebody's not being in a particular place. Present–from the Latin, 'to be in front of'. Loss–the feeling of sadness or emptiness at the absence of something.

My eleven year old daughter is on the phone. It's her bedtime. I've been away from home for two nights.

"I'm afraid we're losing him, my love. He's not going to get better."

"Bring me home something of his," she asks. "A shirt or something."

After a few weeks she gave the shirt to me. For months I, too, would hold it against my face to breathe him in. Three years on the clean shirt lies in the bottom drawer of my filing cabinet. Though no longer him I cannot bring myself to throw it away.

What does writing my father do? What does writing perform? Does it revive him? Does writing making him (more) present? Does it assuage my guilt that I forget him, that my life goes on without him? Does writing about him alleviate my fear? Does it create him? Does writing him create me? Does it perform a revised identity? A 'self' cast in light newly shed by both my words and my awareness of your gaze? Do I feel better? Does it help me to get a hold?

When we were little we–sometimes all three of us–used to climb into my parents bed, in between them, on week-end mornings. We would push my father out, putting our six small feet against his back and inexorably nudging him towards the bed's edge until he would theatrically tumble to the floor.

His revenge–which we awaited with exquisite anticipation–was to move to the foot of the bed, reach for our wriggling feet under the bedclothes and, one by one, pull us down, squealing and giggling, till we, too, thumped onto the floor. My mother would remain serenely under the bedclothes. All very Oedipal of course.

I used to do this with my children. I told them where the game had come from. Grandpa's game. They are all but grown up now.

I remember, the summer before taking up my first teaching post, being at the dining room table. On it were scattered my grandmother's effects. I had not been close to her and had seen her only occasionally her last few years as she drifted into dementia. (I had been occupying myself with the task of being young.) During my childhood she had been a festival visitor–birthdays, Christmas, Easter–staying a few strained days before departing, leaving with us chocolate and discomfort. I had never fully understood the difficulties she caused, as a small child seeing her as intriguing and generous though finding her by then, in my early twenties, curiously disinterested.

Scanning the table I noticed the pack of letters tied with a rubber band. I was drawn to their uniformity and the neatness with which they were folded; and to the familiar jagged handwriting. (At school, every Monday I would receive a letter from him and every Thursday one from my mother, their stories a reminder of where I was. And then I would forget again and be happy.)

I removed the rubber band and took the first letter, postmarked June 1947 from the Isle of Wight. He convalesced from polio on the island for two years at a stately home, Osborne House, converted by the army into a hospital. (Now open to the public, last year I drove past, stopped at the car park and, baulking at the entry fee, attempted to peer through the hedges and fences. I did not see the house and drove on to catch the ferry.) In his early twenties he wrote these letters weekly to his mother. He detailed for her how he was dealing with the occupational therapy–the carpets he had made, the swimming that he was beginning to do again, the discomfort of the callipers, the consultations with the doctors.

I remember his voice in those letters–warm, loving, optimistic–and recall at the time not recognising it. Talking to and about his mother I had heard him only as guarded and resentful. Hurt, wounded.

During his time at Osborne House she never visited. Not even once.

No longer loss.

Absence.

(There is) no longer loss (than) absence.

Back at QI I remember feeling that I was being slightly lazy in sending you "Fathers and Sons". I'm pleased that you ended up liking it but I was aware of sending it to you without engaging fully. This was borne of affect: both anxiety–a restlessness–that we were perhaps becoming entrenched in a way of writing and responding to each other, and desire to fly off in a different direction, trusting that it would take us somewhere. I imagine that this is what might have sparked your disappointment, that you picked up on my wish *not* to stay with the theme (of projective identification) that we were pursuing at the time. However, there's a sense that this very process–of your reacting to my piece with disappointment–

might be an example of both the projective identification that I wrote about and how you mulled it over with reference to Sadie Plant and her 'network of pathways'. Maybe my restlessness was also yours; maybe your disappointment also mine. "There are no individual statements, there never are. Every statement is the product of a machinic assemblage." (Deleuze & Guattari, 2004b, p.42)

I went to Borders one Sunday, on Father's Day, having been taken out to a delightful Fathers' Day coffee by Holly and Joe. I sat down with three Deleuze books that I haven't yet read and dipped into each of them. I 'understood' only a little of what I read but found myself longing to become fully immersed in and familiar with him, to 'work' him thoroughly. I don't feel confident in my grasp of his–or anyone's– philosophy. I noticed that I was thinking that Deleuze, philosophy, and theory are all *your* territory–you're good at it, you know so much–and that my initial impulse is only to try to write evocatively. My inclination is, in part, to leave 'theorising' to you but I also know that I want to find my own place there. I am sure that my feelings about this go back to where we started in my first piece, in that I have insecurity that I am not clever enough.

> "We were never in the same rhythm, we were always out of step: I understood and could make use of use of what Felix said to me six months later; he understood what I said to him immediately, too quickly for my liking–he was already elsewhere. From time to time we have written about the same idea, and have noticed later that we have not grasped it at all in the same way." (Deleuze & Parnet, 2002, p.17)

A Revolt into Style? [11] 2nd July 2006 (Ken)

Again it is a while since I have written to you.

It is a hot humid Sunday morning; I am looking out the window and sense the foreboding of iron grey thunder clouds welling up in the sky above the tree line. I have found myself at this desk. I feel my family crumbling around me and in the lonely quiet of this house a strange gravity pulls me into this little room, full of books, papers; the mess of my 'work'. I have just been reading No Longer Loss, your poems, and I feel quite overwhelmed by this writing.

I have to respond to you.

I usually do this after I have read your writing. As you know my responses to you are often immediate; I am not sure why. Overwhelmed:

---

[11] This is a playful allusion to George Melly's book of the same title (Melly, 1974)

by a tide. It is the intimate intensity of your writing that has really hit me. This great gush of writing and the opportunity that you have given to me to surf the waves that your words create has left me feeling elated and apprehensive. Elated because of the joy experienced through the sheer evocation of the writing, apprehensive because, right now, I am not sure where to begin my response to you. This has left me excited because what you have sent to me has opened up so many doors. In the reading I frequently found myself getting lost and my initial concern about this soon dissolved as I allowed myself to become swept up in your writing. This is beginning to feel like an adventure now; it feels as if this revolt into different styles gives us the opportunity to swing out of the mainstream and into eddies and currents that our distributed selves both inhabit and set up. With this revolt into style we can, in the spirit of Deleuze, 'stutter' in the language, allowing meaning to be continually produced and changed.

I am reading Reynolds' (1998) book on rave culture and there is a passage in the early part of the book that resonates with what I am beginning to feel about our writing and its exciting potential.

> "I finally grasped in a visceral sense why the music was made the way it was: how certain tingly textures goosepimpled your skin and particular oscillator riffs triggered the E-rush, the way the gaseous diva vocals mirrored your own gushing emotions. Finally I understood ecstasy as a sonic science. And it became more crystal clear that the audience was the star: that bloke over there doing fishy-finger-dancing was as much a part of the entertainment, the tableau, as the DJ's or bands. Dance moves spread through the crowd like superfast viruses. I was instantly entrained in a new kind of dancing–tics and spasms, twitches and jerks, the agitation of bodies broken down into separate components, then re-integrated at the level of the dance floor as a whole. Each sub-individual part (a limb, a hand cocked like a pistol) was a cog in a collective 'desiring machine', interlocking with the sound system's bass-throbs and sequencer-riffs. Unity and self-expression fused in a force field of pulsating, undulating euphoria." (Reynolds, 1998, p.xvi)

Experiencing the different styles and stutterings that are present here has given me this 'rush', this great sense of liminal potential that the many thresholds of our collective writing seem to possess. Your use of different poetic representations are like the many 'tics and spasms' of our writing and encourage me to think about the massive and exciting collaborative complexity of the whole. Writing in these different ways offers the opportunity to engage and re-engage with what we have begun, to stimulate new ways of thinking and new approaches to the way we might write in the future.

I loved reading your writing about caring for your dad and the earlier memories of your life with him. How much a part of you is that?! Reading this has encouraged me to think again about my dad and how so much of the way he was becomes me now.

So ... whether intended or not, this was a wickedly evocative piece of writing for me.

Relationship troubles (Jonathan)

Is this how it starts?

A thread we can't help pulling
As the cloth of intimacy unravels

A scab we can't help picking
Until the skin of love is raw

We pull the thread and pick the scab because
That is what we are doing

Our imagination fails us when we most need it

Mount Alvernia Hospital, Guildford 17 September 2003 (Jonathan)[12]

He lies unconscious. It is morning. My sister and I are 'getting him up', she washing him and straightening his bedclothes, having delegated the task of giving him a shave to me.

I notice how surprising I find it that, even at the end of life, such processes as hair growth do not slow.

He uses a brush and cream to generate a lather. He has always done so, and I have never. I am in a lather of my own, struggling to create enough soap and then managing to apply it not only to the beginnings of his beard but also to his nose, ears, hair and neck. He breathes on, slowly and rhythmically, seemingly oblivious to the mess I am making. My sister laughs at my attempts.

---

[12] A version of this brief piece forms part of Wyatt (forthcoming, 2009)

Sad Poem for Happy Summer Night: (Ken)

(18th July 2006: Remembering my mother's birthday)

Love drifting
through waves of sound,
cool waters lapping my feet,
spray wind coming off the water.
I dance with you
as skin tingles
in fresh hand glow,
knowing love
traces strange
feelings;
like the sea
like the sea.

I have to learn,
to learn how to thrive
on those moments
when,
on the beach,
my son, Reuben,
looks in my face
and says
"Hey Dad, you've got
salt crystals on your eye lashes!"
His warm hands
on my shoulders,
his face intent,
smiling into mine.
We laugh,
I rub my face,
we pull the boats
up the shingle
and lash them
to the granite posts
at the Cleave.

Drinking
cold delicious beer,

leaning on those posts,
with Reuben.
We look out to sea,
our beach, cooling now
as the sun goes down,
across the bay,
still light, bright,
shining fields and
crystals dancing off ships.
Reuben digs in close,
tastes my beer,
grimaces
but says,
"Yeh, its cool–good taste"

We walk up
through the village,
bare feet on
warm stones,
the streets
now deep in shade.
Our conversation is deep;
we discuss ground lines,
camping on the beach,
bait.
I soar with my son,
we share that
beautiful languid,
end of summer day sun.
This is precious to me
I know this is something
we share:
Dad
Son.

We return
to the house,
those pure crystal moments
dissipate
An Other presence
permeates,

is in control;
all other emotions
are subsumed
in this presence.
Orders and commands
make adult
this casual world of fun.

Creatures of the sea
return to their shells,
like hermit crabs on the beach.
Predation, stalking,
as individual gain
threatens
community and sharing.
Life sulks.

The river beach, Le Minier, France. 10 August 2006: Jonathan watching his twin nephews watching Joe and friend

Their pale backs are towards me. They lean back in parallel, hands in the gravel sand behind them, faces to the water, watching their cousin swimming, receding, with Clare.

The boys are silent. They look at each other occasionally.

The lost boys, confused by Joe's betrayal.

I've got to go ... (Ken)

Happiness (is)
captured in fleeting moments:
laughter in pubs,
smiling at a baby's face,
singing aloud.

These images, these joyful realities,
are not dissolved
by the over-riding weight
of this imposed agony,
these selfish controls.
The naturalising function

of Oppression
leads to forgetting,
to forgetting what
happiness can be.
Happiness
now is only glimpsed
- oh there it is! –
the elusive shooting star
of fantasy.

Tonight
sitting (smiling?)
with people
who seemed
stuck in their worlds
managing identities
coping with Others
stuck with:
the same jokes
the same songs
the same sadness

I've got to go …
time is running out
love is absinthe
sharp, unique, voluptuous.
It is becoming rare,
lost in lazy doorstep sips,
the emptying bottle,
captured only in frozen
moments of time.

I see those
sad people
people of my generation,
my birth.
I see that I share
so much with them
and that I don't.
(Tonight)
my laughter

came from them
and yet
it drags me down;
their creased red faces,
their watery eyes,
their repeated jokes,
their steady,
insistent drinking of red wine.)

In my life
there would be
the perfect Karaoke;
The Kinks'
You Really Got Me.
not tired, not sad,
but perfect, strident guitars
spitting out chords,
insistent bass-lines,
drums snapping the rhythm.
Me singing,
head up to the mike,
knowing all the words,
certain of self,
certain of song,
identity wrapped
up in the song
rapt delivery:
not hollow sad,
fuck-up energy
of pissed Saturday night
but there in that moment,
committed to that sound,
that moment of
clear
pure
happiness.

I've got to go …

Beginning to Mourn a Daughter's Growing Up (Jonathan)

I open the door and step into the room

She is talking to friends,
Silently,
In an animation of multi-coloured writing

I can pick out the occasional word as I approach the screen

She turns towards me, smiles and touches my arm to steer me away
Back the way I came

I kiss the top of her head and turn towards the door

When I glance back
She has already resumed her conversation

About the party next week?
School?
Friends?
Boys?
The intrusiveness of parents?

I will never know

I remember how, years gone by,
She would crave attention from me
And be eager to intrude upon my conversations

I miss it being that way around

Bringing Dad to life: June, 2007 (Ken)

I shared a coffee and good conversation with a friend in a café last week. Catherine. We do this regularly but not frequently. She has surprised me by wanting to keep our meetings going. She is always the first to make contact and to suggest a few dates for us to negotiate the best time in our respective busy work schedules. I have known Cath for maybe ten or fifteen years. She is a little younger than me, not yet 60; on the surface we seem so different and yet we share so much and have many interests and feelings in common. Our conversations are lovely; she listens and wants to hear and I find myself being warmed by her humour and by the resonances that our stories seem to set up.

I greet Cath like a lover, like someone I haven't seen for a long while, someone whom I have greatly missed and yet it is none of these. She always remembers who bought the cappuccinos on our last meeting and I am happy to go along with her confident judgment. Part of me doesn't care who paid and the other part enjoys her care and her thoughtfulness in doing this. It makes things special, etched, remembered. We sit, smile at each other, busy ourselves with spoons, sugar wrappings and stirrings and start to talk. We have no agenda: the words flow. There is never any stopping, any thought about what to talk about; any hesitation. We turn-take, although sometimes she might say more than me or the other way around.

Last week we found ourselves talking about education and class. Not surprising, really, both of us having similar backgrounds of activism, studying sociology, growing as children of the 60's. I found myself talking about my dad, as I often do when this subject becomes the focus of my interest. My reflections on my dad have been rehearsed so many times, I feel confident; this is a knowing. My dad, born in 1919, his stories of growing up as a child in a very poor family between the wars, joining the army as a teenager, sharing his memory of the thrill of eating bacon and having sheets on his bed for the first time, are very sharply etched into my soul. As a child Dad attended National School in Launceston in Cornwall and was in the same class as Charlie Causley[13]. As I described these things to Cath I could sense her attention sharpening. This was a narrative that I had offered to others before but somehow Cath's concentration upon my words was drawing something out of me.

I recounted my memories of Dad, throughout his life, religiously preparing himself for his Friday evening visit to the library: changing out of his dusty work clothes, shaving, putting the heavy hardback books into his bag and disappearing for an hour, maybe two, to a world that was wholly his. For all I knew he could have been making regular visits to the moon, he might have been sharing hurried tender love making with a mistress: it didn't matter. That was what happened on Friday nights. I marvelled at the transformation that my dad enacted in those Friday night rituals. He would come home from work dirty, smelling of sweat, full of

---

[13] Charles Causley, teacher, poet, historian of our town, was known to all of us, except his pupils, as 'Charlie', a sign, perhaps, of his very real belonging to the town. Even at the height of his fame he was always approachable, friendly and very much a part of the town.

the stories of the day, hungry, teasing my mum, eager to enjoy his evening meal, 'tea' we called it. And then, as Mum and I cleared away the plates and cleaned the pans, he would wash, change and reappear, fresh smelling, his newly shaven face shining as he readied himself to go out.

When he returned the chemistry altered; it was as if with the sun going down the mood in our little family became more serious. I remember Mum sewing, pumping the treadle on her machine, tidying, cooking perhaps. I would play at the table with my toys, an old army blanket covering the proudly polished grain, protecting its sheen from the warfare of tanks or the skidding of high speed racing cars. Dad would sit in his chair and read. Avid, intense, completely focused: I knew he was in his own world. I know that feeling, with a new book, the desire to hide myself away, to bury and to immerse myself in that intense secret imagined world of words, to become lost in those imaginings. I learned to try not to disturb him, not because of fear of reprisal but because his expression would indicate absorption, that he was somewhere else and that he was not entirely with me. Perhaps more than any other this memory of my dad stays with me. I see him in his chair, his library books around him, at peace.

It is hard for me to capture the intensity with which Cath's sharp attention upon my words drew the telling of these stories of my dad from me. As I recounted how my dad, Charlie Causley and another boy had passed the 'matriculation' to go to Launceston College but Dad couldn't go because his family could not afford to pay for his school uniform, I was aware of Cath's eyes filling with tears. I have lived with this story of my dad's life, almost taken it for granted; it is a part of our life together, it has always been there: fabric, texture, reality. I have lived with its inevitability, its layering of normality: this is how it is.

Now I am here writing because of Cath's tears. I am writing this because of Cath's tears and for my dad. I am writing for my dad to honour him but also to shake my complacency, to rattle the discourses that made that story an accepted part of my life, a story whose origins became concealed by the insularity of my own social mobility, my preoccupation with my own life. Cath's tears told me then and keep reminding me that I must never lose that image of my dad. I feel with great love and sadness what he was sitting with in that chair in our tiny little cottage in Launceston. Still a young man and yet burdened by the wonder and grief of being that poor small town boy thrust into the horrors of war, spending six years with death, dismemberment and suffering. I see his sinuous, tanned arms, like cables, bulging from the short sleeves of his shirt, his heavy brown hands with stout fingers delicately turning the pages of his

books. He was a grafter, a short but intensely powerful man: I grew up
with his strength and the rate with which he would work. Work, strength
and labour became normal to me too, I found that part of myself through
my dad; that was him. It became me too. This, an embodied sense of
myself: it is only now as I write that I begin to see how this being with my
dad, in that little room, near to him, in his chair, with his books, his
silences, his smiles, the tenderness of his great powerful arms, has
affected me. Cath's tears have brought me to this writing and this writing
brings out the tears in me.

Coda to Bringing Dad to Life (Ken)

I was walking in Totnes on market day a few weeks ago and I came
across a small collection of poems by Seamus Heaney, a poet whose work
I had never read before. One poem jumped out at me and I have to write
about it here. I am taken with these serendipitous moments when events,
without prediction or planning, fill my life with meaning. My reading of
Deleuze should prepare me for such things; I have clarity of thought about
his figure of haecceity where, in a moment, concept, percept and affect all
flash together in the power of one. This sense of meaning has become so
significant for me, rendering other epistemologies with doubt and the
flavour of the abstract, the traditional and, more insidiously perhaps, the
non-reflexive and the discursively constructed. And yet, I am surprised by
these things, these events that capture me in their momentary magnetism.
    The collection was entitled *Death of a Naturalist* (Heaney, 1966) and
with absent-minded ease I lifted it off the dusty shelf and began to shuffle
through the pages. The poem *Digging* was the one that caught my eye and
it has stayed in my vision ever since. I don't think I thought of my dad at
first as I began to read; it was the immediacy of the opening two lines,
where he draws attention to the pen nestling between finger and thumb,
that drew me in.
    The title, *Digging*, and the archaeological metaphor of using the pen to
dig down for meaning, perhaps in a Foucauldian sense, was the initial
lure. Although I now hesitate when I am faced with the apparent
structuralism of Foucault's archaeological approach to the construction of
meaning, identity and practice style, the subversive tendency inherent in
the imagery of uncovering and exposing layers of hidden meaning attracts
me. I sense the archaeologist at the dig, scratching away at the earth with a
trowel, gently exposing a hidden fossilised form and gradually laying its
shape and content bare to a new world. It is at that point of discovery that
new meanings begin to emerge, conditions of possibility shift and

meanings become re-constructed. So the pen resting snugly becomes implicated in such actions; the writer with the pen, like the archaeologist with the trowel, has the power to engage, to uncover and to challenge.

So opening the book and starting to read that poem's first few lines was the hook; the lure had been set and I was drawn by the moment. It was only as I became submerged in subsequent lines that the image of my father began to appear. Slowly, as Heaney reveals his father, digging below the window, whilst Heaney himself engages in the writerly task of constructing his poem, I began to feel my dad's presence in the lovely poetic stanzas formed by Heaney's words and lines. Does he, in becoming aware of his father working as he looks down, begin to engage us in a reflexive, evaluative task as we read the poem? Is he suggesting in the positioning of the two of them that there, at his desk, peering down somewhat self-consciously at his father working outside, he is somehow above his father? Is the writer, located in a hierarchical elevation above the raw physicality of the task of the digging man, engaged in the kind of tasks that his writing appears to be taking him away from?

I can see my dad, working hard with a pick and shovel; I can see the rhythmic way in which he seemed to work effortlessly, digging a trench, a hole or perhaps, more peacefully, turning the ground in the garden for next summer's crops. I can see my dad engaged in actions of this kind; the picture is vivid in my mind, as if it were day. He is long gone from my life but his spirit lives on in me. I dig with his long handled spade, worn smooth at the edge by his labours. Every time I put my weight onto its lug, drive it into the soil, pull the smooth handle back, lift and turn the soil and start again, his presence is with me. Heaney states that he does not follow such men in wielding a spade. I am not sure that is the case with me: the palpable feeling of connection with my dad, there with me as I too dig down in the soil, is powerful and it is sometimes as if I lift that spade just to be with him. But there is something else. There in the shady recesses of that bookshop, the poem read and the book held a little loosely in my hand, I am with my dad. Heaney's final lines, where he draws attention again to holding his pen, ring in my head. Unlike my dad or Heaney's, I do not have to dig with the spade to live. I can live with the pen to write. In living like this I also live with my dad. He would be pleased to see me digging in this way.

"Bringing Dad to Life": a response July 2007 (Jonathan)

As you bring your dad to life
You hold him in your arms,
Slowly walking towards me
And, close enough now,
I can touch him
See him,
Smell him,
Feel him.

As you bring your dad to life,
I am able to hold him myself,
Hold inside an embodiment of him,
Have a sense of him;
His pain, his dreams, his life.

Bringing your dad to life,
You have brought him
To me,
To my life.

You have brought your dad to (my) life.

This feels unusual in our work so far and I feel excited by it: here I am with a personal piece of your writing, a profound autoethnographic story, which I am now responding to. It seems to have emerged from the raw experience of living, from a place in you that you sometimes, in our writings, guard well. (Is that right? Is that fair for me to say so?) I have experienced this 'Ken' before mostly in your poems, and also in some of our collective biography exchanges (Gale & Wyatt, 2008b), recently in Secrets and Desire[14], and through the 'Ken' in Therapy[15]. But this current piece feels different again: unexpected, not written in direct response to me. It takes me by surprise.

I find myself drawn both to the portrait of your father and to the textual performance–to, for example, your choosing to tell a story about your father through your encounter with Cath. I am awed by the responsibility I feel for honouring you and your writing with my response,

---

[14] pp.210-212
[15] pp.165-196

and am struck by how skilfully and respectfully you have written in response to me in the past. I am thinking (again) of narrative therapy practices, of *definitional ceremony* (Myerhoff, 1982; White, 2000, 1995) and of witnessing, and want to respond accordingly. I want to situate my responses "'within the context of my own personal experience, imagination, purposes, curiosity" (White, 1995, p.5), which doesn't suggest that I necessarily write about *me* in response to you, but that I write performatively and from the body. And I want to "orient to mystery" (ibid, p.7).

You have written about your dad before. I have the picture of him in your living room in the house where you grew up, turning off the television because Jagger and his mates are on (Gale & Wyatt, 2008b). I have had a sense of your affection for him, and also of your battles with him, the length of your hair a regular site of conflict. I have also an awareness from before, echoed here, of the journey away from his and your wider family's working class culture into the middle-class, learned culture that you now inhabit, a journey brought into relief by your experiences at family events where family members gently mock your bookish life[16]. Yet I note, in this space, that you identify with your father the 'grafter', a habit/practice/quality that is familiar to you too.

New to me, though, is how your writing draws me to his physicality: this man, with "arms like cables", echoed in the Heaney poem by men who could handle spades and dig the ground. I am drawn to the vividness of how, on Fridays, this vital, physical man shed the garments of hard labour, left behind both the world of men and that of domestication– women, children, home–and, like Clark Kent spinning in the phone box into Superman, transformed himself into this unexpected man of books, books into which he would (continue to) dig. As you now do.

What image is it that you must not lose? You seem to possess so many images of him. I think that the image you have in mind is the man in that chair, the man whose dreams of education were thwarted and who saw more suffering than he could bear. (Am I right? Is it this image? Maybe there is not only one.)

What is it that you must not lose?

Your connection with him?

This sense of whom and where you have come from?

And why now? Why has this surfaced now, I wonder?

These are not questions intended to demand answers from you. They are questions whose mysteries I am enjoying.

---

[16] See p.56

And as I move from my focus on him–this has felt like witnessing your dad, as we did when producing our collective biography pieces (Gale & Wyatt, 2008b)–to another layer, I turn to what I have termed the textual performance. (Do you know, I am finding this difficult? I am doing what you normally do: our customary roles are reversed. It's good.) You tell me of your dad through the story of an encounter with Cath, your old friend. I reflect upon this haecceity, this moment of telling; sharing with a friend, a witness. She is someone who encourages you to tell your story, who cares enough to make the effort to make contact, who knows whose turn it is to treat the other to coffee. I sense sadness in the fleeting nature of these occasional encounters with an old friend. She brings warmth, attention and care into your life–of which there is usually, I sense, not enough–and then is gone. It is through her interest–her love?–in/for you that you re-experience your dad.

It seems that you wish to move towards a different knowing of your father, to write a new story, altered from the well-worn tale you know too well. You say that the story was renewed in its telling to Cath: "(her) concentration upon (your) words was drawing something out of (you)"; her "intensity" elicited some new quality from the telling of familiar stories. You were aware of her tears, and you were drawn to write "because of (her) tears"–first–"and for (your) Dad". It sounds as if it was Cath's tears that "shook your complacency", that shifted you into a fresh position from which you can experience your dad differently. Her tears brought you into changed awareness of (the meaning of) your dad, in that chair, in that small, familiar cottage, and of both the peace his books brought and the pain he bore. The process of writing, prompted by Cath's tears, takes you closer to the impact of your father on you, brings you to your tears.

There are your shifting, somewhat troubled memories, there is the context (your old friend, the occasional, anticipated meeting), the telling there, Cath's tears, the writing (to me) of this. All of these (and more) contribute to a re-storying of your dad, and a re-storying of you.

Layers upon layers.

No,

An "entanglement of fibres" (Deleuze & Guattari, 2004b, p.475).

Felt.

So, what am I saying? What am I doing here? Am I simply repeating what you have already said? Am I rehearsing the same script that you have already performed? I am, in a way. I offer you an echo. Perhaps I am performing the same script but slightly differently. I have Michael White and *outsider witnessing* (White, 2000) in mind. I have Cavarero in mind–

you as *unique existent*, with a friend, Cath, whose embodied and imagined presence co-writes your story. The presence of the other(s), to whom, with whom, you narrate, changes, refreshes the story. Cath and I are the 'others', without whom you are unable quite to see your (always-changing) *daimon* (Cavarero, 2000), though you perhaps sense 'him'. Cavarero uses an Italian word that does not easily translate but its nearest English correlate is 'sense'. She suggests that we have a 'sense' of ourselves being narratable, and that this sense is to do with being familiar with oneself *bodily* rather than intellectually (Cavarero, 2000). You are not oblivious to your daimon; you sense that there is something on your shoulder that you want to see differently.[17]

I am writing about my father again. My mother says that she can't believe it. She is pleased but doesn't understand how there could be more to write. It is his physicality that I am writing into, an interest generated in part from the experience of performing him recently at conferences.

My voice, my body; his voice, his body.

These are brought to mind by a sense in your writing of yours and your dad's voices and bodies. This is (some of) the work that your writing does. It evokes. It writes against its own containment (Pelias, 2007)[18].

What is it about fathers? What is it about our fathers? We have both written about our mothers in our collective biography paper but I experience, I think, more yearning in my writing about my father than I do in writing about my mother. It could be that this is because my mother is still alive, of course, but I think it is not only that. These days I am with Pelias, who writes that his father:

"...is a centre of my affective life. I am always writing him, even at times when I do not recognise that I am doing so. He is always present, always watching, as I am watching him." (Pelias, 2004, p.74)

Like Pelias, I sometimes think that I am becoming who I am "by writing, over and over again, my father." (ibid, p.77)

---

[17] See Narratives and Sanity, pp.202-2-5
[18] See Ron is Here, pp.217-221

WRITING SPACE TEN

TWO MEN TALKING
(OCTOBER 2006–MARCH 2007)[1]

In the previous writing spaces we have not considered explicitly questions of gender. In Gale & Wyatt (2008b), written during the same period of time as we were writing this space, we began to explore our process of "becoming men". We exchanged stories from our childhood and early adulthood about boarding school, hair, sexuality, mothers, relationships and more. After Butler (2004b; 2006), we discussed the provisional nature of gender, and how in our collaborative writing–our "collective biography" (Davies & Gannon, 2006)–the experience of writing to and with each other about gender was central to our process:

> "Because of what has gone before, and because of our shared present and prospective shared future, we can perform these versions of our masculinities today." (Gale & Wyatt, 2008b, p.251)

Here, we continue our Deleuzian dialogue about being, not being, and becoming men. Jonathan begins.

Two Men Talking 1: December 2006 (Jonathan)

I have stories to tell you, ones that I have thought about sharing with you before now but have held back from. They feel like they are risky:
Tessa more than once, has said to me, about you and me:
"If Ken were a woman, I wouldn't be happy."
I have taken this to mean that she perceives an intimacy between us that disturbs her.
Once, while I was in Bristol meeting you, I failed to contact her during the day. I was caught up in our discussions, preoccupied with you and me

---

[1] This writing space was originally published in the journal *International Review of Qualitative Research* (Gale and Wyatt, 2008c)

and our work together. Later, she and I spoke on the phone. She asked me, lightly and with humour,

"Where were you? What were you up to? Were you having sex with a furry Cornishman?"

She calls our writing (affectionately) 'up-your-bottom stuff', referring to its theoretical content and to its focus upon ourselves. Our work is up itself.

Earlier this year (2006), back in about June, as the summer holiday was approaching, Holly (who was 14 at the time) and I were talking. She was asking me what all this writing and reading and talking to you and going to Bristol was about, and what was a doctorate anyway. I was telling her about the writing that you and I were doing together at the time. And I also mentioned that we (the family and you) were going to meet during the summer while we were on holiday. She asked me, with that slightly sneering directness that teenagers seem so adept at: "What is it, Dad? Are you and Ken gay or something?"

Jane[2] has often commented how she experiences reading our writings as 'ear-wigging', a rare opportunity to listen to two men talking. She has used the word 'voyeuristic' in describing her sense of this experience.

When I told Tessa that you and I were doing this piece together about being two men talking she pointed out: "But you and Ken don't count. You're not proper men."

I have 'mates', male friends, maybe half a dozen. Most I have known for years, two for well over a quarter of a century. With some I email, and before email we would exchange letters. I meet my friends for nights in the pub. I have been on holiday with one, both when we were single and now with families. My friends are important to me and I would be happy to describe my relationships with them as intimate, but my intimacy with them has not provoked the kinds of questions from the two women in my family–taunting? joking? uncomfortable?–that I have outlined above.

What is it about our relating to each other, about being two men talking–or, more accurately, two men *writing*–that is disturbing, I wonder? And does it disturb us?

Two Men Talking 2: January 2007 (Ken)

Well! This is funny. Two Men Talking 1 has been sitting in my files for quite a while. I have read it a number of times and do you know, each time I read it I laugh! It is lovely that I know Tessa and Holly and can

---

[2] Jane Speedy, our doctoral supervisor

really sense them saying these things. Is it odd that I find their responses
to us endearing and amusing?

You have prompted me to write here today. I have been grappling with
body-without-organs, connectivity, multiplicity: Deleuze is always there,
inspiring me, making me feel uneasy, pushing me to write more. But it is
hard. The ideas I am working on here are challenging me and I am
struggling to find my voice in this writing. I have found myself using the
words of others, impressed and awed by their ideas, eager to immerse
myself in them, work with them and then to create my own. Inspiration.
These ideas have been with me for a long time and each time I read
another Plateau or listen into a Dialogue with Parnet, they become shaken,
I am stirred by what these ideas do to me, how they capture and incite me
to think differently. I am desperate to do this collaborative work. Our
process makes me think about something Bronwyn Davies (Davies &
Gannon, 2006) says about her collective biography process and how the
'Swedes' who became involved wanted to have a plan, they wanted to
know what the writing was for, what the direction was, and Davies could
only say 'Let's see what happens, let's see where it goes'. The nomadic
nature of our inquiries into writing seems to be like this. It seems that our
lines of flight trace new shoots and pathways in the rhizome; I am always
aware that we or I might be going off in another direction. What feels
good about this is the feeling of trust that I have in doing this. I have a
feeling; no, it is a knowing, that it will all come together. I have a sense of
what we are doing and it convinces me of its worth, it encourages and
motivates me to do more. This coming together is the becoming that
Deleuze talks about, the folding and the unfolding.

So our becomings as 'two men talking' fills me with anticipation,
good humour: I sense a certain lightness of being. I don't know what I am
going to write but I know that I am going to write from this sense. Like
Bacon it is quite possible that my bird will become an umbrella [3]. The
morphology of my writing is not spurred by intention; at the moment it is
not even writing as a method of inquiry, it is writing as expression. Let me
see what becomes. What is this, our becoming?

Two men talking: what's so unusual about that? Is it what they are
talking about? All that 'up yer ass' stuff and not about 'wimmen', or
football, or telling racist or homophobic jokes. Is it that? Is it because it

---

[3] Of Bacon's *Painting 46,* Ficacci talks of "a mysterious adventure of
modifications during its realization" and of various figures within the painting, a
bird of prey, a chimpanzee, a field, changing and gradually re-forming and
becoming "incorporated in other ideas or indistinguishable impressions" (Ficacci,
2003, p.23)

does not conform to the stereotype? That seems too simple but Jane's sense of being the voyeur, Holly's acute teenage observation and Tessa's mature inquisition all tell us something about what we are doing. They are performing their selves to us, they are reading us in particular ways, they are curious. Is this because we are two men talking in ways that surprise them, that encourage them to express forms of disquiet? Jane almost appears gleeful that she is able to peep in to see what we are doing! Tessa's enquiry suggests a reading of us that is perhaps a little threatening: threatening because it is unusual? Women looking at men. Women who care about these men? My partner does not express one jot of curiosity. She encourages me. She asks occasional questions about what we are doing but she never looks at our writing or shows much of an interest in it. If she thought that I was having sex with a tall sensitive (male) therapist she would probably say "Well done"!

And what does this say to something else that Tessa said: "If Ken were a woman, I wouldn't be happy"? It is almost as if our friendship, our writing together, our intimacy, would mean something different if I were a woman? If I were a woman is it likely that you would be having sex with me!? Odd though it is we can be trusted as two men talking; we are not going to engage in anything amiss, we are only having 'up yer ass' conversations! But Jane, the self-confessed voyeur, feels that she might be party to a party! She appears to sense that she is becoming privy to intimacies that are, perhaps, suggestive of something more, the mysterious, exotic (erotic?) frisson of two men talking.

Two men talking: what do I think about that? You talk about other relations you have had with men and observe that it is not like ours. I can similarly reflect upon my friendships and agree with the tentative conclusions that you are making but this does not surprise me.

I sense bodies-without-organs. I sense an emerging reluctance to talk about these generalised gendered wholes, these 'men', these 'women'. I sense a uniqueness in you and me. I know you inhabit a male body, though, as Judith Butler points out, "sexual difference is not a given" (Butler, 2004b, p.178). However, I do not feel that this is leading me to talk generally about you and me as two men talking. It feels to me we are talking; there are verbs and the nouns are not necessary. I recognise you as a man, I recognise me as a man, but I do not therefore feel that this alone inscribes you in a special relationship to me. It is true we are 'two men talking' but it feels to me that the 'men-ness' of this is subordinated by the 'talking-ness'. I am not sure if I want to compare you with others. As I write I have started to do that in my mind, I have started to try to uncover diversities, my friends, lovers, other 'men', other 'women', and all that does is to provide me with rich complexity, thickness of description, multiplicity and connection but little gendered generalisation.

I am being drawn to your final thoughts and curiosities. You say: "The question is, what is it about our relating to each other, about being two men talking–or, more accurately, two men *writing*–that is disturbing, I wonder?" and I think, yes, this is an important question.

Tentatively I am going to suggest that 'two men talking' is disturbing to others because of the way in which men (and women) are constituted as gendered wholes. We are familiar with Foucault's discursive effects, with docile bodies and the hegemony of type and specification and it feels to me that what we are beginning to do here is to disassemble all that. If gender as discourse, gender as text makes our talking and writing together in these ways 'disturbing', then that is part of what we are doing and this will involve us in troubling the ways in which sex and gender (whatever they are and however they are related) are always brought together into categories, types, or what Foucault prefers to call, 'species' (Foucault, 1998b). We are 'male' or 'female', 'masculine' or 'feminine', 'heterosexual' or 'homosexual': it is always nouns. It is always presented as black and white. I can't stand it: it all seems to be so shallow. The processes at work here are all to do with the idea that we can somehow discover identity rather than about engaging in a consideration of the way in which these identifications are made up at different times and in different places. We have here a set of constructed categories of knowledge which appear to govern us, establishing patterns of conformity and framing our norms, values and beliefs, so it seems to me very exciting to be disturbing these things.

Two Men Talking 3: February 2007 (Jonathan)

I am energised by your writing: by the humour you refer to–I too catch myself laughing at the 'furry Cornishman' every time I read or think of it. I am energised by your strength of feeling, your passion, in resisting being 'noun'-ed. It's this that I would like to respond to particularly, by telling you a story. It's a recent story about a moment when, as St. Pierre says, I think that I "got" Deleuze (St. Pierre, 2004), profoundly: a haecceity. I plugged him in.

I attended a group relations conference in November (2006). Thirty-three participants and ten staff–from the UK, the US, the Middle East, Africa, Scandinavia, and France–gathered for a week to explore what happens in and between groups and organisations. Such events have a long tradition in the work of institutions like the Tavistock and Grubb

Institutes (the Grubb Institute ran this conference). Group relations draws from psychodynamic and systems theories about human beings' behaviour in groups.

The conference was structured around a number of different 'events', where different configurations of the membership (participants and staff) met, always with the same underlying purpose of experiencing and examining the here-and-now of the occasion: what feelings do we notice? What sense do we make of these feelings? What meanings do we attach? How might we articulate these? How does what is happening here connect with the whole? The staff role is to act as consultants to the various different groups, to notice and draw attention to behaviour that they see as being significant in helping them to work with their own dynamics.

One such event was the Large Study Event, which took place each morning for ninety minutes. All participants attended, with three staff as consultants:

It's the fifth morning. I choose to sit near the middle. The chairs, as always, are in a spiral. As the room fills around me I can see the backs of some people's heads, the faces of others. Still others I have to shift position to see. One consultant, who has been waiting outside, enters the room at the designated start time of 9.30am, draws the door shut behind her and finds a seat. This signals the beginning of the event. (Working with the time and other boundaries is a motif during the conference.)

There's silence at the start, which is familiar. Today, it feels to me that the silence suggests a need to digest. There have been struggles over the week about who we are to each other and how to be in this group, how to find a space, a voice. Race, sexuality, politics have been named: one morning the Palestinian (gay) man sat next to the young–Jewish, lesbian– woman from Jerusalem, who in turn was alongside the London-based South African, white, Jewish woman consultant, and this configuration was a focus for passionate, painful discussion about violence, oppression, diaspora, and loyalty. The quasi-political affiliations of those who are involved in the rival Tavistock Institute have been identified as a present, live issue in the room. Male sexual attraction to women has been made explicit: an older man expressed the longing he experienced as the youngest woman in the group moved to sit next to him, during the session, in the empty chair at the centre of the spiral. More than once the three out gay men have spoken to their sexuality. Rivalry, hate, competition, love, desire–all, if not identified as such, have been expressed.

I have spoken most occasions. Some people rarely do; others do so frequently and easily. My heart always races when I speak. I like it but I find it difficult. Two mornings ago–it was a morning when the group was struggling with personal memories and experiences of political and sexual oppression–I noted my awareness, in the room, at that moment, of my middle-class, Oxford-connected, straight, Englishness. I spoke about this, conscious as I listened to myself of my accent and manner. In amongst the effort to identify who we are in this context I found myself cast in this role, moulded. Yesterday at this event I remained feeling stuck in this persona and could not break out of it. The past twenty-four hours I have been straining against this sense of being typecast. I am aware that I have bought into it; I do not blame the group, but nevertheless I see it as something I am 'carrying' for the group. During other events yesterday I felt that I had lost my voice, unable to break out of a straitjacket that I had donned. (And if I have both been placed and placed myself in this straitjacket, I have wondered, haven't others too–as 'gay', 'straight', 'Jewish', etc.?) I understand this as projective identification (see Bion, 1961; Klein, 1984; Ogden, 1986, etc.), that I am carrying for the group the meanings attached to middle-class, Oxford, straight Englishness that others do not wish to own: Privilege? Authority? Up-tightness? Likewise, I am colluding in disowning parts of myself and ascribing them–putting them into, even–others[4].

Last night I did not sleep well. I was fired by remembering, as if from nowhere, an ancestor–Thomas Wyatt–who was an Elizabethan poet and, even more powerfully, his son (also Thomas Wyatt), who led a rebellion against Queen Mary. It was not a successful rebellion, it has to be said, in that he thought that he had mustered many more supporters than was actually the case and marched on London expecting to be joined by throngs of fellow rebels angry at Mary's plan to marry a Catholic. Sadly (for him) there was not much more than a smattering of fellow rebels when he reached London and he was promptly captured, arrested, imprisoned and, within a short time, executed. His dismembered body parts were displayed in various London locations in a bid to warn others not to do similar. So, a rubbish rebel but a rebel nonetheless.

Full of my rebel and my poet, I stayed between waking and sleeping most of the night.

There are exchanges in the room about an empty chair: who is missing? Where is she? How do we experience her absence? What does she, and her absence, represent for us? Again, this is familiar discourse. The energy seems flat. One of the two women consultants, Mary, sitting

---

[4] See Intersects, Rhizomes and Haecceity, pp.94-99

directly behind me, intervenes. She offers a hypothesis about what the discourse thus far might be hinting at, and she finishes with a challenge:

"There are many voices that we are not hearing, parts of ourselves that are not being given voice, that will say something important to this group, this system, here, now."

Full of my deliberations last night, and restless to find a way in, I seize the invitation:

"I am going to take up Mary's call because I'm conscious of parts of me that I have not expressed here. But what I'm most aware of first is that I have lost my appetite. I usually eat well but these past couple of days I have not wanted to eat and I don't fully understand why, but I connect it with this: that I've felt stuck in a position here of casting myself as English, middle class, Oxford. I can't digest it. And I'm tired by this, and tired of not being hungry. It's not all of me. I have an ancestor who was a poet and another, his son, who was a rebel. He was hopeless as a rebel but he had a go. I feel that I've probably given my poet some space at this conference but today I want to speak up for my rebel."

I notice that I am looking directly at Steve, a young, Irish, gay man to whom, at an earlier session, I expressed anger and with whom I have had no contact since:

"And Steve, I've hardly spoken to you. But I have Irish blood in me too and today I wish to own my Irishness."

He is surprised by my making contact with him like this. I go on:

"And what frustrates me is that I also wish to tell you that I find you an interesting, attractive man but I feel inhibited in doing so. Because here we have to label, we have to box ourselves in. If I tell a man here that I find them attractive I will become one of the gay men. We have conveniently located all the 'gayness' in the out gay men. The 'straight' men do not speak of their attraction to each other, nor much, it has to be said, do we do so to the women here. For fear of what? Being ascribed an identity, I think, or of generating confusion about our identities. I am party to that. But no, there is a multiplicity of feelings, thoughts, desires, that flow through me. I am struggling, but I do not wish to be boxed in as straight or gay, English or Irish, middle class or working class, or whatever. I will not be."

I didn't say all of that final paragraph. I wanted to and I should have but I was afraid to. I said some of it, and more of it differently a day or two later, at a different, smaller group.

I understand this experience in different ways. I can see it, from one point of view, about becoming conscious of what had hitherto been unconscious. I was not (fully) aware that, at times, I felt rebellious, angry, and desiring of (forbidden?) intimacy. These feelings came into view as I worked with the genealogical metaphor of my internal ancestral rebel, my Thomas Wyatt, and I had to work out how to understand and what to do with them: Were these feelings mine? To what extent were they, unconsciously, being projected into me? Towards whom or about what was I angry and rebellious? What kind of intimacy did I want?

At the time–and for the twenty-four hours leading up to it–I was, however, mostly aware of multiplicities. This is Deleuze, I thought. This is something of what he meant. It was exciting. Deleuze and Guattari's writing about how to make oneself a body-without-organs provides insights: my experience was a noticing of a "connection of desires, conjunction of flows, (and) continuum of intensities" (Deleuze and Guattari, 2004, p.179). I sensed that I was "lodge(d) on (the) stratum" of English, middle-class, straightness, and felt impelled to "experiment with the opportunities it (offered)" (p.178). I managed to find "an advantageous place on it", to "find potential movements of deterritorialisation" (p.178) away from the fixities of given or claimed identities. I sought possible lines of flight, experienced them, produced "flow conjunctions here and there", tried out "continuums of intensities segment by segment", and, in speaking up as I did, found "a small plot of new land" (p.178). I needed to be troubled by where I was, enough to examine the detail of what I was experiencing so that "through a meticulous relation with the strat(um)" I could succeed in "freeing lines of flight, causing conjugated flows to pass and escape and bringing forth continuous intensities for a body-without-organs." (p.178)

Maybe Butler brings these together–unconscious processes, multiplicities, BwOs–when, in writing about Braidotti, she notes that for Braidotti,

> "(M)ultiplicity is a way of understanding the play of forces that work upon one another and that generate new possibilities of life. Multiplicity is not the death of agency, but its very condition." (Butler, 2004b, p.194)

For Butler some of these forces are unconscious but they all work through the body, so when something new happens, "it is the result of an activity that precedes the knowing subject, but is not, for that reason, fully external to the subject." (ibid., p.194)

Something new happened for me at the conference. The embodied awareness of multiplicities–some of which, though in me, were not all of me–drew me into performing new possibilities.

So where does that leave us and our work, and being 'two men talking'? It leaves me seeing us less as 'men'–as nouns, as static–and more, as you draw attention to, as being verbs, as becomings (each of us) and as a becoming (the two of us), seeking–being–conjunctions, connections and continuums.

What I have not addressed in this piece, but which I am aware of at this moment, is how *writing* is doing this, and how the process of writing to *you*, now, here, is (or is not?) contributing to our multiplicities, our BwO.

Two Men Writing in (Smooth) Space: February 2007 (Ken)

As is so often the case now, I am writing and I don't know what I am going to write. I have read your last piece again and am invigorated by what you have to say there. Your writing comes off the page, enters me: affects. 'You' is indeterminate, your writing, your 'doing' is tangible; it is the action of you to which I am finding myself responding to here. Inter action: responding to your writing. I am now bringing my writing to you. I feel as if I am writing in the space of the other. I feel very troubled, my life is hurting me and as I write I am wondering what that 'I' is, what it means to me, what it means to others. Therefore, I am trying to put that aside, I am trying to write; perhaps to be in the writing. It feels like being in the writing is about embodiment, soul, about self coming through, about being recognised. Becoming in the writing feels more like living in the writing. Is this a life in the writing? Is there a sense in which being and becoming intersect and are connected?

Richardson has spoken of her experience of rejecting some writing of Virginia Woolf's that had influenced her, "like a mantra", for a long time: "I find it now, behind the guest room door, propped on the floor, braced by the wall: Virginia's facing the wall' (Richardson, 1997a, p.174). Talking further about her reflections on her own writing and her 'rejecting' Woolf, she said: "I wanted to write through the 'personal' binaries (me/them, good/bad, for/against) that were my walls, invisible to me then, bracing and constraining." (ibid., p.174). This 'writing through' is what draws me in here; it feels Deleuzian, like a line of flight, like the creation of a concept which is an event, mercurial, connected and multiple. You talk of your fear of being "ascribed an identity" but then, as resistance, you say: "But no, there is a multiplicity of feelings, thoughts, desires, that flow through me. I am struggling but I do not wish to be boxed in ..." It feels as if Richardson's 'writing through', her writing as a method of inquiry, becomes us in powerful ways. It feels as if, as you "give your poet some space", as you "speak up for (your) rebel", you begin to dissolve the constraints of those categories; you allow yourself to write through them, to write as becoming. Braidotti talks of nomadic inquiry in similar ways; for her the nomad is only passing through: "s/he makes necessarily situated connections that can help him/her to survive, but s/he never takes on fully the limits of one national fixed identity" (Braidotti, 1994, p.33). This is it, isn't it? Never fully taking on these "limits" but at the same time struggling with the forces that seem to want to fix us in these ways. I am not sure that those "feelings, thoughts, (and) desires" that you talk about, "flow through you": it feels more as if you are them, that they are becoming you. The 'you' that you talk about being flown through is indeterminate: "poet"? "rebel"? "middle-class"? "straight"? As you say: "I will not be". You were feeling, you were thinking and you were desiring and, if anything is to be essentialised, it is these doings, these actions, if you like. Right now I am writing and I am struggling with this writing; this feels far more important, in terms of what we are doing, our writing, than to say "I am Ken", or "I am a man" or whatever. The writing and the struggling is me.

I have been thinking about Deleuze and his writing, that the 'body' of Deleuze's work is a BwO: Deleuze and his work are not fixed; they are becoming. We recognise the 'body' from the way in which the familiar concepts as organs are related to the whole, they link together, the connections are there, but, crucially, it is us who makes the meaning of all this. Because "(t)here is no heaven for concepts" (Deleuze, 1994, p.4), concepts are events, being created, shifting form and meaning. We can only gain or temporarily have a sense of haecceity, or multiplicity, or faciality. The 'organs' of the Deleuzian 'body' are not constitutive because they are always re-forming, being re-used, drifting from tangibility to intangibility and simply shifting in sense and meaning. Our thinking about Deleuze, our use and application of his figures in our writing is also a territorialisation, a political act, where we take his ideas and use them; we plug them in (St. Pierre, 2004). As Massumi says:

"A concept is a brick. It can be used to build the courthouse of reason. Or it can be thrown through the window. What is the subject of the brick? The arm that throws it? The body connected to the arm? The brain encased in the body? The situation that brought brain and body to such a juncture? All and none of the above. What is its object? The window? The edifice? The laws the edifice shelters? The class and other power relations encrusted in the laws? All and none of the above." (Massumi, 1987, p. xii-xiii)

And this of course is a signifier for what we are railing against here. We are concerned at being named, of being given a gender, a class, a sexuality. Whilst we have been active in this we are also aware of the discursive forces at play and which act upon us, constituting us, making us up and fixing our identity. It feels that in the chaos, interconnectedness and multiplicity of Deleuzian thought and feeling we are de-centring ourselves and displacing the self-conscious 'I'. By drawing upon Richardson's inducement to use writing as a method of inquiry, we are acting transgressively, preparedly unaware of beginnings or ends, opening ourselves to what emerges and being ready for the unlikeliest of consequences. I have a note here from a workshop run by Bronwyn Davies at QI2006[5], which may not be directly ascribable to her but which seems relevant to what we are exploring here: "writing is a place that is blind, where strangers and unfamiliarities meet". Nomadic inquiry can take us through the plateaus and territories of Deleuze and Guattari's topographies of space, resisting the certainties and stabilities of the logos of striated space, where language is only interested in the closure of the denotative utterance, and exploring, through the application of strategies of territorialisation, the doubt and uncertainty of the nomos of smooth space, where language celebrates the openness of the connotative utterance.

> "There exists a nomadic absolute, as a local integration moving from part to part and constituting smooth space in an infinite succession of linkages and changes in direction. It is an absolute that is one with becoming itself, with process. It is the absolute of passage." (Deleuze & Guattari, 2004b, p.494)

I am going to find that famous Barthes quotation where he talks about the texts that are written rather than the author that writes.

Postscript to Two Men Talking in (Smooth) Space: Losing it!? February 2007 (Ken)

I have read Two Men Talking so far, your contributions and mine, and I am left carefully pondering the question you left at the end of your latest writing:

What I have not addressed in this piece, but which I am aware of at this moment, is how *writing* is doing this, and how the process of writing

---

[5] 2nd International Congress of Qualitative Inquiry, May 2006, University of Illinois at Urbana-Champaign

to *you*, now, here, is (or is not?) contributing to our multiplicities, our body-without-organs.

This is troubling me. My previous piece touches this question, skirts around it, like a nervous animal unsure of its prey but does not fully connect with what it is asking. I remember a long time ago coming to Derrida and Foucault in my studies and finding myself wondering where all this thinking about language and meaning was connecting with the phenomenologies of self that I had grown up with. My reading of Sartre and Merleau-Ponty and then Heidegger familiarised me with the idea of a 'being', of dasein, of being-in-the-world (Merleau-Ponty, 1962; Heidegger, 1962; Sartre, 1973). I began to develop an understanding of a self going through life, as Sartre says, of "surging up in the world" (Sartre, 1973, p.28) encountering the world and changing with experience, abandoned to the angst of individual decision making, with no one, no God, to help me make up my mind. I therefore found Heidegger's device of placing being under erasure useful and, similarly, when I found Derrida using the same device to explain the endless play of signifiers (see Derrida, 1978; Derrida, 1976), I felt equally at ease. As I reflect back upon this time, I am aware that I shelved what now seems to be an uncomfortable binary: border crossings to be made, perhaps. Boundaries to be dissolved.

My reading of Judith Butler has helped and I feel that, so far, our writing, up to the point of your question, has taken us to a similar way of thinking that is expressed in the following assertion from *Gender Trouble*:

> "Clearly this project does not propose to lay out within traditional philosophical terms an *ontology* of gender whereby the meaning of *being* a woman or a man is elucidated within the terms of phenomenology. The presumption here is that the "being" of gender is an effect, an object of a genealogical investigation that maps out the political parameters of its construction in the mode of ontology...As a genealogy of gender ontology, this inquiry seeks to understand the discursive production of the plausibility of that binary relation and to suggest that certain cultural configurations of gender take the place of "the real" and consolidate and augment their hegemony through that felicitous self-naturalisation." (Butler, 2006, p.45)

We seem to have been working toward and with the 'doing' of gender and what Butler calls its 'effects'. We haven't looked directly at power and, in particular, at the way in which Foucault talks about power as actually forming the objects of which it speaks. It seems to me that Butler makes this point well in this book; she takes Simone de Beauvoir's profound and direct assertion that "one is not born a woman, but rather becomes one" (de Beauvoir, 1978) and advances it into a detailed and challenging piece of rhetorical writing. She emphasises how language works to fix and establish ontologies of gendered self but as I write now to inquire, I am searching for a sense in which her writing addresses the question that concerns us here.

It is fascinating in the quotation that I have used from your last piece that you have italicised the words 'writing' and 'you': this is the binary, here is the boundary; this is the border that needs to be dissolved. Is this somehow a phenomenology of language? In the *definitional ceremony* (Myerhoff, 1986; White, 1995, 2000) of our writing it is becoming increasingly clear to me (in existential or phenomenological terms but not in epistemological terms!) that whatever 'I' is for me is also the writing. I have grappled with the embodied nature of what we are doing. When I first read Davies and Gannon (2006), their use of the embodied self in relation to memory work troubled me. I was trying to understand it and couldn't. I was searching for a meaning and I couldn't find it. But now as I write I am increasingly gaining a sense of what this is. I am feeling a sense of needing to write, of struggling with the writing, of searching for help in the writing. More, perhaps. My being in the writing? My being is the writing? We seem to be performing our selves in the writing. I know that I am writing to you but increasingly this is feeling like I am writing with you. If writing the self is about performance I have a growing sense that this performance is characterised in an embodied way. Stanislavski's idea of method acting, where the actor as person becomes the part and the part becomes the actor, not just in the 'performance' but in life in general, seems analogous to this.

I have been struggling now for days; wanting to write, not knowing what I will write, not knowing if I will be able to write but, somehow, knowing, sensing, that this is me, this is what I want to be doing, what I want to be, where I want to be. Here at this desk, tapping these keys, looking at this screen, my glass of water, books, the silences of this house. This is my sense of self, embodied in the writing. The bigger picture of my life remains troubled and as I write here now anxieties and sadnesses pervade my sense of self; I feel as if I am identifying myself through this but this identification is not working in a Foucauldian sense. I don't feel 'constructed' by circumstance, by the naturalising forces of discourses. I know that these forces are there and that they have in the past and are now playing a part in my life, in the formation of self; but that is not what I feel captured by here and now. My energy, my life force seems to be in this writing.

I know, when I have thought about Bacon and his painting and his life, his process, the way that he worked (Deleuze, 2004; Ficacci, 2003), that senses of self will change. My senses of self will become apparent and then, perhaps, diminish. Or explode! My 'painting' will change, the duck that I drew will become a rabbit[6], but, as Deleuze encourages me to think, I am becoming through and in the writing. Like Bacon when he died, there will be many canvases 'unfinished', stacked in the kitchen and the hall, the line between him and the canvases blurred, erased by the vibrant processes of his refusal to be a 'painter' and yet inextricably fused to that becoming self that I am reading now and attaching such significance to.

Clearly, Bacon is defined by his work and yet I remember that when he died people spoke with surprise and in wonder about the unfinished paintings: 'How odd that he didn't finish them: how strange'. This misses the point: the 'unfinishedness' of those paintings characterised the way in which he worked and, therefore, in this sense, characterised him. For me, in so many senses, none of his paintings were 'finished'; I know that they hung in galleries and were exhibited but they always seem to carry with them the potential for change, to be changed.

This is how I feel about our writing. I know that we too have 'finished' pieces, and that is great; it is good to have our writing published–out there, so to speak–but at the moment, for me, it is the 'in here' that is important and the sense that the 'in here' is also now, as I write, becoming me and becoming us through this process, our exchanges, our dialogue, our 'between-the-twos'. I am not writing: I am becoming! Have I overstepped the mark by saying this? I found myself laughing as I wrote that, seconds ago! What am I saying here?! Are you with me? I want to be cheeky. I want you to smile too. I want your sense of self to smile with this embodiment that I have just sensed. I am in the writing: the writing is in me. As I write here I am also defining myself but the figures that I produce to do this are elusive: will you get them? Yes, of course you will. You will get them. Your getting them is also about dissolving that you and me binary. Two Men Talking is about (our)selves. It is talking, it is writing, it is becoming.

---

[6] Wittgenstein used in his lectures at Cambridge what became the very famous ambiguous figure of the duck-rabbit. The figure can be seen differently as either a duck or a rabbit and the point that Wittgenstein was making through the use of this figure is that of 'seeing-as'; the figure is representational, it is interpreted by the person who 'sees' it. At this stage in his work Wittgenstein was influenced by the work of the gestalt theorist Kohler and both of these thinkers were influenced by the morphological studies of Goethe. For an extended analysis of this see Monk (1991).

I am going to stop here. I have started to worry that I am losing it! I started to think that I had better write some more analytical material and be more reflexive about the representations of self that we are working with here. I am wondering if I should be asking questions about my narrative work as therapy. I am thinking that I should consider the processes that 'define' us here; that I should go back to Foucault and power and look again at the ways in which discourses produce us; that I should think again about gender and self, which doing collective biography (Gale & Wyatt, 2008b) encouraged us to explore. But I have just seen Bacon's studio in South Kensington and all those unfinished canvases stacked in the hall and I am feeling OK again. I don't think I am losing it yet!

Reeling and (W)riting: February, 2007(Ken)

Sometimes I think I will
Then again I won't
Sometimes I think I will
Then again I won't
Sometimes I think I will
Then again I won't
Well ...

(Chuck Berry - Reeling and Rocking)[7]

> We notice, in this exchange within Two Men Talking, that there is a series of pieces by Ken before Jonathan responds. Ken mostly writes fast and plentifully. Jonathan less so.

I keep reeling back to this writing: the writing seems to keep reeling me back to it. Again I am captured by not knowing what this means; as I write I am fascinated by these words that inscribe me. Those words that I have just written that have been and are so important in my life: 'knowing', 'mean(ing)'. Words that you are going to read as these exchanges, these between-the-twos, continue to engage us. Words that now I am challenging and that are challenging me. As I read again what I wrote to you/with you last week–Losing It–I feel a great reflexivity about

---

[7] B-side of Sweet Little Sixteen, originally released in January 1958 on the Chess label. Written and performed by Chuck Berry; produced by Leonard and Phil Chess (Berry, 1958)

our 'process', about the different ways in which we represent ourselves to each other here. I am also reflecting upon the way in which we perform ourselves through the writing and the nature of our intentions as we write.

Here I feel myself being washed into the turbulent waters[8] of sense; wanting to be immersed in, what we could call, a phenomenology of writing, being in the writing. This sense is constant, though mainly indeterminate: it seems to have a kind of self-presence; driving me to write, frustrating me when I have so much else to do that I can't write and being with me when I am actually doing it, being in the writing, like now. My consciousness keeps reminding me of Heidegger and then Derrida, of placing being or meaning *sous rature* and how the space that is opened up here is a space that is at the same time a space of both necessity and inadequacy. As Derrida says:

"Without the possibility of differance, the desire of presence as such would not find its breathing-space. That means by the same token that this desire carries in itself the destiny of its nonsatisfaction. Differance produces what it forbids, making possible the very thing that it makes impossible." (Derrida, 1976, p.143)

So I was also struck by your recent e-mail to me when you said:

"Love what you say about how you see/feel about writing these days. I'm with you. Differently, but with you. I'm preoccupied at the moment by wanting to write *stories* - stories about some counselling incidents that have happened recently, and a story about Joe and me falling out. What's that about? Why stories? I'm feeling tired of reading Butler and others at the moment - she's doing my head in. Too much 'cerebral epistemological' stuff as you might call it. Makes me want to read Pelias. And I'm listening to Zadie Smith's 'On Beauty' - it's great. …Still writing away, slowly but getting there." (E-mail from Jonathan to Ken 1st March 2007 10:09)

This is important in terms of what we started to do when we began our writing–where we reflected our different writing styles–and it is interesting to see now how things have changed through being in the writing, through actually doing it: writing. It seems as if this began with an awareness of my 'cerebral epistemological' approach to things at the time and your preoccupation with "wanting to write stories". As I am wondering now about this and what it means to me I also realise that again I am getting

---

[8] Deeply affected as I write by the terrible news this morning of two people being swept into the sea by the storms down at Mullion: the great force of the water, the heaving desperation of abandonment in the waves.

back into that disciplined analytical thing, when actually what I have really learned through this writing is how much I love writing 'stories' too. So maybe it's that our stories are different, that we write them in different ways and that we are being in them, becoming in them, in different ways.

So in what ways are we the subjects of our writing? Our writings provide the spectacle of us. Are they are also imbued with the ways in which we want to represent ourselves? I am beginning to feel that your "wanting to write *stories*" (your italics) is different to me 'wanting to write'. We are read. We read each other. Others read us. Žižek argues that

> "(T)he subject is usually reduced to so-called subjectivation, he is conceived as an effect of a fundamentally non-subjective process: the subject is always caught in, traversed by the pre-subjective process (of 'writing', of 'desire', and so on), and the emphasis is on the individuals' different modes of 'experiencing', 'living' their positions as 'subjects', 'actors', 'agents' of the historical process." (Žižek, 1989, p.174)

Further, it seems to me that he hasn't yet talked about the discursive and hegemonic effects of culture, as we have begun to explore here in Two Men Talking. In what Žižek says here I gain a sense of Althusser's (2001) idea of interpellation, where a particular style of writing and an attraction to a specific subject matter 'hails us'; we are drawn to it.

There is desire expressed in your e-mail that you want to write stories. That process is drawing you. My visceral, 'phenomenological' sense of writing and the feelings associated with it are similarly seductive: in the moorland of sense, what is the spectral allure of the siren that is drawing us? The magnetism of this allure seems to be different; the energies that pull us seem to be particular to our respective selves. To repeat Žižek phrase, we are "caught in, traversed by the pre-subjective process (of 'writing', of 'desire', and so on)" and this has the effect, he argues, of producing our subject position of, in this case, writer. Therefore, as a discursive effect, we seem to be the subjects of and therefore become, in a Foucauldian disciplinary sense, subject to the signifiers we use. This only follows, however, if we allow these subject-positions to become established, as we become antithetical to our own becoming and allow ourselves, our each others, and others, to construct us in this way.

I feel so powerfully then that it is the writing and not the writer that I want to see becoming: in this sense I will never become a writer but my writing will always be in state of becoming. As species we are endangered when we become the subject of the signifiers we use, so I agree with Torfing when he says:

"(The subject) strives to inscribe itself as a signifier in the symbolic order, but cannot find a signifier which represents it. The subject is therefore penetrated by a constitutive lack. The subject is this lack, and the subjectivation of the subject through the identification with different subject positions is merely an attempt to fill it." (Torfing, 1999, p.57)

Who are you? "I woke up in a Soho doorway/the policeman knew my name" (Townshend, 1978). Pete Townshend was mortified by the 'subjectivation' that his fame and notoriety had given him; he was subject to the policeman's recognition of him. His identification as a writer, a performer, a guitar player and, in this case, a bon viveur, necessitated a disciplinary effect. As Althusser claimed

" ...the hailed individual will turn around. By this one-hundred-and-eighty-degree physical conversion, he becomes a subject. Why? Because he has recognised that the hail was 'really' addressed to him (and not someone else)." (Althusser, 2001, p.174)

So, I am nurturing a reluctance to be through the nouns that 'hail us' in particular ways. Now, I am writing but I am not a writer. Tonight, I shall be teaching but I am not a teacher.

Two Men Talking 5: March 2007 (Jonathan)

I have taken longer to write this than I can remember doing with others. It has not been the struggle that other writing has been, but I have only been able to write in small doses. It is as if the writing is inviting me to take care. It may be that this is because it is risky: there is much at stake.

I feel relieved to be writing again. Writing like this to you, though this implies the me/you binary that we have been developing away from.

As I write:

I am thinking about: this, here, now. What this is like. Pen in hand, in a café in Oxford. The shape of my body, the angle of my pen. (And written again, here, now, as I type my handwritten text.)

I am asking myself, why do I now enjoy writing long hand, whereas until less than a year ago, I only used to write at the keyboard? Something is freed by the holding of a pen, the inscribing of ink onto a page in the red and black note book (see Cixous, 1991).

There is more though: I am questioning why it is not only the writing by hand but the setting in which I am writing. I enjoy writing–I am unable to write in any other context, it seems–in 'in-between' places, mostly cafés but also at, say, railway stations, airports. These public, in-between places are settings where people are passing through. Here, there is the noise of people talking–the students discussing their music lecture–and there is movement as people arrive and leave; buses pass, babies chatter, milk is being steamed. So I wonder about this need to write in such settings–amongst movement and transience–and think that these features are perhaps echoes of my internal writing world. If I think of "flows (that) pass and escape" (Deleuze & Guattari, 2004b, p.178), how writing is an attempt to disappear (Deleuze & Guattari, 2004b), then my need to be in places like these begins to make sense.

This, here, now, writing to you. The you-ness, again, of this writing, and how different this sense is from, say, when I write with a more generalised audience in mind. This latter audience feels to one side, where I can glimpse it. Here, the you-ness is in front. I'll come back to this. Others' witnessing of our writing feels increasingly important, but there is a difference.

I am aware of Joe and the now resolved falling-out with him that I have told you about in passing. Not so much the experience itself (whatever an "experience itself" might mean) but what it means to want to write about it to you. Writing into an empty space would not be the same. Writing to you means it is going somewhere; it is directed–into the "collection of muddled lines between us" (Deleuze & Parnet, 2002, p.viii). So, if I were to write about Joe now, it would involve writing within the multiplicity we are creating and are being created by, and adding to our collection of muddled lines. It is writing into inhabited, rather than empty, spaces.

I also notice myself thinking about what you have brought us back to. You seem to say that the writing and the subjectivity are 'one'. It is not I (subject) who writes. The writing is me. And more: the you and me and the writing and subjectivity are all 'one'. I use the word 'one' as meaning not that they comprise a 'whole', but that they are inseparable: felted (Deleuze & Guattari, 2004b).

I feel dizzy. I am unable to hold any of this still: you, me, writing, our inquiry, my gender, your gender, my sexuality, yours–nothing is fixed, it feels, even for a moment. These are all flows and intensities... and it seems too much. I long for groundedness–but as soon as I say the word I am destabilised by questioning the metaphor and its implicit binaries (ground/air, low/high, earth/sky). I feel destabilised.

In this frame of mind, and trying to allow myself to stay destabilised, I go back to how you write about writing. When I write, I write with you in mind. You are in my mind, in me. I have a picture of you reading as I write, in your office at home, or, having printed my writing out, in your kitchen with a coffee. I imagine how you might be responding–how you might write in the margins, handwriting at an angle to the text, words, phrases, question marks. I imagine your wanting to rush to respond, trying to find space amongst the demands of your children, your work, and your relationship. I have all this–you–in mind; I have my experience of the writing, feeling, thinking Ken within me. And therefore, this is one way in which "we" write together, even when we are apart. Without you–or Ken-ness? Or is it Ken-ing, the verb?–there would not be my writing.

So here is another take, then, on the 'disturbance' that our relationship has engendered (an interesting word!) in my family, where Tessa asks "were you having sex with a furry Cornishman" and Holly asks if you and I are gay: I would suggest that our writing together is indeed a kind of love-making. I think that this is what Deleuze means when he says:

> "Writing carries out the conjunction, the transmutation of fluxes…one only writes through love, all writing is a love-letter." (Deleuze & Parnet, 2002, p.38)

WRITING SPACE ELEVEN

THERAPY:
A PLAY (MARCH 2007–JANUARY 2008)

In this writing space, we experiment with form. We imagine that we are engaged in a therapeutic relationship–Jonathan as therapist, Ken as client–and explore how our dialogue in this fictional setting takes us into different terrain.

We wrote the contents of this writing space, in prose form, as a variant on our between-the-twos, each of us picking up the emailed story from where the other had left off. We each, respectively, wrote the sections where our 'character' was talking and thinking.

One interesting aspect of this process was that the fiction allowed us space to work at our conflicts via both our fictional selves and the other characters who enter the story. We don't usually find ourselves in conflict. The 'selves' we become in this space give us freedom that we do not customarily allow ourselves.

We also find ourselves employing magical realism (see Bowers, 2004; Faris, 2004; Speedy, 2008) to assist us. "Employ" is too functional, deliberate a term: our characters came upon us–upon Jonathan–as he/we wrote, as the "demarcation lines between the layers of reality" (Speedy, 2008, p.171) blurred.

In the redrafting process we have adapted this into play script. We have found that this form allows more space. The density and intensity of the script is relieved, both by the stage directions and the movement of bodies.

This writing space allows–to an extent–for the pain and sadness in Ken's life, alluded to in passing during this book, to be articulated more fully.

***

The room is too full. Too many books–most unread. The shelves are crammed, with volumes placed horizontal on those that stand. Too many papers on the desk (but neat, in piles). An old leather sofa dominates, with an armchair (from a different set) at an angle. A Persian rug, the only feature of genuine taste, red, with intricate patterning, lies central.

A large sash window looks out onto the street. It's open. Traffic passes but rarely intrudes. The room is too high up and the vehicles occasional. The drunks that gather offer a greater obstacle to the work that takes place here.

Jonathan–tall, angular, around 50–welcomes Ken into the room. He motions towards the sofa and folds himself into the armchair. He considers his client: 60s, tanned, fit, medium height. The day is warm and Ken (K) wears a T-shirt and long shorts.

Jonathan (J) notices Ken's long, looked-after nails and the striking coat of hair on Ken's limbs. Esau, eat your heart out.

J: So, Ken, what's going on for you? What's brought you here?

K *(looking up):* I never know where to start. I know that you are going to ask me something like this … the Morcheeba song seeps through my consciousness … 'it's all part of the process'. It's what you have to do; to get the ball rolling. I know. I understand. I am driving here; my head is bursting with ideas and sensations that come out in half formed sentences that I am going to express to you. I want to open out. I want to reveal. I want to feel that I can say something to you that will enable you to help me. I want you to be able to say something to me that will help me feel better. How sad is that!? Why am I saying that? That's why I am here after all. That's why I am paying you £40 for this hour.

God. I hate to sound so aggressive: so challenging. Is that unusual? The way we are; the way we change according to where we are. Just before I came into your door just now I half recognised a woman walking down the street; she totally recognised me. Her eyes briefly lit, she was going to speak; I averted my gaze and walked on. I didn't want to talk to her. I knew her as a student from a course a number of years ago. I remembered me; confident teacher, erudite, urbane, full of witticism and knowledge. I remembered her; mature student, adult returner, somewhat in awe, enraptured by the excitement of the teaching and the learning. I didn't want to talk to her. I didn't want her to meet me, the person who was coming to meet you. Here is me now, that person who is fragile, prone to depression and irrational bouts of anger, wanting and needing help, keen to lay bare and expose the nakedness and rawness of the hurt that is gnawing away my energy and my life. For that brief moment I didn't want that woman to see me. I didn't want that bubble to burst. I wanted to preserve that identity that had become me with her; I wanted to remain the person that I felt that I was in her eyes.

But … here I am now … here I am now, talking to you. Trying to construct something else; feeling that I want to 'lay bare' myself in order that you might help me but concerned in another part of myself that I might be making me up for you, just as I did as a teacher, making myself up for that woman who was my student. I might 'confess' something to you, in order that I might try to enable you to 'see' something of me, a deep 'hidden' part perhaps. I tell you about some misdeed, some affair, some apparent weakness which displays my openness, my 'desire' to come clean about something, to confess, to offer something up to you so that you can help me. But what is that? Why do I do that? Am I really trying to achieve some kind of transparency as part of this process? Perhaps I am showing off; perhaps I am telling you this, this fiction, in a way that will help to normalise us, will help me to identify myself in your eyes in certain ways, so that will I feel good about myself. I want you to see me in this way.

I am so exhausted by all this. I find it so easy to work with this cerebral stuff. I like to think. I don't mind crying. My desire is for insight. I want to open out. I want to give as much as take. It is all so complicated, so rhizomatic; the complexity draws me in many ways but leaves me stranded on a rocky beach in another very profound way. In many ways my deep desire is for love, for passion: I feel myself, in my imagination of course, absorbed, immersed, in a deep, powerful surging current of love, that transports my body in such a way that my feelings drift, my world is of dreaming and of lightness. I am tingling warm, wonderfully drowning in a deep swirling glow of intense love.

Sorry…I drifted off there. That was amazing! I was so conscious of my whole body then. I felt whole in those moments. Not thinking, not feeling as separate entities of my being but for a few brief moments I had a total sense of self. It was both where I wanted to be and where I was. It's a bit hard to come down to earth: I need to stay with this for a moment.

Jonathan looks at Ken, respects the silence. He turns and speaks to the audience, aside.

J: What do I feel? I feel sadness. I feel confusion. I feel energy.

What can I say? I don't know yet. I'll stay quiet if I can, if I can allow myself not to jump in.

There's so much here. I'm overwhelmed at the moment.

Was there resentment in Ken's voice about paying? Was it the amount that was the issue? £40? No, I don't think so. Maybe it's a challenge: will I come up with the goods? Shall I say something about this? No, no. That won't be helpful.

He needs something from me. The quiet has been long enough. To stay quiet for longer may seem, I don't know, rude perhaps.

I'll go with what's captured me, I think. I'll go with that.

J turns back to K.

J: The picture that's stayed with me from all that you've said…the picture I want to ask you about it is the rocky beach that you feel stranded upon. You said that this complexity leaves you stranded on a rocky beach. Tell me about this beach. What's it like?

K: So often in my speaking and writing I find myself in water. Water, or perhaps more specifically, the sea, has a powerful effect on me. Physically, swimming in the wild sea around the coast where I live, losing myself in the surf, actually feeling myself being swept, actually taken, by the waves is one of the most exhilarating feelings that I have experienced in my life. Perhaps that is why I can say here that I often 'find myself in water' when I speak and write about my feelings, my emotions and the things that energise me. You remember my poem that I showed you some time ago?[1] I know that that writing was about transport; it was to do with actually being on the beach with Reuben but it was also about the way in which those images of the sea were able to take me to places in my heart that felt tender and raw because of what was happening to me in my life at that time.

So, you are asking me how this complexity leaves me stranded on a rocky beach. How do I respond? You would ask me that! I told you that I often find myself in water and clearly finding myself on a rocky beach is part of the same thing. It is not a good place to be.

Last Saturday I went swimming on an isolated beach, on my own. There had been storms and the sea was very rough. I felt excited, a little apprehensive, about going into the water; the tide was coming in and I knew the beach, there were no rips. It would be OK. It was fantastic going

---

[1] See Writing the Incalculable, pp.77-79

into the sea, it was boiling; I didn't need to go out of my depth to be immersed in the raging water. It was so exciting. The waves were breaking over my head; it was exhilarating to make a couple of strokes and feel myself taken by the wave on a wild racing ride. But then, within minutes of being there, I suddenly felt a huge force and found myself being lifted right off my feet by a great swell of water. Panic. Immediately I had an awareness that this is what drowning is going to be like; I could feel the water taking me at will, a mere cork bobbing in its great surging energy.

For a few moments I felt that I was going to be swept out to sea and drowned and then, as quickly as it happened, the heaving groundswell subsided and I was back within my depth, on my feet, being buffeted again by those waves.

I struggled out of the water as fast as I could. The backwash from the huge waves was really powerful, knocking me off my feet as I forced myself back up to the beach. High tide: a rocky beach. Relief. I sat on that cold beach with my heart heaving, both from physical exertion and from fear. I sat looking at the huge, surging sea, wondering what had happened to me, what it was that had nearly drowned me. Then I saw what I didn't see when I first raced into the water: the great volume of water on the high tide was being magnified by a cross tide, caused by the waves being trapped within the headland on my left. So, when a particularly big wave came in, the little bay was too small to take it, causing a cross wave to combine with the incoming wave to create an irresistible, surging mass of water. I realised that was what took me by surprise and made me feel that I was going to drown.

Why am I telling you this?

It was being on that beach after my scare. Although it welcomed me, it was not like a summer beach. It was cold, the rocks were icy and wet and the sand stuck to my body like a rash. Being there was a disappointment to me. I felt washed up, unable to go back into the water; the place where I am normally confident and ecstatic had become too much for me: I couldn't go there. That was a 'real' rocky beach.

How does it connect with the image of the rocky beach that you picked up on in what I was saying earlier? I don't know.

Yes, I do. It feels to me, now, that what I was trying to say by using that image was that I am at ease with talking with you, or perhaps with others that I trust, about the complexities of my life, in particular about the unhappiness that I am experiencing in my relationship. I want to be open, I want to share; it feels to me that if I do that with someone I trust something good will come of that, something will come back: words, thoughts, feelings, gestures. It is like talking to you now. I am fascinated, drawn, by the intricacies of this. I enjoy trying to work things out. I suppose also it appeals to my vanity: we are talking about me! It is also good for me to talk with you, to feel a sense of companionship, even though you are a therapist and I am your client. I feel that I am able to open out to you because I trust you and feel respect for what you give back to me in this relationship. But as I said before, it is complex: the thinker in me enjoys this. The thinking, in one way, makes me feel good but, in another, leaves me stranded.

I have just been hooked by a line from that fantastic Polly Harvey song, 'This is Love'. How does it go? "Why does life have to be so complex/when I just want to sit here and watch you undress?[2]" In that line she has captured something of what I am feeling here and why the 'rocky beach' is such an uncomfortable but profoundly significant place for me. I can do the thinking, I can open myself out, I can reason and I am happy to try to expose and share the things that are in my heart. In this sense working with the complexity that I was talking about is something that I can do but at the end of the day where does it get me? I am aware of the simple, the profound, unthinking sensuality of love. Something elusive. This is what I want and it is not there. This feels to me like the rocky beach.

That took a lot of getting down to. Do you understand what I am trying to say here? It feels like I have been the therapist. I have had to do all the working out!

Have I made any sense at all?

Jonathan looks at Ken, attempting to convey calm. He is taken by Ken's energy. He notices his envy: of Ken's ability to articulate, yes, how words flow so easily. But also he is envious of Ken's sea.

But this will have to wait. He is distracted by something more fundamental. Jonathan can't speak. As Ken has been talking he's been aware of his uneasiness about this process. Ken and he here, doing this. He hasn't been able to identify the source of his discomfort. But now he understands that he can't go on; in this moment, in this lull after Ken has finished talking so powerfully, he knows this. He says to himself:

J *(to the audience):* I can't maintain this attention to Ken. I am thrown by the impossibility of having this role whilst knowing that it is a lie. This

---

[2] This is Love by PJ Harvey from the album Stories from the City, Stories from the Sea. Written by PJ Harvey, produced by PJ Harvey, Rob Ellis and Mick Harvey. Island Records, 2000 (Harvey, 2000)

is weird. Ken is my friend, my peer, my writing partner. He's not my client. I can't do this, not even for our writing. I can't be a character in a story that Ken and Jonathan are writing where we pretend that he is client and I am counsellor. I am not going to let them do this. I can't be the trusted person Ken is treating me as–the therapist. I feel impelled to rebel. This is not fair on me and not fair on Ken.

Turns to Ken.

J: Fuck this.
K: Pardon?
J: I don't mean fuck what you've said. At all. Nor you. What you've been talking about makes sense and I'm interested in it and want to talk with you more about it. But not like this. I mean this can't work, Ken. I mean fuck them. Fuck Ken and Jonathan. This is too much for us. I can't pretend to be your therapist. I don't know why I agreed to do it. It's unethical. I know too much about you and you know too much about me. I can't maintain my 'stance'. Please don't think that this is about you or about what you've been talking about. On the contrary, it's *because* I want to engage with you about all you've been saying that I can't maintain this pretence. It's simply too weird.

Silence. The two men are still.

A second Ken, Writer Ken (WK), and a second Jonathan, Writer Jonathan (WJ), enter from stage left and right respectively. WJ squats on the floor stage front and looks out over the audience. WK approaches, talking to him all the while. The lights focus on these two. The 'original' Ken and Jonathan are in shadow behind them. WK speaks quickly, forcefully, his voice raised slightly. He walks slowly around WJ as he talks.

> What follows is Ken's writing. In the process of writing Therapy, Ken came out of the story and out of role at times. Jonathan did not. The characters of WK and WJ embody this. WJ says nothing. We're interested in this. Was it to do with Jonathan's need to stay with metaphor? And/or Ken's passionate immediacy? Jonathan's sense of being constrained by the boundaries of the conceit? And Ken's unwillingness to be so?

WK: It's three months since you sent me your latest writing. It is summer, although it doesn't feel like it. Veering irrationally from ennui to anxiety, I find that my ability to control these feelings is becoming less and less. Lines of flight image themselves in my mind but I am too scared to flee; I return to coping, getting on with it and hoping that waking up tomorrow will be to a brighter day.

In a recent emailed reflection on our writing process you said:

> "We have talked about how you write fast, perhaps impulsively, fluently; how no sooner have I sent something to you than you excitedly (it seems) reply."

I am aware of this. There is normally a great urgency to respond, I am so taken by something in your writing that my mind starts to race, my feelings bubble over, everything is put to one side and I just have to write. I have learned to put your attachments to one side, perhaps for few hours, at most a day, before I open them because I now know what will happen. It is as if I anticipate my own eagerness, I know what is coming so I ensure that when I open, read and reflect there will be some space there for me to write. This time it was different and I am not entirely sure why. The latest text that you've written has been in my writing folder now for over 4 months. There have been many circumstantial events that I could cite to explain my lack of response but of course this will not do; I have written other things to you, we have talked. No: this is an intentional, avoiding, lack of response. I didn't know what to write back. I don't know what to write back. In the spirit of our writing over the last few months, in the context of writing as a method of inquiry, in the light of so recently finding myself actually in the writing, I am going to try to write myself into a response.

Am I writing as Ken the therapist's client or as Ken conversing and diversing with you? I don't know. This is partly because I don't know how you were writing to me. It feels to me that in those last paragraphs you wrote yourself out of our fiction and I think it's that Jonathan whom I am addressing here. But I am not sure. Where shall I start?

I know that when I was talking to you, the therapist, (*he points towards therapist Jonathan*) what I was saying was simply coming out of me. What a phrase: "simply coming out of me"! Uncrafted, uncharted, with little forethought. This is often the case when I write and 'talking' to you in that 'session' was no different. When I was talking with you about that experience in the sea, I was there. I have just re-read that piece and I can feel my feelings, feel the fear of the great surge of the water and sense the coldness of the rocks on the beach. So although the therapist/client interface that we set up could in many ways be seen as an artifice, the 'me' that was in there was qualitatively the same kind of 'me' that you are getting now. I know that we are still grappling with 'me-ness', 'nouns', 'selves', 'subjectivities' but I know that over there, (*he points again*) I was engaging in a similar set of feeling, thinking, sensing actions as when I write to you 'normally'.

So what about your response? I felt unchanged by the 'Therapy' process, in that I found myself acting out the same kind of writing that I have come to enjoy sharing with you: increasingly this seems to be what I do. This to me seems to be what our writing is becoming: becoming through the writing. So now I am concerned about you. When he (*pointing*) said "I can't pretend to be your therapist", I didn't realise that you were pretending. When he said "I can't maintain my 'stance'", I didn't realise that you had one. I am becoming fascinated by this; I am becoming drawn into this as an intrigue draws in a reader of crime stories. I thought that Therapy, just like our other writing, was part of that large rhizomatic theme that we have begun to explore, two men talking. I can see that in a way there's an imbalance in our contrived relationship in that, generally, I believe, clients do more talking than therapists. This had concerned me. I remember thinking, as we began those exchanges, this is not going to be fair on Jonathan because I get to do all the talking. I began to become concerned that the therapy/client artifice could lead to self-indulgence, only focusing upon me. I didn't have time to think myself out of that: your final piece shook me out of that reverie.

WJ continues to gaze across the audience, still. He is not looking at WK. His look, though, conveys concern, worry, anxiety. He is affected by what he is hearing. WK continues:

You say: "It's unethical. I know too much about you and you know too much about me." Am I naïve? Am I gullible? I sometimes think that I am; I have become aware that sometimes I play the naïve, gullible person to facilitate a dependency, to encourage others to help me. But this is not the case here; I simply thought that we were providing opportunities to write in different ways and to use the writing, nomadically, to explore the processes and emergences of selves. I thought that the 'knowing' about each other was part of the processes of becoming that also included the feeling, the sensing, the intuitive, the soulful, the mythical, whatever. As our writing has come to re-territorialise these spaces that we share, my writing seems to move further and further away from the telling, confessing the congealed vagaries of an essentialised self, to becoming a performance of self/selves, within these spaces. This writing as performance is a way of knowing. When Ron Pelias talks of "performance as a way of knowing" he says:

> "We just knew it was true. We knew it in our bodies, from the daily work of performance. We knew as we talked with one another about our performance experiences. We knew it personally when some performances would live with us, like old friends or enemies, inscribing their images and spirits on our psyche. In other words we knew this as sensuous beings, somatically engaged in performative events. Such knowledge resides in the ontological and is perhaps best expressed in the poetic." (Pelias, 1999, p.ix)

It feels to me that our writing works like this. The 'knowing too much' that you refer to here suggests quantities of knowledge that I am not comfortable with: increasingly I am becoming used to knowing as a performative process in which the quality of knowing shifts incessantly and is being constantly folded into a rich seething mix with feeling, sense, intuition; all the ingredients of body and soul. You can know all of me in one performance and nothing in the next.

But I am still troubled by what that Jonathan *(indicating the seated, therapist, Jonathan behind)* has just said and done. I am worried that I am not getting something. Of course I could call you up and we could discuss this piece and sort out the meaning. We could use our elaborated codes and 'find out' exactly what is going on. Such an approach would of course commit the sin of phono-centrism with the assumption of locating presence in the horse's mouth of the spoken word.

Still no response from WJ.

Perhaps you are tempting me to perform myself within the script, to be that client…

And, with that, WK turns on his heels and walks off whence he came. WJ stands slowly, heavily, and exits too.

The lights come up on Ken, the client, and Jonathan, the therapist.

Ken looks aghast at Jonathan. The therapist has just cast the chess men off the board and kicked the table to one side. Jonathan's arms are folded, long legs stretched out from his chair. The weight of the silence between them is heavy.

K: Do you know I had forgotten the 'relationship', the 'client' and the 'counsellor'? I had lost any awareness that I might have had of 'stance'.

I come along here because of the conversations that we have.

I come along here because the opportunity to talk is good for me. I find myself talking; it is almost as if I am talking with you rather than to you. I am aware of you there and that awareness seems to facilitate something. "Facilitate", "opportunity": these seem to be strange words within the context of our talking together but they are words that begin to describe, in pragmatic terms, what enables me to talk to you.

I wasn't aware that you were taking any 'stance', as you put it; I know you are the 'therapist' and I am the 'client', but somehow or other that seemed to dissolve. I forgot that you had this professional identity. I found myself able to talk and that was good.

I have been quite voluble; I have found myself keen to talk about myself, it has been an indulgence for me.

I suppose that it makes me feel a little sad, therefore, when you say things like, it is a 'pretence' or a 'lie' or that 'It is simply too weird'. I don't know much about the way in which these kinds of relationships are put together but it seems to me that it could possibly be a good thing to forget your 'stance', to get to 'know' each other (whatever that might mean).

Ken is looking intently at Jonathan as he speaks.

I wonder how easy it is to try to put parts of self in relief, in relation to one another; to do something or be somebody here and then do something or to be somebody else there. As I am thinking about this I am drawn back to rhizomes and what Deleuze and Guattari refer to as "the principle of asignifying rupture" (Deleuze & Guattari, 2004b, p.10) to describe the viral, perhaps unnoticed, transversal communications that take place between us as we move from place to place, situation to situation, conversation to conversation. Try to thin out your iris plant! Throw the unwanted pieces away! Watch them grow on the rubbish heap! The rich, complex intimacy and multiple interconnectedness of rhizomatic relations means that even the fragmented pieces that are removed contain energy, vitality and the features of other chains of signification. Even though there might be an absence of presence in those pieces that are tossed away, traces remain.

I remember being chilled by the final scenes in Ridley Scott's *Alien* (Scott, 1979), when Ripley was escaping in the shuttle, beginning to relax, on her way home, all thought of danger past and, suddenly, that 'thing' was still with her.

Then you talk about ethics, when you say that what we are doing is 'unethical', my understanding is tested to the limit.

He is near exasperation now.

I don't know what unethical means. I know all about the Consequentialist ethics of the Utilitarians, the Deontological ethics of Kant, Aristotle's Virtue Theory and the Emotivism of the Logical Positivists. I can think of all the different ways in which these can be applied, but I also know all about reflexivity and I therefore always have to question the basis of any ethical statement or stance. MacIntyre partly addresses this when he says:

> "(E)very moral philosophy offers explicitly or implicitly at least a partial conceptual analysis of the relationship of an agent to his or her reasons, motives, intentions and actions, and in so doing generally presupposes some claim that these concepts are embodied or at least can be in the social world." (MacIntyre, 1982, p.23)

Morality, ethics, they are all made up. As Deleuze says, "Concepts are not waiting for us ready-made, like heavenly bodies. There is no heaven for concepts." (Deleuze & Guattari, 1994, p.5).

Off stage, outside the window there is the faint sound of raised voices. An argument.

So if you say to me that something is unethical then I have to ask all kinds of questions: why? Who says? For how long? There is a politics here and I can't help railing against the transparency that claims to ethical status often try to make. As a Foucauldian, I want to know the conditions of possibility that have allowed that code of ethics, as a moral technology, to exist and to function; as a Marxist, I want to know the ideological grounding of that morality and who benefits from it; as a Constructivist, I want to know how that code was constituted. I can't let it stand. I find it hard to live with statements that appear to be resisting reflexivity. You know that collection of papers that Gubrium and Holstein (Gubrium & Holstein, 2003) put together ? I find them influential in relation to this, because although they are mainly talking about interviews, what they have to say is challenging in relation to the conventions of this form of human interaction and I think that this is relevant to us in our therapist/client relations. I know that you know all this stuff but the attack they make upon the formal hierarchies of the interview relationship in terms of validity claims, lack of response, the nature of 'data' and so on has to have some significance if we are going to talk about what we are doing in our sessions.

The voices outside are becoming louder.

Hey, I had better stop. You'll think that I am losing it (again)! My life has always courted trouble when I have allowed my heart to rule my head, so I will just take a shot of rationality, calm down and let you say something. You are still here. What do you think?

Jonathan closes his eyes for a moment, then places his hands upon the arms of his chair and, with a sigh, levers himself up. Ken watches him walk to the window and look down. For the past few minutes, as Ken has been talking, Jonathan has been aware of the raised voices outside.

Angling his head to peer past the window ledge he sees a woman in, probably, her early twenties raising her finger at what he takes to be her partner, a squat, spike-haired older man. (They are positioned, silhouetted, back stage.) She is arraigning him with accusations of infidelity, finger wagging close to his face, and the man stands there, hands on hips, defiant. In the window two floors up, Jonathan, tiring suddenly of the fruitless, clichéd argument outside and aware that by being away from his seat and disengaging he is further transgressing boundaries already crossed some minutes ago, he pushes down on the sash and lets the window drop.

Jonathan walks slowly past the seated Ken towards front stage. He stops and looks at the audience.

He is on the back foot, and his face is troubled. He had hoped that moving away from the you-and-me-ness of sitting opposite Ken might have released some of the tension that he was experiencing. He is profoundly unsettled by Ken's response. He expected Ken to have acknowledged the–as he saw it–problems with being placed in a story by their writers; yes, in roles, he as counsellor, Ken as client. He had expected Ken to say, "OK. I can see that. Let's head down the pub." Instead, Ken mobilised the writer-Ken to enter the story with a lengthy, powerful aside, before challenging him strongly here in the room.

Jonathan is aware that he caused damage and realises that he was clumsy. His own confusion interfered, and he has not honoured Ken's profound account of the swimming, the sea and the beach and their symbolism. He doesn't yet know what to say, but decides that a prolonged silence while he formulates words will be unhelpful and that, instead, he will take the risk of talking himself into understanding. Talking as inquiry.

He sits again, looks up at his client–his friend–and notices, in the eager tilt of his head and the raising of an eyebrow, the other man's robust puzzlement.

J: I don't know quite yet how to respond, so I am going to talk, to go with where the sense takes me. So, at this moment, I am aware most that I *am* performing a role–one assigned me by the authors of this piece–and one which I am seeking to carry out authentically. Isn't that what we all do, all of the time? Are we not always in role? Does not the performative imply role? I have Moreno and role theory in mind here (Moreno, 1946).

Having roles does not imply pretence to me, but highlights context, purpose and audience. What I am saying, perhaps, hidden behind my counsellor-speak about ethics, is that I'm not happy with this role here, in this context. I feel constrained by it and want to step out of it. If I am your therapist then it's you who is the focus, and I who am helping you to explore and reflect upon you and your life. It's rightly not about me, but that means I can't be reciprocal. That's what I'm finding difficult. I don't want to be your therapist. I want to be your friend. I am your friend. I can't forget the relationship between us here, as you say you have, the 'client' and 'counsellor'. In this chair, in this room, my consulting room, I am your counsellor. This hasn't dissolved for me as it has for you. This is a performance and with a performance there is a front stage and back stage (Goffman, 1959). A role. A stance. One I can't ignore.

You say,

> "I know that when I was talking to you, the therapist, in those sessions what I was saying was simply coming out of me…This is often the case when I write and 'talking' to you in those 'sessions' was no different."

Now, to me that seems difficult to hold: you talked freely, openly, prompted by my question–as your therapist–about the beach: "Tell me about this beach. What's it like?" You spoke to me as a client, opening up in the scope provided by this setting, me, this room, this time, your time. Haecceity. It would have been different if we'd been the writers Ken and Jonathan, not characters–us–in a story in this setting. When writer-Ken and writer-Jonathan meet–in Bristol, on planes, wherever, Ken doesn't talk like you just have. He is reticent, unwilling to take up too much space for himself within the friendship, hinting at some difficulties within his life but seemingly conscious of the limits within the unspoken contract that he and Jonathan have. You are asking me to believe that what has happened here is no different from other interactions that Ken and Jonathan have and I am not convinced. I don't buy that. I do not recognise the dissolution of roles and boundaries that you propose has taken place.

As for ethics, it is difficult that you have challenged me in this way, but you are absolutely right to do so. I presented it as unproblematic: "it is unethical", I said, as if it were fact. Well, I don't know the ethical traditions that you cite–my God, you know so much! I enjoy (and envy) that in you–but I do know this: speaking within my ethics, then, though I know that there are constraints on my agency, I feel uncomfortable with being in a job–a role–where I do not have the capacity, the resources, to do it well. And my internal resources are not up to this: they are deployed elsewhere as Ken's friend and writing partner. And I therefore have to say that. I can't not. It saddens me, because at the moment we are distracted from where you were–the sea, the swimming, the rocky beach.

He stops. Talked himself into understanding? He is not sure.

The noise from outside is louder still, despite the window being closed. The quarrel between the couple below the window has developed into shouting and name calling. (Both enter, back of stage, right, arguing. They are visible to the audience but not to K and J.) Both Ken and Jonathan glance at the glass pane, eyes averted from each other for a moment, both frowning at the intrusion this brouhaha is causing. They hear the woman (Finger) shriek:

F: I have had enough. It's over.

And the man (Spike) obdurately respond,

S: No, it's not.

To Ken and Jonathan it is as if this spat is coming closer as its volume increases, the protagonists floating up from the road to continue their contretemps in the room with them. The two men look back in unison at each other, realising, too late, that this is exactly what's happening. Confused, they have no time to react, no opportunity to attempt to avert the threat they sense approaching. They are frozen just as each reaches to stand.

Finger levers the window open from outside, pushing it up with a flourish before climbing through, closely followed by Spike, who turns to let the window plunge. Ken and Jonathan remain motionless. The strangers brush themselves down and straighten their clothes, smiling.

S: That took some doing. *(His voice now soft.)*

There is no indication from either party that they have only recently been at each other's throats. Each calmly surveys the room, taking in the carpet, the books, the pale walls, the soft furniture, and finally, the two men, sat in suspended motion, one facing the other, anxiety conveyed in the tilt of bodies ready to rise.

The young woman, standing taller than she seemed outside, hair in black curls falling to her shoulders, circles Ken and Jonathan as if examining a frieze, before perching on the arm of Jonathan's chair and jabbing a finger playfully into his unresponsive shoulder. She looks up at her partner.

F: So what do we make of what's been happening here?"

S places himself neatly opposite her, sinking onto the sofa next to Ken.

F: Well, they seem to be at some sort of impasse.
S *(laughing)*: Like we were.
S: Yes, like we were. We were good, weren't we? That finger wagging…I thought I might lose an eye.

They smile at each other, congratulatory.
Spike turns to Ken again, then faces the motionless Jonathan.

S: An impasse.
F: I'll tell you what: We have conflict here. That's obvious, but that's unusual for these two. There's edge. Temperatures are raised. Most of the time they are so full of generosity and affection towards each other. And relentlessly complimentary.

She turns away, grimaces in disgust, moving two straight fingers in and out of her open mouth in a gesture of mock auto-vomiting. They chuckle.

I know it's genuine, that generosity, that affection, but this–this is good. They're on to something significant here. Important. How will they deal with this? There's energy in the room. I like it.

Spike places a hand on Ken's bare arm.

S: And the edge might go something like this: Here, I have the "furry Cornishman"–*stroking Ken's hirsute arm gently*–who has thrown himself into this encounter, as he does the boiling sea, immersing himself in the moment, the experience of being here. Its sense. He follows the logic of sense; this is how he writes about writing and it's manifest here. He powerfully resists being placed in the box of 'role', does not wish to see him and Jonathan constrained by fixed notions of humanist subjectivity. He is driven by a desire to embody multiplicities, to step into the flows of Deleuzian concepts and figures. In claiming that there are no roles here, he is echoing how Deleuze asks whether an encounter with someone you like is,

> "(W)ith the animals who come to populate you, or with the ideas which take you over, the movements which move you, the sounds which run through you? And how do you separate these things?" (Deleuze & Parnet, 2002, p.8)

He is resisting the separateness that Jonathan is drawing attention to.

F: And here, *(Finger looks to her side at Jonathan)* you might be saying that the lanky Jonathan is, to be slightly uncharitable, being driven–because he is under stress–by an entrenched belief in the humanist subject, and–not unrelated–by the authoritarianism of his psychodynamic therapeutic training.

S: Yes, that's uncharitable, though it contains an element of truth. It's uncharitable only because it's more complex than that, I think.

Finger turns, still on the arm of Jonathan's chair, and picks up one of the books on Jonathan's desk. She seems distracted.

F: It is. It's much more complex.

She stands and, still holding the book, walks around to the other side of the desk to the chair where Jonathan writes. She idly sifts through papers in front of her, waving her hands across them, only superficially interested. She is thinking.
She abruptly becomes still and fixes on her companion, book hanging.

F: It's much more complex. This situation is illustrative of the differences and the contradictions–perhaps 'paradoxes' is better–that they are working at more generally, beyond here, outside this room. We're wrongly positioning them in binary opposition. Jonathan might analyse it as projective identification: he is carrying, perhaps, the need in both of them for the clarity of the therapeutic 'frame', for boundaries, for a division (to an extent) between self and other that he would argue was part of healthy early development, and Ken is currently holding their resistance to any clear, humanist demarcation between self and other. After all, this is something that together they have been working on for a few years now: understanding how, as Deleuze puts it, the 'between-the-twos' happen, experiencing how the grass grows between, thinking about Josephine Klein's *intersects* (Klein, 2005). But it's not just Ken who owns this; it's Jonathan too.

I think that, although Jonathan is at this moment full of the strictures of psychodynamic counselling practice, he, if he had the mental and emotional space, would have Deleuze and Guattari in mind as well: that you have to have sufficient "rations of subjectivity" (Deleuze & Guattari, 2004b, p.178) in order to get by. And he would bring to mind Derrida's view that, though decentred and unstable, "one cannot get along without the notion of the subject" (in Macksey & Donato, 1970, p.271) and Cavarero, whose desire is not to lose sight of the uniqueness of the human subject (Cavarero, 2000). These takes on the subject and those that emphasise the nomadic and the fluid, and smooth, unstriated space (Deleuze & Guattari, 2004b), are not oppositional in themselves but, here, where there is conflict, they seem to become polarised. Jonathan appears to be saying, "Ken, we can't function without 'skin'" , because this is his *valency*, to coin Bion's term (Bion, 1961), and Ken is responding with "but skin is permeable", because this is his *valency*. Both are 'true'. As Ken has written elsewhere: "They are shifting, changing parts of the whole"[3]. They are part of the changing, flowing assemblage. But there is a block here, one they need to overcome, and it is not easy.

Spike grins at her.

S: Pardon?

They laugh.

F: No, I don't understand it either to be honest. I'm just making it up as I go along.

---

[3] p.208

Spike claps his hands together. He is energetic, restless.

S: Come on, let's leave them to it. We can always come back if we're needed. I'm bored now–I want to see what they do from here.

Finger looks reluctant.

F: Well... No, leaving might be premature. Why don't we stay for a bit? In the background, so they can get on with it.
S: They'll be fine. Let's go. I'm itching to resume our fight, myself.

Finger's interest is kindled.

F: You're on. Let's get a cup of tea first, though.

She tosses the book onto the chair behind the desk.
The two visitors step towards the window, ignoring Ken and Jonathan now, their attention elsewhere. Finger lifts the sash by the brass hooks at its base, motions Spike through the gap then follows, smoothly negotiating the manoeuvre before holding the weight of the window from the other side and allowing it to lower gently behind her.
Silence.
Ken and Jonathan relax into their chairs. It is quiet outside.

K: I'm glad they've packed that in. I couldn't hear myself think with that shouting.
J: *(he has already moved on)* I know what I'm going to try.

He gets up from the armchair, moves purposefully around his desk and pushes his desk chair round next to the armchair. A book slips off as he does so. He looks down, puzzled, but leaves it where it falls. He sits on the newly-introduced seat.

J: When I'm here in this chair I'm out of 'role'. I let go of my counsellor. I will return to that chair when I need or want to pick it up again. So, sitting here, as not-your-counsellor, I want to go back to what you were saying about the sea and the beach. I could say so much. But mostly I remember how you talked about the "profound, unthinking sensuality of love" and likened the rocky beach to the opposite of that. Have I understood you right? I don't see love like that. It's always messy to me. It's just as complex as anything else. It has rocks. There is always the risk of undertows and tidal pulls that threaten to overwhelm. Aren't you idealising love?

And why couldn't I say that from the other chair? I don't know. I feel freer here, though.

WK and WJ emerge from the wings, front of stage, as before. The lights are on them, shadows behind. WJ remains standing this time, and, though silent, makes eye contact with WK as WK is speaking.

> Writer Ken returns. Finger and Spike were introduced by Jonathan and they surprised Ken. He needed to step back again from the story.

WK: I have been struggling with the concerns of Becoming-Jonathan (Therapist?) and Becoming-Ken (Client?). I spent a large part of yesterday wanting to write back to you, to respond to your last 'Therapy' piece, which I received the night before. It was a struggle; words didn't flow, I found myself going back over our writings, reading and re-reading Deleuze, Pelias, Cixous, playing with ideas, trying to immerse myself in the energy and flow of our writing, unsure where to go, hoping that the writing would take me. Then, seemingly unprompted, a thought, no, an image, came into my head.

I have a student, let's call her Tanya. I was having a tutorial with her a few weeks ago and she was struggling with an assignment on professionalism and values. Her struggle was not an intellectual one; she is very bright and she brings a tenacious wit and intelligence to everything that she does in her graduate studies. It was, in a sense, an ethical struggle.

It was clear to me that she had grasped all the conceptual material to do with the study she was undertaking but that she was unhappy about where it was leading her. We talked about altruism and public service, about duty and codes of ethics. She understood the idea of and the need for professional knowledge and so on, but still I could sense that something was wrong. She is a mature woman of great integrity; she has had recent experience of illness and trauma and her past life of travelling and performing has left her with a sparkling countenance, a wickedness of spirit and a fierce commitment to succeed in her life. Her appetite for learning is voracious and as she satisfies her hunger she respects the menu but is always looking to question and to trouble what it represents.

This is desire. It is a productive desire, a desire to know and to learn.

I offer her snippets of Deleuze or Foucault; she takes them away with her, with a furtive hunger, like an animal secreting her prey in her nest, then studies them, digests them and draws them into herself. So it is not enough for her to simply read about the professions, to examine different perspectives, to engage in critique and to then produce an accomplished academic piece that will gain her good marks. This seems to render the object of her study as lifeless for her; as if, paradoxically, in her digestion of the ideas, she wants to breathe new life into them by infusing them with her own energies and life blood. I feel the word 'authentic' welling out of me; it is how I sense her achievement in doing this. She seems to possess an embodied sense of self. She cannot distance herself from that which she studies; in devouring the words she reads and hears she gives them vigour and vitality, a meaning that is profoundly relational to this sense of self.

In the agonistics of her struggle to acknowledge the public meanings of the academy at the same time as giving life to them for herself, she produces rich and vibrant writing. She works to create a synthesis of meaning, knowledge and sense within which she can claim herself, within which she is prepared to claim her own identity. So, in coming to terms with professionalism and values, she was not prepared to allow public knowledge to stand alone or to speak for her as a working woman, a teacher, a 'professional'. For her the values of her life spread in fluid, capillary forms across all that she does; "transmutation of fluxes". She seems to have a sense of her own wholeness; she resists the dislocation of the professional self from the self that is also mother, wife, student. She is unable to accept the conceptualisations that isolate the 'professional' from the other trajectories of her self.

In this tutorial she was passionate about what she sees as her firmly rooted ontological sense of self. Her deep hazel eyes flashed: "I can only see myself as a professional as I see myself", "What I do as a professional is what I do as me", "If I have professional values then these are my values". Her willingness and ability to express herself with such commitment and within the context of such a profound sense of human subjectivity seems to be grounded within an intense ethical sensitivity. It is her values: they are possessed, they have tremendous phenomenological force.

I feel respect for this. I can rationally contextualise my feelings here in relation to her vibrant and vital past and her willingness and desire to construct herself in relation to this, to the courage with which she dealt with her serious illness and in the committed way in which she approaches her study. However, it is the sense that I gain of her, a complex assemblage of shifting indeterminate elements that seems far more powerful than all the rationalisations that I can conceive put together. Body-without-organs. For me Tanya is a haecceity.

This energetic commitment to life, her own life, has both troubled and impressed me but in doing this it has drawn me back to the 'therapist' and the 'client', to 'Jonathan' and 'Ken', to the uneasy couple now sitting side by side over there *(he points).*

WK turns to face the therapist and client behind him. He pauses, then turns back to WJ.

I have painted this picture of Tanya because I wanted to express her in ways that help me to come to terms with what you have to say. As you can see she is special but like Petra[4] and Janice[5] before, here she will come to be a representation, her multiplicities and her connectedness will assemble and re-assemble as she appears and re-appears in these narratives. I want to honour and not simply use her; that is why I have written about her here. I think that I could simply have constructed an argument to say what I want to start to say here, but I wanted her to be in my narrative and, perhaps, she will help me to say more than the argument will struggle to achieve. This is what the tutorial is like.

"The plane of consistency contains only haecceities, along intersecting lines. Forms and subjects are not of that world. Virginia Woolf's walk through the crowd, among the taxis. Taking a walk is a haecceity; never again will Mrs. Dalloway say to herself, "I am this, I am that, he is this, he is that." (Deleuze & Guattari, 2004b, p.290)

Tutorial? Walk? Therapy session? Can this be what the therapy session might be like?

Tanya did not, could not, see the professional Tanya, as being in any way separate from Tanya, the mother, the wife or the student. As I look into these reflections I notice Finger's observations of Cavarero's need not to lose sight of the uniqueness of the human subject, Derrida's (surprising?!) admission that "one cannot get along without the notion of the subject" and your attachment to, what Finger describes as the "humanist demarcation between self and other".

I was talking with some students yesterday about Derrida and the deconstruction of binary forms of meaning. In this discussion I became struck by the tendency to read a binary existing in Derrida of absence and

---

[4] See pp.205-208
[5] See pp.68-70

presence; that whilst the rhetoric of *differance* argues for an absence of presence, can we really accept that this is the case? If, in the endless chains of signification that Derrida's work asserts, there are traces between one signifier and another then surely this trace contains some presence, some sense of identity, meaning or knowledge? Would we find DNA in a footprint? Apparently molecules on geckos' feet become part of the surface that they touch. In what sense can we absent 'Jonathan' from the presence of 'Jonathan the therapist', or 'Ken' from 'Ken the client'?

Tanya is troubled by the notion of her professional identity as something that is seen as being unique or at least separate from what she sees as the authenticity of herself. I sense you feeling the need to achieve some kind of separation here, perhaps through the delineation of the role of therapist and the ethical guidelines that are associated with that, whilst at the same time being unable to resist the allure of the unique human subject. In what sense do we have a structure and agency binary here? In what ways do the requirements and constraints of what you describe as the 'role' of the therapist impact upon the kind of human subjectivity that you are working with here?

Finger seems to be saying something similar when she suggests that you are at the moment "full of the strictures of psychodynamic counselling practices" but by citing Deleuze and Guattari and the need for "rations of subjectivity" to get by she is also aware of the sense of agency that you feel residing in you. I want to work with this; I want to work with Deleuze and Guattari's development of the figure of haecceity. I don't want to forget

> "Deleuze and Guattari's notion of the body as "a discontinuous, nontotalised series of processes, organs, flows, energies, corporeal substances and incorporeal events, intensities, and durations." (Grosz, 1994p.193-4)

I was surprised to find Finger and Spike entering our sessions; I would be interested to meet them again. I want to talk to them about their troubles, about their relationship. I have something to say to them, about their intrusion into our space and their uninvited presumption that they can offer opinions and assertions about you and me and the nature of our relationship.

With echoes of Tom emerging from the screen in *The Purple Rose of Cairo* (Allen, 1984) Finger and Spike have had enough of their own argument, they have become fascinated by the discussion taking place between our protagonists and decide to take part themselves. They have emerged from their own kitchen sink drama to offer astute and sometimes challenging views on the agonistics and dilemmas we are grappling with. I have listened carefully to what they have had to say and it is interesting that their 'outside' commentary has touched me, has encouraged me to address what Finger talks of as our "block", "one they need to overcome". Deleuze and Guattari are right,

> "(W)e must avoid an oversimplified conciliation, as though there were on the one hand formed subjects, of the thing or person type, and on the other hand spatiotemporal coordinates of the haecceity type." (Deleuze & Guattari, 2004b, p.289)

Finger's final remarks about working with the skin as valency seem to be illuminating, providing the light to shine in a new direction to follow. I am curious to see what happens after this intervention, as Finger and Spike climb back into their movie.

He waits. No verbal response from WJ, so WK turns and exits left. WJ looks towards the audience. He looks towards where WK has just gone, makes as if to call out, but doesn't. Exit stage right.

Lights up on the client and therapist.

Jonathan has created a new space by moving chairs and has asked a question–"aren't you idealising love?"–that seems to infuse the liminality of this new situation. There is a tension in the room that is eventually broken by Ken's response.

K *(laughing)*: Am I idealising love? Yes, I am sure I am. One of my faults I reckon. But I think that love *is* profound, unthinking and sensual. Maybe it is a lot of other things as well but this is what it seems to be to me. I don't think that I carefully selected those words before I expressed them but now that I reflect upon them I am not uncomfortable with what they represent.

Ken leans forward and starts rummaging in his bag, pulling out notebooks and pieces of crumpled paper; he is clearly focused. There is something on his mind.

Bear with me a minute. There is something that I want to read to you; it is something that I wrote to a friend … well, I suppose I should call her a lover … it is part of a correspondence we shared and I think that begins to say what I am trying to express here. Ah! Here it is. Let me see. Can I read it out to you? It is only a short piece; a kind of love note.

Jonathan nods and leans slightly forward in his chair, as if he is finding it hard to hear.

Ok, here it is.

Ken clears his throat and reads.

"You know that I am drawn to Irigaray's lovely image that spells unity and ambivalence in one lovely poetic concoction, where our touch is not the person touching or the person being touched: it is our embodiment in the touch. With you I feel fused by our touches, captured in webs that we spin like erotic insects. When we last met you told me that you had dreamed me and how that dream was charged with our energies: I so much wanted to hear you telling me that dream, to feel a part of the telling, like the touching, would be a further union of you and me. I know that in you performing that dream to me and in me, drawn to you in my hand holding listening, we would fly into new spaces, inhabit new dimensions of the selves that we are becoming."

Pause. Jonathan appears moved. Ken seems a little embarrassed but eager to try to press home the point.

I wanted to read that to you. I wanted to try to convey the way in which I see love. The rocky beach that I referred to earlier and which you asked me about is not, as you seemed to want to suggest, opposite of that; it is part of that, part of its wholeness. Sure, I suppose it can sometimes be messy and, as you said, it can be complex and rocky. The undertows and the currents are always there but knowing that still does not, for me anyway, detract from the quality, the lure and the intensity of love. Yes, I might be idealising love but if I did not do that then I might as well die.

Look … when Foucault (1986) talks about "other spaces" in relation to our situated selves he refers to the topos in *both* utopian and heterotopian ways. If you like, the utopian is how we conceive of that space, perhaps how we wish it to be or how we think it is: the heterotopian is more phenomenological, to do with how we experience it, how we might 'live' in it. But I don't think that Foucault is engaging in a form of binary thinking here, he is trying to trouble the Cartesian dualism of the worlds of the mental and material. In a way Butler (2006) does it even better when she offers a deconstruction of what she calls "the spatial distinctions of inner and outer" (ibid., p.182); her writing is so brilliant in the way in which she exposes the interior/exterior distinction as a trope. Look I've got my copy of *Gender Trouble* here; I'm going to show you.

Ken is animated. There is a sense of urgency about his return to rummaging in his bag. The floor is now scattered with papers and books; marker strips become freed from the restraints of tightly pressed pages, Ken's scruffy writing marks everything, as if an agitated child had been let loose with a pen. Eventually he surfaces with a bent and crumpled copy of a book, on its creased cover a strange sepia tone picture of two children dressed in elaborate frilly clothing, their gender difference made indistinct by the ambiguous nature of their dress.

Here it is … let me read you this.

Then, looking across to Jonathan, his face anxious.

Is this is OK? Do you mind me reading things out like this?
J: Well, I'm in this chair. I'm not being your counsellor here. You're my mate getting excited about theory.

Ken has settled into his reading. He has found the page and he is clearly scanning the words to pick out the exact passage that will convey what he wants to say. He is wearing his glasses and his urgent rapid movements have given way to a more studied and relaxed sitting position.

K: OK, here it is, this is the piece I wanted you to hear:

"Regardless of the compelling metaphors of the spatial distinctions of inner and outer, they remain linguistic terms that facilitate and articulate a set of fantasies, feared and desired. "Inner" and "outer" make sense only with reference to a mediating boundary that strives for stability. And this stability, this coherence, is determined in large part by cultural orders that sanction the subject and compel its differentiation from the object. Hence, 'inner' and "outer" constitute a binary distinction that stabilises and consolidates the coherent subject. When that subject is challenged, the meaning and necessity of the terms are subject to displacement. If the "inner world" no longer designates a topos, then the internal fixity of the self and. Indeed, the internal locale of gender identity, become similarly suspect." (Butler, 2006, pp.182-3)

At first Ken slumps back in his chair, both pleased and exhausted, as if he has just achieved some great feat, but then pulls himself forward again.

You see I might be idealising love, as you suggest, but that is how I am. I find it so hard to curb this 'idealism' with practical rationality or the pragmatics of decision-making. Of course I do these things. That is not the point: I am influenced by a logic of sense and not one of rationality. We cannot allow logos to be a distinct order; it is fused with mythos, ethos, eros.

> Ken – as both client and writer – has occupied considerable space in this writing. Jonathan's sudden refusal to continue with the conceit of the therapy setting (an interruption that we did not discuss as 'ourselves' outside the writing), his introduction of Finger and Spike and his decision to move chairs, seems to have released energy in both of them, but the 'setting', even though Jonathan at this stage is not in the therapist chair, gives Ken permission to be expansive. Jonathan (the writer) received these current words, both as WK and as the client, all at once from Ken. The occasional responses from Jonathan have been added to break up the Ken-flow.

Do you know that amazing quotation from Jeanette Winterson's *Written on the Body*? It's alright, I can remember this one; I don't have to go looking for the book! Listen to this!

"Why is it that the most unoriginal thing we can say to one another is still the thing we long to hear? 'I love you' is always a quotation. You did not say it first neither did I, yet when you say it and when I say it we speak like savages who have found three words and worship them." (Winterson, 1993, p.9)

Great quotation don't you think?

J: Yes, not bad, not bad. I don't know how you manage to remember them.

Ken seems more relaxed, his body less tense. His gestures become expansive and less agitated by the concerns that he seemed to be grappling with.

K: I have been doing lots of reading about performativity and I have been drawn back to linguistic philosophers like Austin and Wittgenstein and his theory of language games and also the way in which Lyotard works Wittgenstein's ideas into his representation of the postmodern condition: it's compelling.

Lyotard (1984) says that the distinctive feature of the performative utterance,

> "is that its effect upon the referent coincides with its enunciation" and in this respect is "not subject to discussion or verification on the part of the addressee, who is immediately placed within the new context created by the utterance" (p.9).

It seems to me that when we say "I love you" we are making a performative utterance; it is, as Austin (1962) would describe it, a *speech act*. I also think about this in relation to something bell hooks has said:

> "Like desire, language disrupts, refuses to be contained within boundaries. It speaks itself against our will, in words and thoughts that intrude, even violate, the most private spaces of mind and body." (hooks, 1994, p.167)

That's great isn't it? "The most private spaces of mind and body", mind and body. It seems that hooks is also wanting to dissolve that binary. I don't feel that I am idealising love any more than I might be dealing with it in practical ways. It's true: love, whatever way we look at it, does seem to have got me into all kinds of messes in my life but I don't think that necessarily means that I have idealised it.

Ken's is deep in his chair apparently immersed in thoughts and feelings. Jonathan, also, is quiet. They exchange glances and Ken is unable to leave the space between them empty. He starts to talk again, this time he focuses sharply upon Jonathan's face. His expression regains some of his earlier intensity and he begins to question his friend.

I have talked loads today and it is interesting that this seems to have occurred in a slightly different setting. It seemed to be important for you to change chairs; you said,

> "I feel freer here … When I'm here in this chair I'm out of 'role'. I let go of my counsellor. I will return to that chair when I need or want to pick it up."

Have you reached that stage yet? I seemed to have challenged you on that. Is it possible for you to return? Do you remember what I said about Tanya? Is her experience relevant to the Jonathan that is sitting in this chair? You thought that I might perhaps be idealising love; do you still think that is the case?

Sorry, I shouldn't be asking you all these questions.

J: No, it's fine. It feels like you successfully keep putting me back in that chair (*pointing to the armchair*), but I'm here still, not your therapist. Your friend.

K: Look, I'll stop now, but is it OK if I leave you a couple of pieces of paper? I have another fabulous quotation from Judith Butler which, I think, says a lot about the way in which we talk together. Here it is:

> "(V)erbalization entails a certain dispossession, a severing of an attachment to the self, but not for that reason a sacrifice of attachment altogether. The "relational" moment comes to structure the speaking, so that one is speaking to, in the presence of, sometimes in spite of, another. Moreover, the self in its priority is not being discovered at such a moment, but becoming elaborated, through speaking in a new way, in the course of conversation. In these scenes of speech both interlocutors find that what they say is to some extent beyond their control but not, for that reason, out of control. If saying is a form of doing, and part of what is getting done is the self, then conversation is a mode of doing something together and becoming otherwise; something will be accomplished in the course of this exchange, but no one will know what or who is being made until it is done." (Butler, 2004b, p.173)

Our conversation today around the idealising of love has prompted me to share one of my poems with you. Sorry about the corny title. It comes from an exercise that I did in a workshop entitled Heartbeats that was run by Mary Weems at QI2006[6], which is when I wrote the poem. Here.

He gives it to Jonathan, who takes it from him and starts reading. Ken interrupts.

K: I'll let you read it, and head off.
J: Oh, OK.

Jonathan stops reading and stands, as does Ken, gathering his stuff. They hug.

K (*whilst they hug*): Therapists don't do this, do they?
J: I'm not your therapist.
K: Oh, yes, I keep forgetting.

---

[6] 2nd International Congress of Qualitative Inquiry, University of Illinois at Urbana-Champaign, May 2006

They part, and Ken exits. Jonathan, still holding the paper that Ken has left him with, walks again to the window, opens it, perches on the sill and reads Ken's poem aloud.

J: "What is love?" by Ken. My friend.

What is love?
Is calm,
love is calm:
calm sea,
that lovely warm,
languid
place …

That place
I look out on;
its smooth, oily waters
draw me in,
absorb me,
transport me,
take me there.

That place
where
I lose myself.
That place
where
my thoughts disappear.
That place
where I float,
where I am supported,
where I dream.
That place
where I am loved
where I love.

We float.
We float, then submerge,
eyes open, we see ourselves
dancing in the swim,
laughing, we gyrate

in the water:
warm, happy, free.

Dancing is watching,
Not watching.
Dancing is spinning,
Not doing.
It is abandonment
to and with the music.
Together.
Dancing together
with smiles,
with laughter and tears.
This is love.
This is love.
This is love.
Nowhere else to be?

(To the absent–but present–Ken.) Dude. Thanks.

> 'Dude' is our customary term of greeting. It conveys affection,
> humour and a certain cool (in our eyes, at least).

He picks up his notebook from his desk, slots the poem inside, grabs a pen and his coat.

Right. Coffee and writing. Let's go.

Exits.

In the open window, the heads of Finger and Spike appear. They glance around the empty space then climb in.

F: That didn't go how I expected it to.

She snorts, coughs up phlegm, and spits back through the window.

S: No, but they've got time. There's more to come. The conflict is there, on the table–to be continued.
F: Love, love, love.

S: Ken wasn't just talking about love out there, was he?

F: No indeed. Two Men Talking started it, and here it is again.

S: Well, actually, it started way back, but TMT named it.

F: Yes, you're right. Love and friendship. This is what they're doing here. It's both what they are developing and what they are doing. It's what they're working at. They'll come back to it.

Finger drops onto the leather sofa and drapes herself. Spike perches on the therapist's armchair, then moves to the office chair, still adjacent where Jonathan left it. He looks up, stroking his chin in mock puzzlement. Then moves back. And again, back and forth.

S: Therapist? Friend. Therapist. Friend? Therapist. Friend.

They laugh.

Curtain.

WRITING SPACE TWELVE

ALTERITY 3:
DELEUZE, PELIAS, 'PETRA', GOD, AND MORE
(MARCH–JULY 2007)

This is our final series of between-the-twos and explores ourselves in relation to each other and certain others. Initially, Ken loops back onto some writing of Jonathan's in Therapy, and Jonathan refers to some of Ken's writing in Two Men Talking, in a process of folding and unfolding.

Towards the middle of the exchange we 'move'. We create a fictional setting in which our conversation continues. As with Therapy, this fictional device–which we did not plan–creates a different energy.

Diary of a Madman (Ken to himself and to Jonathan, 26th March 2007)

Can I talk about madness?
My madness?
What sense does it make to talk of this?
Is this talk of possession?
Possession of
some thing ,
some body,
this person,
Ken,
Being possessed by some thing that I call mine.
Madness.
It is the word 'my' that signifies here.
It is the observation that 'I' am talking about 'my' madness.
I am not sure about this.
This talking's difficult.
This talking is possessed.
My talking.

My words.
Possessed.
Possessions.
I own these words and yet ...
                    as soon as I write them
and share them
they are no longer mine
they become,
they are a part of the person who reads them.
Dispossession.
I become dispossessed through my desire to express these words.
Why do I want to speak these words?
Why do I want to talk?
This talking that is not mine.
This talking that is not owned.
Talking to myself.
Talking to myself?
Is this sanity?
Is talking to myself not performing myself to another?
When I talk to myself
(like a madman, ha!) perhaps I am not talking to myself?
Is this writing honestly not talking to another?

In the film *Betty Blue* (Beineix, 1986), Betty, the main character, tried to take Zorg's words and type them out. She believed him to be the greatest writer; she typed and typed those words that he seemed to write just for the sake of writing. His writing was for himself, his diaries, his quiet words, written in silent moments; he stored them away, not to hide them but just to keep them somewhere. It was as if he had to write those words and once he had written them that was that. His little notebooks piled up, forgotten perhaps, until Betty found them and read them and tried to turn them into something else. She wanted to use Zorg's words to make him something that he hadn't thought about being. He hadn't thought about his 'being' in that way, he just wrote. Betty, in her loving madness, wanted him to 'be' in a way that she envisaged, in a way that she saw him, in the way that she saw him. She wanted to type him in a way that she saw him, she wanted to create the him that she saw in the writing that he had simply written. His writing was writing: just writing. A doing.

Those wonderful filmic moments captured her trying to make a *him* out of those writings; she saw him in those writings, something that he hadn't thought himself to be: He wasn't writing to be: he was in the writing, the writing was him. He couldn't understand her wanting him to be through his writing, his writing was writing, something, an event, in itself, a happening, a simple line of flight, a trajectory with its own force and momentum, its own energy, not possessed by anyone, not wanting to be possessed.

Writing is something of itself. All it is possible to say within the context of thought that tries to contribute to meaning and that does not exist in the world of sense is that the possession of writing is temporary, momentary but not illusory. This writing is a line of flight that incises, cuts through, burns with incendiary force: it is an event.

So is this writing cultivating madness? This writing, with its lines of flight, its senses of direction, its conceptual events, makes all these bodily structures and frames unstable and liable to shift. This body-without-organs

> "... is an intense and intensive body. It is traversed by a wave that traces levels or thresholds in the body according to the variations of its amplitude. Thus the body does not have organs but thresholds or levels. Sensation is not qualitative and qualified, but has only an intensive reality, which no longer determines with itself representative elements, but allotropic variations. Sensation is vibration." (Deleuze, 2004, p.44-5)

This madness has such liminality: as the writing moves subjectivities and senses of self through space and time, new doors open and these familiar constructions and conceptions can be looked at from the perspective of the new or simply forgotten. Writing releases those selves from their habitations and their colonisations, nurturing their existences in multiple, diverse and temporal forms but in so doing producing texts which are read and which lead, in a wholly Nietzschean way, to nowhere in particular.

You have been writing into the frustrations and uncertainties that you have felt in corresponding with me in Therapy. I want to respond to your most recent writing in that piece, where you rebel against our conceit ("Fuck this…This is too much for us. I can't pretend to be your therapist, etc.")[1]. There seems to be a co-respondence here; something in your writing seems to connect with my writing here.

I have thought long and hard about this piece of writing and I am enjoying doing this on a variety of levels. Now it feels as if I am in a mine. I have descended the main shaft and now I am not sure which level

---

[1] p.171

to go in at, where the best lode is likely to be located, which vein I shall tap into and excavate. So much liminality pervades my senses; I hang here on the edge of this writing, getting ready to go in, about to write, on the threshold of some new journey, some new space which will captivate and capture me for brief, incendiary moments: immersed in the writing. Where shall I start? Your writing jostled me. I am still reeling from this, asking, 'Where is this coming from?' but, as I begin to write here, as I start to write this through, I am happy to abandon this inquiry and simply write, write to you. I am not worried about my position in this because I am going to lose my selves in this writing, maybe only for brief moments. (Today my back aches, I woke up feeling tired, my office is full of the work that I 'should' be doing: marking, session plans, e-mails to answer and so on. Outside the sun is shining, the sky is iridescent blue, I want to walk in the air, feel the warmth on my body and the breeze on my face). You say:

> "I am thrown by the impossibility of having this role whilst knowing that it is a lie. This is weird. Ken is my friend, my fellow student, my peer, my writing partner. He's not my client. I can't do this, not even for our writing. I can't be a character in a story that Ken and Jonathan are writing where we pretend that he is client and I am counsellor. I am not going to let them do this. I can't be the trusted person Ken is treating me as–the therapist. I feel impelled to rebel. This is not fair on me and not fair on Ken."[2]

I am glad that you "feel impelled to rebel". That is what is necessary here. Your rebellion is what is connecting with me here. Perhaps 'rebelling' is a form of madness. I hope that rebelling will involve you and me in a challenge to all those identities that are revealed and that seem to be causing you so much concern in your writing: 'friend', 'student', 'peer', 'writing partner', 'client', 'character in a story', 'counsellor'. Even now as I write this I am not sure who I am as I respond to you. Am I one of those identities that I have repeated here from your writing? As I write am I seeing myself as one of these identities? Is there congruence here? Are you seeing me in the same way? Do you know, I don't mind?! As I write I am happy and mad to be in what Deleuze calls, above, the "intensive reality" of a world of sensation, "which no longer determines with itself representative elements, but allotropic variations" (Deleuze, 2004, p.45). So, to my world, I will live in more than one form, this is my allotrophy. I will be 'friend', 'student', 'peer', 'writing partner', 'client',

---

[2] p.171

'character in a story', 'counsellor'. But it is in this writing that these forms crumble and disintegrate and lose established meaning.

So, I am more concerned about the writing. Perhaps it is a rebellion in the writing: transgression, madness. I have travelled back to the writing that I have sent to you and which forms a part of Therapy. I have read that correspondence through again and all I see there is writing. I don't see 'you' or 'me' in any of those identities that you have mentioned in this piece; all I see there is writing. The writing. I know that what I wrote there in that piece I simply wrote. I know that I am moving toward writing and I know that I am feeling less and less 'I' as I write. I know that is bizarre, I am using the word 'I' here all the time as I write to you now but I am feeling more and more in the writing. Now this seems to me because of the writing and of somehow becoming through the writing. I am back to Deleuze and Guattari's 'between-the-twos' again. I am writing in this writing, in this writing that we are sharing, that we are doing together. I don't feel as if I was writing in Therapy in the way in which you appeared to feel concerned about; this didn't show in your writing there. I don't feel that I was writing in a way that might have revealed 'parts' of me that would not hitherto have been revealed because of the parameters that we had set for this writing. You are right. We used a dramaturgical conceit; we thought that it would be a good idea, a means of setting up another dimension within which to write. And of course it has! Ha! Instant reflexivity!

This reflexivity does not expose any concern or worry about what I have written. I was looking forward to writing in this way but I was worried that this might be a little self-indulgent and that you would have nothing to write about, except me! So there is no confession here and, even if there is, it is all approved by me. I am happy to write. In this writing, to use Foucault's words, there is no *scientia sexualis* (Foucault, 1998b); for me, there is no sense in which I feel engaged in a scrutiny of my thoughts, feelings and emotions. There are things that trouble me in my life but I feel, in these between-the-twos, that I am not constrained by any particular notions of 'identity' or 'role'. I am happy to write; it is the writing that is pleasurable, in itself, of itself. So, rather, for me, it is an *ars erotica*, I am enticed and drawn to indulge in the sensuality of this writing, nurturing a sense of multiplying pleasure as I write. I'm coming out in this writing!

Let's just stay with Foucault for a bit. In *The History of Sexuality* (Foucault, 1998b) he wants to lay bare the discursive construction of selves, the way in which power and authority creates and legitimises sexual practices in relation to each other. Through the confession, heteronormativity becomes established; species are created. I like what Davies and Gannon's approach to 'collective biography' (Davies & Gannon, 2006) offers, what Haug's espousal of 'memory work' (Haug et al., 1999) suggests and the way in which Butler's work on the becoming nature of gender (Butler, 2006) helps us to deconstruct and destabilise fixed notions of (gendered) subjectivity. It feels to me that our writing between-the-twos can be a part of that. It is as if we are taking Richardson's canon of using writing as a method of inquiry to challenge and disrupt those discursive processes that work to fix and congeal us as 'friend', 'student', 'peer', 'writing partner', 'client', 'character in a story', 'counsellor' etc.

You talk about 'fairness' in this writing; you are concerned about "having this role … knowing that it is a lie" and I think that it would be worrying if our writing did not have an ethical sensitivity within it. Everything we write has a value orientation; we are positioned by what we say but it feels to me that these positionings must be transitory and indeed transgressive. As we write we are becoming; perhaps we are becoming-writer, becoming-Ken, becoming-Jonathan. I don't know, but I am happy with this nebulous, dynamic and ever shifting state.

I am happy to try things out in this writing, I am happy to be in different ways in this writing, I am happy to be writing.

So I think that it is good to express your concerns about 'lies', about 'fairness'. It is not as if you are writing me in ways that are going to found and establish me, or that my response to you here is going to do the same. I don't feel that we are writing in the way that Betty Blue was writing Zorg, with an idea in her head of what she saw him to be, what she wanted him to be, or perhaps by how she was constrained by certain norms and values to see him. It feels like we are writing in, what Richardson (1997a) refers to as "sacred spaces", places where we can safely "err, transgress, because there is a space for tensions and differences to be acknowledged, celebrated, rather than buried or eaten alive." (p.186)

Haven't you noticed, it is the place where I can feel quite comfortable to be mad?!

Narratives and Sanity–May 2007 (Jonathan)

You and I have just returned from the heady experience of QI2007 and, full of that experience, I am re-engaging with our most recent writings, and yours in particular–Losing It, Reeling and Writing[3], and

---

[3] Both in Two Men Talking, pp.144-164

Diary of a Madman (above). I have not yet fully responded to them. Reading again it is almost as if I have not read them. I am not sure where I was (mentally, emotionally) when I did: lost in our preparations for going to the US? Focused on making the space to go? I am taking them in very differently now. I am stunned by their richness and by their (healthy) demands on me.

You write, in Losing It, that

"(I)t is becoming increasingly clear to me (in existential or phenomenological terms but not in epistemological terms!) that whatever 'I' is for me is also the writing."[4]

And

"(I)ncreasingly this is feeling like I am writing with you."[5]

And again:

"(I)t is the 'in here' (of the writing) that is important and the sense that the 'in here' is also now, as I write, becoming me and becoming us."[6]

It seems to be that you are saying that you lose yourself–lose your self–in the writing. The writing is you; the writing is us.

In Diary of a Madman, you write:

"Writing is something of itself. It is possessed by everyone and therefore it is possessed by no-one."

And:

"I know that I am moving toward writing and I know that I am feeling less and less 'I' as I write."

There is something of this at the end of Two Men Talking, where you note Deleuze's de-centring of ourselves and the self-conscious I.

In Diary of a Madman you refer to my 'rebellion' within our Therapy piece as a "form of madness", one that you identify with and exhort us to use to continue to challenge fixed identities.

---

[4] p.157
[5] p.157
[6] p.158

I have all these thoughts in mind. I remember how we talked outside the Illini Union that afternoon at QI preparing for performing Two Men Talking (Gale and Wyatt, 2007a). We discussed the paradox–or is it the contradiction?–contained in the ending: you have earlier written about warming to verbs rather than nouns and you have passionately challenged the way in which identities become congealed–"I can't stand it!". I responded by writing about the Ken(ing) I have in mind when I write. Does the latter (the Ken(ing) in my mind) contradict the former (your desire not to be noun-ed)? Do I want to noun you? Or can these two desires, longings, be held together?

I write below about Petra, a counselling client. I have had to. You refer to Althusser's 'interpellation' (Althusser, 2001): to misappropriate this term perhaps, Petra's narrative(s) has/have been calling me. For months. She has formed me. Your "visceral phenomenological" sense of writing is calling you. As you write, we are subjects of and to the signifiers but we must resist this subjectivation. You are "nurturing a reluctance to be through the nouns that 'hail' us", but I am nurturing a desire for the 'other'. Is it, as you write, that our stories are different, that we write them in different ways and that we are being in them, becoming in them, in different ways? Or have we encountered a contradiction that we must resolve? Or a paradox, different parts of which we are each holding, that we have to live with?

The other. Writing the other.

I have in mind Cixous' assertion that:

> "(Writing is) the passageway, the entrance, the exit, the dwelling place of the other in me - the other that I am and am not, that I don't know how to be, but that I feel passing, that makes me live - that tears me apart, disturbs me, changes me." (Cixous, 1994a, p.42)

This has been something of my experience of writing Petra: I have had to write out of myself and into her; though also out of myself and into myself, differently; I have had to write through. As Gannon writes, of Cavarero: it is "storytellling in particular that changes us, the desire for narrative, specifically the desire to be narrated by another" (Gannon, 2006, p.4) I am writing Petra in order to re-write myself.

I feel we only make sense in relation to each other. Like you and me. Ken. Jonathan. You-and-me. Judith Butler argues that our intelligibility as human subjects is reciprocal (Butler, 2004a; see also Gannon, 2006).

Gannon, again, states:

"...I privilege the view of the writing of narrative as a means of thinking beyond our selves and towards another fictive other, as a relational strategy, as an act of rigorous imagining that might begin to open thought. Always partial, always situated, perhaps even always doomed but also, more than ever, absolutely necessary." (ibid., p.11)

Doomed or not, I have a go. I can't not.

A Counselling Story: Petra–May 2006[7]

I tell Petra that it's been a privilege. She looks down for a moment, then lifts her eyes–hazel, intense–her long hair slipping back slightly in the movement. She mouths the words 'thank you', and I quickly say, "So, I'll see you in a few weeks then", as cover for the tears I feel gathering at my eyes. And I wonder to what extent my suggestion of meeting again in a few weeks' time, when today was our final session of six, was to address my need as much as hers.

When she leaves I remain standing, looking out of the window at the September afternoon. The view, of bushes littered with fast food containers and cigarette packets, a quiet suburban road and houses behind, is drab; the sky, grey. Today is indistinguishable from yesterday and will probably be so from tomorrow.

I cannot face writing notes yet. I carry Petra's story. I long to write it. I am full of her. (The notes will feel routine, a chore, and I do not want that now.) Today–again at my prompting–we have talked about her writing her story during the time before we next meet. I hope that she writes. I already want to read the outcome, though I have kept this desire to myself.

I replay our fifty minutes in my head: Today is Wednesday. She came at midday. She was low. She described how, on Saturday, she had been at home in her flat, waiting for her younger sister–Petra is twenty-eight–to arrive from abroad. She waited all day. Her sister did not arrive and she received no word. They had not seen each other for many weeks and Petra was looking forward to their meeting. Although she had woken determined to be positive, to make something of her day, she found herself sinking. Her sense of loss, a constant presence this past year, rose to meet her.

Her sister did not contact her until Sunday morning and arrived, eventually, later that evening. Petra told me that she was not angry with

---

[7] This story became integral to Gale et al. (2008), a writing group that we have the continuing honour to be members of.

her sister–this is how it is and she is used to it–but, by then, having again
spent the day alone, she was close to despair.

A knock at my half-open door. I turn from the window and Susan
gives me a message about someone I'm seeing later that day. As she goes
I notice a steady stream of older clients heading to and from the nurses'
room for flu jabs. One man, uncertain about which room, turns towards
mine briefly before registering, from the posters offering advice on breast
feeding and healthy eating for children, and my lack of uniform, that this
is not the place. We smile at each other and he moves on. I look again at
the posters. On other days this room is used for the baby clinic. The
posters cover the boards and walls: a series of smiling mothers of different
races and ages, babies latched on, feeding happily; salutary cartoons
alerting parents to hazards in the home, like the father carrying his baby
who trips over the unseen dog and topples in mock horror; and a selection
of grinning, toothy children and instructions on how to preserve baby's
teeth. I sit down in shock. Did Petra notice? Of course she did. How could
she not? She is not the first client whom I have seen who has lost a baby
and I have often worried about the reminders that this room must carry.
With Petra this must have been cruel. She made no mention, nor did I see
her notice them.

Ever since she had been a young child she had known that she would
never have children. Her medical condition, which she continues to
control through heavy medication, meant that she could not consider it an
option, with the consequences for her, and for any baby she might bear,
being too dangerous to contemplate. She had therefore grown up
preparing herself for this reality and apparently reconciled to it. It was as
if she had managed to close the lid on that part of herself and place the
box into the archives.

Then, at 27, she met someone at work and the relationship progressed.
She conceived.

Initially, aware of the implications, and afraid, she considered a
termination. But something beyond the biological had been born inside
her. The archived box had been retrieved.

Her partner accompanied her to endless consultations with her
specialists.

At eight weeks she had a scan.

Her baby had died.

Four days later, a Sunday, she had a brief operation to remove the
"genetic material". Next day she rested at home, alone. She had told her
family about neither the pregnancy nor its loss. Her partner was at work.
On the Tuesday she too returned to work.

Over the weeks that followed she experienced her partner as unwilling or unable to communicate with her. He ended the relationship. They continue to see each other in the office every day.

I stay seated and my door remains open. In a few minutes I will need to vacate the room for the doctors' monthly meeting. This space is the largest in the building and sees heavy and varying traffic. I gather my laptop and other items together. I will be back later this afternoon for two further clients.

I carry Petra with me into the greyness outside. This 'possessing' of her is a good feeling that I am not anxious to be rid of. I am aware of resonances, and why, in part, she stays with me: the vivid memories of fifteen years ago, of to-ing and fro-ing to the hospital, of raised hope and fierce sadness before, finally, relief and joy. But the echoes do not account for all of it, for this powerful need to tell a story about Petra.

Armed with notebook I settle to coffee in town and, as the small, blond boy next to me in the blue tracksuit talks to his attentive mother about Mrs Honey, his teacher at playgroup, I begin to write my way into Petra, and into me; and the scrawled beginnings of a narrative become another way in which I will continue to bear her until I see her again.

Six weeks later, I am outside my room, looking the short distance up the corridor towards the glass panelled waiting room door. (I always wait here rather than inside. I think it is a gesture towards connection.) She will open the door and see me. I will probably become aware of her first, notice her walking towards it through the glass.

I am expectant.

Expectant.

I see her. I can't tell, initially, from her face, gait nor quiet greeting, how she is. I know that she planned to take a month's leave to return home to the north-east and head, alone, for the Northumbrian coastline she loves.

We sit, catch each other's eye and I wait for her to begin:

My child is named.
He is formed within and I have named him.
I have carved him into the packed, damp sand,
Gathered fingers feeling him form in the roughness,
Water collecting in the furrow of each letter.
I have sat on rocks, drawn my coat around my belly against the cold,
And watched the incoming tide inexorably approach,
Water sweeping in to shroud him.
I have written him and I have written to him:

Of the hopes and plans that I had for him,
Of how I would have been for him,
Of the love I would have given.

When she leaves I shut the door and, standing, close my eyes; then
settle to her notes.
I prepare myself for my next client. I think that I am ready.

Obsessions and Desire–12th May 2007 (Ken)

I always (re)cognise you. When you write to me or with me, when I
meet you at the airport or we talk on the telephone. I always (re)cognise
you. Each time I know you differently although I have a sense that it is the
same you. This cognition, this knowing is not good enough. It is the
knowing of the noun. It is not the knowing of sense, of moment, of
haecceity: that seems to emerge in the writing. I do not deprecate this
knowing, I deprecate its dominance in the discourses of self that culture
forces us, everybody, to inhabit. It feels to me that our writing works to
transgress and transcend these simple classifications of self. You refer to
our discussion about the 'paradox' at the ending of Two Men Talking: you
say, "or is it an inconsistency?". I am not sure that it is either a paradox or
an inconsistency. The more I feel myself in this writing the more I feel we
are writing within similar senses of shared selves. I am trying to grasp the
self that is me in the writing. You are trying to grasp the 'other' to whom,
or with whom, you write. I now contend that they dissolve. Not easily,
readily and consistently. Perhaps it is better to say that in our writing, our
process, they are shifting, changing parts of the whole: transmutation of
fluxes. As Deleuze suggests, perhaps the single smallest unit is not the
idea, the concept, the words, but the assemblage that surrounds them and
merges and folds them into one: we observe these as haecceities.

So, in the paragraph of hesitation, of wondering, in your last piece,
you concern yourself with a binary, or perhaps it is a dilemma. This
seems, on the one hand, to task you to trouble the difference between the
(re)cognised 'Ken', the one who rails against 'nouning' and the
congealing effects of the denotative utterance and, on the other, the
(re)cognised 'Jonathan' who associates the writing with the 'Ken(ning)'
the desire to see, the reluctance to ignore, the 'other'.

I don't think that you should be troubled by this. I feel that we work
with this writing in different ways. You refer to Butler's suggestion that
our intelligibility as human subjects is reciprocal: for me this is an
intelligence of the senses more than an intelligence of the mind.

I sense this also in your writing about Petra. I sense urgency in what you do here. Where the obsessional leap into the unknown pleasures of writing entices me and I just have to write, not knowing what I will write, or how it will come out, just writing because something in your writing has provoked me, pushed me, caused me to think and feel, your writing is often connected with 'other' and it is this other that seems to drive you, create passion in you. It is perhaps what Deleuze calls a logic of desire. As Due says:

> "A logic of desire is different from a logic of sense in that it takes place on the level of affect and sexual energy, considered as a field within which a human being is connected with its environment. Desire is organised into a 'logic' because different kinds of relationship are coordinated with one another in an ordered way." (Due, 2007, p.69)

At the end of Two Men Talking you say:

> "I have my experience of the writing, feeling, thinking Ken within me. And therefore, this is one way in which 'we' are writing this now. Without 'you'–or Ken-ness? Or is it Ken-ing, the verb?–there would not be this writing; and without the you-in-me there would not be this writing."[8]

At the beginning of Narratives and Sanity you say: "I carry Petra's story. I long to write it. I am full of her". I remember the importance for you of 'Janice' in Writing the Incalculable and of the effect that seeing Rachel again had upon you and where that led you in your writing[9]. The imagery of self that is so powerful in your writing is also connected, perhaps as Butler says, in a reciprocal sense, to others; it is as if you see yourself in others and perhaps, in part, want to find yourself there. This feels to me like the kind of desire that Deleuze and Guattari talk about. It is not the desire of or for the object; rather it is a flow or a process, a constant becoming. Desire is free-flowing and nomadic, it both territorialises the self and the other in multiple, interconnected becomings. It is not that the spaces of desire that we inhabit remain smooth and unstriated; in these processes of de/re/territorialisation blocks will occur, hesitancies exist and senses are often frustrated by the presence of unknowing. But remember where 'Janice' took us! Remember the soulful concerns to do with aging and mortality that Rachel's reappearance caused! It seems as if striations appeared, regulating you and constraining

---

[8] p.164
[9] See Alterity 1, pp.85-103

you within particular patterns of thought and feeling, but then our writing seemed to take us off on lines of flight and some of the blocks to the free flow of desire that were emerging dissolved as new spaces were opened up in the process of the writing. In describing the principle of asignifying rupture of the rhizome Deleuze and Guattari talk about the way in which

> "A rhizome may be broken, shattered at a given spot, but it will start up again on one of its old lines, or on new lines … (e)very rhizome contains lines of segmentarity according to which it is stratified, territorialised, organised, signified, attributed etc., as well as lines of deterritorialisation down which it constantly flees." (Deleuze & Guattari, 2004b, p.10)

There seems to be no doubt that we are writing here to open up lines of flight, but the 'fleeing' that Deleuze and Guattari refer to here and that which we seem to engage in together takes us in many directions and in numerous new, unfolding spaces. I find writing often takes me 'inwards', inquiring into my writing self as the writing unfolds on my page, folding in new, different and diverse thoughts and feelings. In writing, you are often taken 'outwards' to others, to me, to Janice, to Rachel and now to Petra. You find yourself absorbed by them and you live through and with these absorptions and they live within you. We are not different; these are not inconsistencies because what my previous sentence has not yet written is that these 'inward' and 'outward' flights are always and increasingly connected by the sharing and the intimacy that our writing is becoming.

Secrets and Desire–18th May 2007 (Ken)

> "The secret is not at all an immobilized or static notion. Only becomings are secrets: the secret has a becoming." (Deleuze & Guattari, 2004b, p.317)

How you felt for Petra. How her story is in you. It feels as if the writing in the sand is etched on your soul. Your words on paper. It has taken me so long to be with those words: to let those words enter me. I have already written in response to the piece you sent to me with Petra in it but I have not really written to you and your writing of Petra. What is this about me? I remember doing this with Janice, wheeling and dancing with haecceities, leaving both of us (and Ron[10] as well, as I remember, when you gave him our piece to read) that she had been left, abandoned by our great desire to write, to be in our writing.

---

[10] Ron Pelias

So here I am writing about Petra: your story, your writing, your heart on the page, your sadness spilling over, touched, immanence, flow, transmutation, fluxes, movement between us, indiscernible, order lost, haecceities: I seem to have entered that world of sense again. Did I ever leave? Is it that I forget? Is it because I use those reasons (or are they excuses)? Work? Marking?

Petra. Petra. That name has been with me. I know it is a pseudonym. I know you would use this to protect. I envision her. She has begun to reside in me; through your writing. Your writing. Its evocative power. It gives to me. I take from it. I am disturbed by its energy. I know that sense of loss. It has been mine: a resonance, another story perhaps.

But I must go back to the writing, your writing. Petra. I have to shelve myself for a moment. Your writing. Your writing on me, in me. I am disturbed. I cannot review your writing. I can only be through its effect on me. I can retell your powerful imagery, the rooms you inhabit, the posters on the wall, gathering your laptop, the simple evocative power of that phrase, the raw liminal energy of you standing there in that doorway going to her, thoughtful, wanting to meet, to extend a hand, to give your heart, a loving gesture, so much of you in there. Jonathan. Disturbed by that anguished story of loss, so adrift in the professional identity that you inhabit and yet have to vacate as the busy traffic of the counselling room is taken over by another therapist and you de-robe, close your laptop, reconstruct yourself, go for a coffee and write.

My writerly friend, I sense you writing and re-writing, territorialising and re-territorialising those spaces that you create so vividly on the page. Is this an expression of your desire to remain in the flow of feeling and emotion? Never sure where your writing is taking you? Never sure if the way in which you have written will capture a fleeting moment of pain or a subtle movement in your heart. Transport. That harsh angular, exhaustive word; in many ways so improper, but I have to use it. You have taken me there. You have taken me there, to the world of feeling that you inhabit as you reside in Petra's story, her life, her sadness, her loss.

As I write now I feel so insecure. I can't help it; I have to write through my emotions too. I sit back in awe of your words, I connect with this story, this Petra, this pseudonym, this cipher, this image on the page but all the time I am finding you, finding you through the sadness that your story represents. I am drawn by your sadness, I know now the sensitivity that resides in your heart and that tumbles out in your words.

How I know your dad! How dare I say that?! Your dad! But your writing has given me your dad (see Wyatt, 2005a, 2008). I can say this because I know you understand: this knowing I have is a knowing of sense; I am not going to try to articulate, or elaborate: no intellect tonight. I know through my sense of you. The writing that you have shared with me has allowed me to image your dad. Do you know, my sense of him is so powerful? I could talk and write about him as if I had shared a living life with him. This is a privilege. This is an opening up of a world.

It is the writing that is doing this and tonight I have been trusting you. I have returned to Petra, I have become absorbed in her and what her life and its circumstances have done to you. So, in an odd, perverse kind of way, Petra does not exist for me. She is so important, but just like Janice and perhaps Rachel she represents rather than exists. She has given another part of you to me, told me a little secret perhaps. She is an agent. I know her story but it is your telling that is vivacious. I seem to be moving toward the paradox here.

Through the image of Petra that grows through the writing, I am coming a little closer to the other that is you. You have given me so much of your dad in your writing. He has become visible, tangible, alive in my senses. But in doing that you have given me so much of yourself. The pathos, the sadness, the compassion, the loss that your writing about your dad expresses is you. Whilst I now have these fond images of your dad that will always stay with me, what is so much more important is that I have gained you through your writing about and with him. You have been sharing your dad with me. I have just met Petra and her story touches my heart. She has told me a secret, about you. Perhaps there are many secrets unfolding and becoming in this desire to write.

Writing secrets, writing desire–9th June 2007 (Jonathan)

I am taken by both your responses to Petra, Obsessions and Desire and Secrets and Desire. Your responses take me. You use the word 'transport': yes, they transport me, towards further thinking about writing, about self and other, about ethics, about desire, about the spiritual.

First, writing (though these themes merge):

We have talked about the mild awkwardness and embarrassment that we feel when asked about our writing. "What is your writing about?", someone enquires. We mumble, something like, "Well, it's about subjectivities. We are examining subjectivities." And they say, "Yes, and...?" Today, picking up your lead concerning writing of the senses, I see our project as a study of (the phenomenology of) writing. Writing is our object of study and writing is our methodology. We 'use' writing. Respectfully. We immerse ourselves in it (though it seems we each experience our respective immersions differently) and notice how writing 'uses' us, where it takes us, in the specific, local context of a dialogue between the two of us.

These statements perhaps imply too straightforward a relationship with writing and yet I know that I am ambivalent. I both love and fight writing. I both delight in the paths it takes me and resist its call. We have talked about how you write fast, perhaps impulsively, fluently; how no sooner have I sent something to you than you excitedly (it seems) reply. I, on the other hand, receive your writing and I need to allow it to work its way into me. Weeks might pass before I respond, during which time you might have sent me another piece. My religious past leads me to think of my avoidance of writing–that's what it feels, sometimes–as lack of discipline, of allowing the sin of laziness to prevent me from doing what I 'ought' to be doing. At other times, I tell myself that I am being cowardly rather than lazy, and that it is writing's pain and struggle that I avoid.

However, I wonder if writing is not more like a potential lover whom I might try to–and do, for a time–resist. Writing feels like it calls me: last week, for example, away on holiday with the family, I heard writing sing to me, wooing me, suggesting that I could just check emails first, nothing more; but I knew, once I was captive, that writing would say "Why not write just a few words? Just a few words, then leave it if you want. Come back to it. A little at a time." With sufficient distractions available on holiday I was able to resist, to plug my ears to the sirens' song. But now, I can't. I am home. It is late in the afternoon, the first sun for weeks shining through my window. I have dealt with the household jobs that need doing; I have spent sufficient time with the family to 'earn' some space for writing and, yes, having checked emails, I am writing this for/to you, for/to us. I have been seduced by writing.

And where to start…?

You write to me about how you are drawn in to Petra (and to me-and-Petra); about the extent to which you feel you know my father; how the writing about these others is "an opening up of a world", not to them so much as to me; and how Petra, my dad, Rachel and Janice act as "agents" to bring you "closer to the other that is you". They tell you secrets about me. And you finish Secrets and Desire by saying: "Perhaps there are many secrets unfolding and becoming in this desire to write."

Secrets. This is a kind of secret:

Having wanted–needed–to write about Petra, she has, in the writing, become less the 'real' person I encountered. I mean this in different ways.

I, like both you and Ron Pelias with reference to Janice, want to honour 'Petra', the *unique existent* (Cavarero, 2000) she stands for; but that desire, paradoxically, involves, in a sense, obscuring her. For ethical reasons I have disguised her identity. I have changed her name: at this moment I can't bring to mind her 'real' name. I know her only as 'Petra'. I have adjusted her age, blurred the details of her medical condition, and transposed her home (and the coast she visits) to a different part of the country. These are the usual strategies that one would expect, perhaps. I struggled to square my desire to write about Petra in the first place, and now to share her story, with my responsibility to protect her anonymity and the confidentiality of our clinical relationship. I asked myself whether I was acting in her best interests or, at the very least, doing her no harm.

I wondered whether I should consult her. I imagined how the process might go: I contact her, more than six months after she finished seeing me, to say that I have written about her. Would she like to read it? Would she be happy for me to share the story with others?

Possibility (1): She, meanwhile, has moved on. She does not wish to be reminded and does not reply to my letter. Or she is disturbed by my intrusion into her life and lets me know that she would prefer it if I were not to contact her and not to use her story.

Possibility (2): She is intrigued and interested. She reads the story and is exposed to my unwitting misrepresentations of her experience (which she has the option of asking me to amend), and aspects of my experience of her that she might have preferred not to know. What might she make of my noticing "her long hair slipping forward"? Would she read it as something sexual? Would she be flattered? Or would she, on the contrary, feel intruded upon, that I had overstepped a boundary? And how would she read my impulse to cry, or my "longing" to write about her? How unhelpful might it be to her to know more about her impact on me?

Possibility (3): She responds positively to my initial approach, reads the story, is warmed and supported by both the text and my desire to write about her, and the process is an opportunity for further healing.

Maybe. But I can't be sure and that's a problem.

I discussed these issues at length with my counselling supervisor, and with Tessa; and consulted how others have written about similar dilemmas, both from a counselling (e.g. Bond, 2004; BACP, 2007) and an autoethnographic perspective (e.g. Clough, 2002; Ellis, 2007). Tessa has expressed the view that I should not even have written about 'Petra' without having first secured her permission. What right had I to feel that I can write about her and make literary capital out of her distress? My clinical supervisor proposed some of the changes to disguise her that I outlined earlier but otherwise felt that I did not need to contact her, that indeed it would be preferable that I do not, and that in her view I could go ahead and use it in yours and my work together.

This is the course of action that I am following and, in support of that, 'Petra' has become her own–textual–person and not the original flesh-and-blood woman who came to see me. I have, in a sense, made her up. She is a fiction, though nonetheless real.[11]

However, there is another level to this changing sense of Petra. You refer in Secrets and Desire to how Petra came to absorb you, in the sense of "what her life and its circumstances" have done to me. What draws you in is the part of me that she reveals. The writing, about Petra and me, brings you closer to the other that is me.

I notice, as I read your two written responses, something that I have understood implicitly but have not owned during the process of writing together these past three years. It is an unthought known (Bollas, 1987), to borrow a psychoanalytic phrase: knowledge that we absorb (initially, as we develop as children) that is neither consciously given, nor knowingly received. This is the unthought known: how responses from you to my writing–to me–are vital. That you read me, that you understand, that you come to know me is why I write.

Caverero (2000) proposes that only the telling of our story by another can address who we are. Our daimon–the 'guardian spirit', an idea that Cavarero appropriates from Greek mythology to convey her understanding of identity–is only recognisable by another. In this mythology, the daimon looks over our shoulders from behind and is thus only visible by those we encounter. While Cavarero acknowledges the fragmentary and discontinuous self she holds this in tension with the concept of the *unique existent* with a narratable self who desires that another tell our story. She tells the story of Ulysses, who, in disguise, hears his story recited by the rhapsod–who, in turn, is unaware that Ulysses is present–to the court of the Phaecians. Hearing the story, Ulysses sheds tears. He has been preoccupied with doing great deeds in order to create through them a story that will last forever, and he cries because hearing another tell his story means he is "faced with the unexpected realisation of his own desire for narration" (Cavarero, 2000, p.32) in the here and now.

Cavarero tells a second story of two friends, Emilia and Amalia. After many years of friendship, and after many attempts by Emilia to tell her own story, Amalia writes the story of Emilia's life and gives it to her. Emilia subsequently carries it permanently with her, reading and rereading it. Cavarero writes:

---

[11] In November 2008, Jonathan consulted 'Petra' about the publication of this story. She gave her full support.

"...(T)he who of Emilia shows itself here with clarity in the perception of a narratable self that desires the tale of her own life-story. However, it is the other–the friend who recognises the ontological roots of this desire–who is the only one who can realise such a narration... By writing the story for her (not in her place, but for her), Amalia gives it a tangible form, sketches a figure, suggests a unity. Amalia herself, moreover, finds success in autobiographical narration as well. She even makes her friend weep. Her friend weeps because she recognises in that narration the object of her own desire. Autobiography and biography come thus to confront each other in the thread of this common desire, and the desire itself reveals the relation between the two friends in the act of the gift." (ibid., p.56).

When you write, for example, that you know my father through what I've written, that you could "talk and write about him as if (you) had shared a living life with him", when you acknowledge the 'me' that you recognise through the telling of Petra, and when you say that you find through Petra my secrets (which are–were?–by definition secret from me, too), I hear myself being narrated by you. I experience the relief of knowing that, though I am unable to glimpse it, you are (becoming) familiar with my daimon. This experience is one you offer me. It is, indeed, a gift.

I think again about my desire to write about Petra. I realise how complex this desire is, this impulse that I could not resist. How much was it a desire to write about her? How much was it that she touched a (secret) part of me that I needed to explore through the writing, so that you (and others) might narrate it to me? You write in Obsessions and Desire, above[12], how the self that is you in the writing and the me that is "trying to grasp the 'other' to whom or with whom (I) write" dissolve: they are "shifting, changing parts of the whole: transmutation of fluxes". There feels to be no line to be neatly drawn between Petra and me. I could not write about her without me. I could not write about me without her. And my writing is a performative, expository exercise that invites, in yours and others' practices of acknowledgement (White, 2000), a narration of my shifting, fluid story.

I perform to myself, you and others the secret that is my existential desire: desire, in Cavarero's sense, for narration, and, in Deleuze's, for the multiple, interconnected becomings that territorialise and reterritorialise in constant flow (Deleuze & Guattari, 2004b).

"Desire marks the power of someone to escape confinement in a particular body and encounter other bodies." (Zembylas, 2007, p.337)

---

[12] pp.208-210

For me there is the desire to escape the confinement of my body and encounter Petra, and, through her, encounter you.

I am left considering, as well, the extent to which my writing of Petra had also to do with my client's desire to be narrated, to escape her confinement and encounter another body. My act of writing may be my responding to her unconscious communication of this desire[13].

I wonder whether this narration, this recognition of our daimon by another, is what we seek in the therapeutic–perhaps in every–encounter.

Ron is here–July 2007 (Ken)

At Ron Pelias' workshop at QI2007 I was struck by a claim that he made at the beginning of his presentation: "Performative writing writes against its own containment" (Pelias, 2007). I have worked with this; given it my thoughts, allowed my feelings to play with its implications. I am drawn to the embodied nature of writing, my writing. At first I troubled myself with what this meant; I remember asking about it at a doctoral unit in Bristol when all the talk was of writing from or with the body. I searched for meaning and didn't find it. As that query sat gathering dust on the shelves of my mind I found myself being drawn into Deleuze and sense and, as you know, much of my writing in the last year has worked with sense. I have worked myself into a place where writing is experience; the uniqueness of my deconstructive writing moments has dissolved the binary between thought and word, has blurred the infinitesimal temporal delay between the concept and its expression. I am writing: writing myself.

I am not writing like this now. I am thinking. I am concerned with Ron's claim, thinking myself through what he says, concerning myself with the application to me and to what I do when I write. I think that now, through these processes, I have come to both know and feel embodied writing; writing from and with the body. My body. Your body?

I am writing today to connect with your writing about Petra in Writing Secrets, Writing Desire. At the moment I am writing with thought, I am reasoning, I am considering, I am aware of craft. I am aware of another phrase of Ron's that he used a lot in the workshop when considering a piece of writing: "What work does it do?" I am testing my writing, I am aware of my writing as I write, as I immerse myself in this; I am aware that I am working on the cusp of thought and feeling. Something is brewing. "Performative writing writes against its own containment".

---

[13] See Intersects, Rhizomes and Haecceity (pp.94-99)

Immersion. I have immersed myself in Writing Secrets, Writing Desire. I decided that I wanted to respond to this because I could feel in my reading that you had worked hard to write what you wrote. As I read I could sense you working to give birth to something, wanting to give respect to Petra, having concern (as with Janice) of leaving her behind, fictionalising her, creating an artifice, a living memory to share as support and inspiration for our journeying.

Ron talked of 'possibilising', of making an intervention into the unknown, or the little known, the felt, perhaps, in order to nurture curiosities, to tempt serendipity, to play with suspicions. In this writing you are encouraging, almost provoking, me to 'possibilise'. I have started to think about the daimon and the possibilities of coming to know each other's stories through the tellings of each other that we share. This is rich. I am thinking about the 'unthought known' and I am thinking about our writing in the past where we have paid so much attention to the way in which we perform our selves to each other. I am reading again your sentence: "That you read me, that you understand, that you come to *know* me is why I write".

I continue to be fascinated by Althusser's idea of being 'hailed', of knowing that it is *me* that is being called. I keep returning to this. Indeed it seems that we are hailing each other but that the 'knowing' that you refer to is a shifting, emerging knowing: involving, as we have considered previously, a *re*-cognition perhaps. Each time I 'hail' you therefore, I do it in a different way, from a different place: I have to, each time the knowing is different. I am writing against the containment of my writing. I am not prepared to hold on to the antecedents it presents (and indeed to others).

Reading you writing me tells me about myself in ways that I had not considered myself. You talk to my guardian spirit but talk back to me as if it was me and not the spirit that talked to you in the first place, so I read you talking about me and I see me from a different angle of repose. The daimon was behind me, sitting on my shoulder, talking to you but then you talk back to me in ways that reveal 'me' in certain ways. Is this the 'unique existent' that you refer to in Cavarero? I am fascinated by the sentence that you provide me with here in the third paragraph of page 236. 'Petra' is in speech marks, *'unique existent'* is in italics and you talk about the *'unique existent* ...she stands for'. There is something elusive and mercurial about this. It is not about your ethically sensitive treatment of her that you go on to describe; it is the sense, the scent perhaps, that she leaves behind.

So it feels to me that all that we have left are the footprints, what Derrida refers to as the *trace* (Derrida, 1978). We treasure this. It is as if these emerging fictions are all that we have left. But on page ? you say:

> "Petra has become her own–textual–person and not the original flesh-and-blood woman who came to see me. I have, in a sense, made her up. She is a fiction, though nonetheless real."

It as if you don't want her to go away: she has hailed you and you want her to stay. You are thrown by the astonishing confusions and contradictions that her ghostly presence precipitates; your feelings are awash with doubt: you won't let her go: "I have, *in a sense*, made her up". Perhaps this should be: "I have … made her up."

I understand.

We want the 'flesh and blood' of the *unique existent* but we have found ourselves floundering in those spaces where we seem to have to acknowledge absences of presence. It is what Derrida calls the "desire of presence" (Derrida, 1978). She is hailing you but what is the nature of her call? Is it the lure of the embodied uniqueness of the speaker that Cavarero's writing is pushing you toward? Is it the yearning for unmediated access to something dear, profound and fundamental? Is it love?

In Deleuze, desire is less libidinous and disabling but more productive and enabling and perhaps it is this quest for the essence/non-essence of Petra that is pushing you forward here. I want to inquire into your quest for the spirit or the soul. I want to worry the lingering senses and inclinations of your religious self; I want you to continue to trouble the endless chains of signifiers that our poststructural investigations force us to follow. Is there a theism here even if there is no deity?

I wonder are you going to push us towards finding new messages? Are we going to remain curious, partly inquisitive, partly aloof about Petra, Janice, Rachel and the others that have hailed us in our writing? When we move on will we, perhaps in the future, come back to their 'texts' and read them with enthusiasm, like voyeurs, parasites, eager to devour, with nostalgia, perhaps, the mediated flesh of their empty skeletons, thinking that we remember their bodies and their souls as they were?! Or will we return with calm, analytical, poststructural reflexivity and concern ourselves to dissect the traces that remain, fascinated by the links between various signifiers as we discursively unravel, alert to our rhizomatic tendencies and enthused by the nomadic territorialisations in which we have engaged?!

Did I tempt you into the rhetoric of my binary? Did I tease you to commit? Did I, in full pantomime dame costume, act as a siren luring you into the wickedness of my Modernist trap? None of these I am sure.

These questions draw me back to Deleuze, logics of sense, planes of immanence and becoming. It seems to me that whilst we will never be able to reconcile this binary it is easy to be seduced by it and of course we don't need to be. We can trouble the fixity of the nouns that identify 'Jonathan' and 'Ken' but we can also promote the strangeness that might well be embodied in 'Becoming Jonathan' and 'Becoming Ken'. In thinking about and in feeling and sensing the ways in which Deleuze encourages the territorialisation of space, of meaning and of identity through processes of nomadic inquiry, I become excited by all kinds of possibilities. My desire is nurtured; I want to write to inquire, to sense our relational selves through embodiment and representation, to not worry about those confounding either/or's.

I have been thinking about the way in which Hillman talks about active imagination and the soul (Hillman, 1992) and I am curious to place his ideas in relation to some of the psychoanalytic concepts that you have been offering to me. I have been noticing resonances between his talk of the imagination and the Deleuzian figure of becoming and wonder if this can illuminate our nomadic journeys in particular ways.

Look! An oasis! Shall we stop? Are you hungry? How about a drink? There might be a cafe where we could talk to the local people about our thoughts and feelings; it would be interesting and exciting to think about things in different ways. Look at the moonlight! I love the way that the breeze is lifting the canvas of the tent. Look at those animated and mysterious faces, the low lights, the smoke … ummm … taste that fragrant perfume …! Come on! Let's go there. We could do with a rest and a change of scenery.

Imagine that scene. Can you? Does my writing take you there? We are there sitting on floor cushions, low tables with candles and drapes shading the sharpness of the light into soft, gently moving shadows. People smile at us, we are engaged, absorbed, contented. Imagine the scene.

Performative writing writes against its own containment.

I am wanting to image the world. I am imaging the world as I write to you now. I am performing myself through my imagination. Allowing myself to image the world in this way takes me in the writing, with the writing: through the writing? Is this writing writing against own containment? It feels as if this writing is dissolving the *me*, placing it into the background, encouraging different forms of inquiry, troubling the comfort of the known and creating spaces of liminality. I want my imagining to take you. Imagination as performance.

> "The extraordinary fact of the imagination is just that it is truly extraordinary; no matter how known, it is always able to surprise, shock, horrify, or break into ravishing beauty … (t)he best test of authenticity concerning our disciplines of exploring the imaginal is that the habitual ego senses itself at a loss and is unable to identify with the images. They must be alien even while familiar, strangers even if lovers, uncanny although we rely on them. They must have full autonomy, and the ego enters their realm at first as a stalker, then as their pupil, finally as their maintenance man, performing small adjustments, keeping the building in repair, the fires stoked, warming." (Hillman, 1992, p.41)

Hillman is encouraging the dissolving of vantage points; as we imagine, all those familiar and established points of reference are made strange. Our imagination fights against the containment of the vantage points, in this respect writing is active imagination. As you have written to me, I am imagining you and all the people that you write about, your dad, your family, Janice, Rachel and Petra; it is the warmth and generosity of your writing that allows me to enter your world. But it also provides me with entry into their worlds. But it is not *their* worlds that I enter; it is the worlds that you have created for me. Your writing creates them or you have imagined them in particular ways and in my reading of your writing I too imagine them. This is boundless! In this writing the intense activity of our imaginations not only performs our selves in particular ways, for us, if you like, but also it performs against our selves. Our writing is performative and it feels that in these performances our writing for and with each other does, as Ron suggests, write against its own containment.

And Hélène is here too… July 2007 (Jonathan)

You invite me to sit with you at the oasis. You ask, "Does my writing take you there?"

Yes, your writing takes me there…

Your writing has taken me here, to this (virtual) tent on our nomadic journeys across the ether. I feel the breeze, taste the rich, dark coffee, relish the sensual experience of being in a strange, unknown land, resting. We have been on the move; we have been purposeful; we have sometimes been lost. We are deep into our wanderings. I am here with you. I have so much to tell you, and, caught up in this place that we have come upon, and

amongst the mussitation–look–some people we know–I recognise them–
Ron, Laurel Richardson, Hélène Cixous–she is here too.

I must talk to you about writing.

Do you mind? Can I talk?

I have read and re-read Ron Is Here more times than any other piece
that you've given me.

When I first read it I thought that I was taking it in. After two readings
I told myself, "Yes, I've got this"; but it has drawn me back, and back
again, as I have begun to draft my response to it, discovering something
different each time.

I am tempted now to list the 'issues' and 'themes' I have found
contained within it. "Contained"? No, that suggests an essence to writing.
This is more about alchemy–the magic produced through reading, the
mysterious encounter with writing. Attempting a list would reduce your
writing, reduce you, reduce me, and reduce you-and-me. I will trust that
this writing, my writing, in turn will do its work, and will transcend my
attempts to contain both your writing and itself. Ron-writing. Writing that
writes against its own containment.

You see, I have been interested in, but somewhat detached from, the
element in your writings in recent months where you draw attention to
your experience of writing. I am curious about this detachment. I can't
stay detached any longer: your writing about writing is calling me. It is
seeking to escape the containing that I have attempted.

Here are examples of how you've written about writing:

> "I keep reeling back to this writing: the writing seems to keep reeling me
> back to it." ('Reeling and (W)riting')[14]

> "I feel myself being washed into the turbulent waters of sense; wanting to
> be immersed in…a phenomenology of writing, being in the writing." (ibid)

> "I am drawn to the embodied nature of writing, my writing…much of my
> writing, probably in the last year, has worked with sense." ('Ron is here',
> above)

I've read passages such as these and have registered them intellectually.
I know I have. I have understood what you meant. But I have left them
alone. I have not *felt* them. I have passed on quickly. I have not
responded.

Why? Why so detached?

---

[14] p.159

What is my inattention about? Why gloss over an experience that has clearly so engaged you?

It is as if I have not been interested and have implicitly dismissed your talk of 'being in the writing' as irrelevant. Yet this isn't so: I am interested, passionately so, consciously at least. Writing–how we experience it, where it takes us, what 'sense' we make of it–is at the heart of our journey together. It's what we are searching for in our nomadic inquiry. I am emotionally as well as 'officially' signed up to that. And in our earlier writing together, I, like you, have paid attention to the experience of writing. I've been interested:

> "I have had to fight for words, writing without knowing what text is going to come out onto the screen, frequently going back and deleting, starting again. Even now I am not sure where I am going; I am struggling to hold onto my trust in the process of writing. If we were conducting this interview face to face, I think that I would begin to speak, then pause, then try again and tell you that I wasn't sure what I needed to say. My throat would be sore; I would be losing my voice." (Inquiring into Writing, p.)

> "Writing is physical. It's physical of course in the feeling of fingers on keyboard and eyes on screen." (Writing the Incalculable, p.)

> "(Writing) is...like trying to deal with a blockage in my lungs or in my gut. It requires surgery but my attempt to excise it is clumsy, primitive. I am digging around, trying to locate the clot. But I feel I am f(l)ailing. Words are not coming to mind. I do not know the words so I cannot know the feelings." (Writing the Incalculable, p.)

I have written recently about my ambivalence about writing (in Writing Secrets, Writing Desire)[15], how I experience myself avoiding it, how writing has to 'woo' me. And some time ago on our journey I wrote:

> "Sometimes I think that I must hate writing. If I didn't, why would I find it so difficult to start?" (Fathers and Sons Again, p.)

So what's been going on? Why, when ostensibly I am fascinated by writing, have I ignored your telling me about your embodied experiences? And why my regular struggle to write? Maybe the two are linked.

Come.

Follow me.

It's Hélène we need.

---

[15] pp.212-217

Let's go talk to her; let's listen to what she has to say. She's there–by the fire! The nights get cold, don't they? She will help us, I know. I've heard her talk about this. She believes profoundly in writing. She believes in trusting the body in the writing:

"Writing is a corporeal act, involving the memories and knowledge of the writer's body." (In Sellers, 2004, p.x)

And, again:

"Walking, dancing, pleasure: these accompany the poetic act. I wonder what kind of poet doesn't wear out their shoes, writes with their head." (Cixous, 1994b, p.202)

She only ever writes by hand, because she believes that memories are contained in the body (Sellers, 2004). Write, feel the hand on pencil and page, and the body will find what it needs to say. Ron Pelias, too, "welcomes the body into the mind's dwellings" (Pelias, 2005, p.417).

Cixous refers also to the struggle of writing:

"I feel I only write where I fail, I only write against...I have the feeling that I can't do it - it's not a matter of art, it's really a matter of...it's spiritual....So it helps me to at least confess and note down my weakness, my difficulty, or sometimes the fact that I'm on the verge of giving up: I can't, I can't...It belongs to the state of being in writing...It's really a spiritual struggle against antagonistic forces which I can name - cowardice, and everything that doesn't want to be discovered, shame, fear, all those obscure forces that are stronger than you are." (In Sellers, 2004, p.121)

I feel reassured. Both of these– the embodied nature of writing and how difficult writing is–run through the work of hers that I know. She talks, like you, about 'being in writing', and refers, as I have, to its effort. I understand more why I have let your words about writing run past me at a distance. I understand how it is that approaching writing, and being in the writing, can be problematic. Writing, Cixous would argue, takes us into our unconscious, and our unconscious contains darkness that we would rather avoid (see Sellers, 1994). It takes us close to death as well as life. I avoid engaging with writing for good reason. It is not easy. It involves pain.

Another coffee? Or a beer this time? What do the locals drink? Shall we?

There's more I want to say:

Cixous refers to writing as a "spiritual struggle". You wrote to me, in Ron is Here', in referring to what we make of–and want from–'Petra', who she is, what she is, what she means to us (me):

> "Is it the yearning for unmediated access to something dear, profound and fundamental? Is it love? In Deleuze desire is less libidinous and disabling but more productive and enabling and perhaps it is this quest for the essence/non-essence of Petra that is pushing you forward here. I want to inquire into your quest for the spirit or the soul: I want to worry the lingering senses and inclinations of your religious self: I want you to continue to trouble the endless chains of signifiers that our poststructural investigations force us to follow. Is there a theism here even if there is no deity?"[16]

I want to talk to you further about this. I am ready to talk now about my quest for spirit, my soul, as you put it. I would not talk but this setting, our journey, the lateness of the evening: I think that I can. I want to. It is years ago but part of me now. I think that these travels of ours are a continuation of the same quest. Writing as spiritual quest–*co*-writing as spiritual quest–no, writing to and with *Ken*, you, as spiritual quest: Becoming-Ken-Jonathan is a spiritual quest.

You know some of where I am with this, for instance that I 'had faith' at one point but do not now. There's more. There always is. I have told this story before, though not often, and each time it's different:

I was brought up in a family that went to church occasionally, at Christmas and Easter. I have memories of going to church more frequently as we (my older brother and sister, and I) got older. We clearly identified ourselves as Christian, and Anglican. As you know, I went to boarding school from a young age, where I sang in the school choir, and where there was chapel every day (twice on Sundays). I learned the Lord's Prayer and the Apostle's Creed by heart, and was tested on them; I had to write them out from memory, with the spelling and punctuation exact. I have a vivid memory of doing my homework, learning the Apostle's Creed in silence in a classroom, with the fearsome Mr. Davis patrolling stealthily around us. Occasionally he would pause by my desk, gazing down at my work, standing there silently. Menacing. I found it difficult enough to learn the Creed but it was certainly a harder task for his presence.

I lost my watch once, I remember, at this school. I prayed for God to help me find it, and I did.

---

[16] p.225

My brother, Simon, who is five years older than me, seemed suddenly to become very religious when I was about ten. I was aware of his going to church, reading the Bible and going away during the summer on Christian holiday camps. There were, initially, arguments with my parents about these camps. They were concerned about his burgeoning preoccupation with Christianity and that they knew nothing about the camps he was going to. After telephone conversations with the camp's leader they agreed that he could go, and he went every summer after that.

I followed my brother to public school at 13, though he left just as I started. I again joined the choir and compulsorily attended chapel every day. Everyone had to.

During the Christmas holidays after my first term, I told Simon how my still being afraid of the dark at 13 was troubling me. I needed lights on when I went to sleep, and I hated going outside on my own at night, for instance to put the dustbins out. I asked him what he thought, and he replied that he would be happy to talk to me about it, but that it would involve "talking about God and things like that." I agreed.

I was aware of wanting something that Simon seemed to have (beyond just wanting not to be afraid of the dark); mainly, he seemed unfailingly good-natured and sure of himself. At school, people always talked of him with respect. A fellow (older) pupil once told me that I was not as 'nice' as my brother.

It all seemed so simple when Simon spoke with me that night: humankind was sinful, I was sinful, and Jesus had died for me. I needed only to acknowledge this, and to 'ask Him in to my life'. Simon told me that it wouldn't be straightforward, that there would be difficulties as a result of my decision. I thought it seemed appealing, however, and I was, in the parlance, 'born again' later that evening: I prayed, I 'asked Jesus into my life'.

I wasn't any more comfortable with darkness that night. I felt different, however; calmer. I got up the next morning and went down to breakfast knowing something had changed. It felt very real at the time, and wonderful. I remember seeing my mother that morning and being aware that she knew nothing of my life-changing decision.

I returned to boarding school, and became involved in the Christian Union (CU). As the years passed I went to the same summer camps that my brother had gone to, attended church, and was bullied at school–ostensibly for being a Christian. I immersed myself in the public school, muscular, evangelical Christian sub-culture: sport, no sex, and dreams of heroic, missionary deeds. This third aspect–the heroic deeds bit–was illustrated (as I saw it at the time) by one particular episode at school:

Such was the number of us in my year involved, suddenly, in attending Monday night CU meetings that the housemaster took fright. He told the whole boarding house (about 60 of us) that he was very concerned about this mass religious fervour (which involved, in actual fact, only about a dozen boys), and lectured us on the history of religious fanaticism, witches being burned, and so on. Attendance at CU meetings was proscribed from then on.

Are you with me still? I feel embarrassed telling you this. I'm not quite sure why. I think it sounds, I don't know, faintly ridiculous. Not just the religion but the English public school bit.

Thanks.

I'll go on.

Some weeks after the housemaster imposed this restriction, one night I asked God if He wanted me to go to the housemaster to ask if the ban could be lifted. I decided that, if He did, He would give me a sign. The sign that I asked God to give me was that I would receive a letter from my friend, Peter, the next morning. Peter was still at my previous school. I had not heard from him for some time, and there was no particular reason for me to expect a letter from him.

I went down to breakfast the following day. I could see from the stairs that the post had arrived, with all the letters laid out over the table in the corridor.

There was a letter from Peter.

Even now I find this extraordinary. It does not confirm my belief in a god, but it does make me wonder.

I went to the housemaster, to keep my part of the deal, and he agreed to allow us to attend the meetings again.

This–going to ask the housemaster to change his mind–seemed at the time to be a mildly heroic act.

I maintained my evangelical faith through the rest of school and my first two years at university. My social life there revolved around the CU. I became its Prayer Secretary, which meant that I led prayer meetings. It was, I suppose, my first experience of being in a leadership role.

My faith was characterised by its certainty and exclusivity.

An experience during my second year disturbed this well-established, but brittle, equilibrium:

I was in close contact with one of the leaders at the summer holiday camp. I had visited him and his family on a number of occasions, on my own but mainly with others from the camp. There was a group of about ten of us who looked to this man as what would be termed today a mentor, or a 'spiritual father' in evangelical jargon. I liked him, trusted him, and talked with him openly and intimately about both my faith and me.

This is where it becomes particularly painful to tell. I would prefer us to be talking about Deleuze–to bring him over–might he be here?–or to invite Hélène back. I think that she would be understanding as well as challenging.

It is difficult to describe what developed around this time–I must have been 20–between this leader (I shall call him Mark) and the group of earnest, public-school-educated young men who surrounded him. It involved complete secrecy, a preoccupation with the 'sin' of masturbation, and the deterrence of beatings, administered by him, with a cane. I know: it's bizarre.

I agreed to become involved because I believed at the time that it was 'right', that it was 'what God wanted' for me, and that both God and this man, this friend, had my, and my friends', best interests at heart. I never once questioned his motivation.

Six months later, however, and after two beatings (of fifty and a hundred strikes of a cane, respectively, if I remember correctly, directly onto flesh), I was due to travel to Mark's house–three hours by train, passing my home town on the way–for a third beating, because I had 'sinned' again. So sore had I been after the first two beatings that I had been barely able to sit down. And still I believed that it was 'right' and would make me a better, godlier, person.

During the week leading up to travelling back to Mark's I struggled with the idea that God surely didn't need me to go through with this. I knew that what I had done had been wrong. Was my contriteness not enough?

I telephoned Mark to tell him that I wouldn't be visiting.

During the next two days I was overwhelmed with both guilt and fear. I had disobeyed God, let Him down; every verse I read in the Bible seemed to speak to me of my spinelessness. They told me how God needed me to submit to His will, that He knew best, that He knew what was good for me, that I had to trust Him; and that in disobeying Him I was betraying myself.

I felt almost immobilised and, though I played football, studied and went to a concert, all the time I was aware, in my body, of my terror. Nothing I did distracted me for long.

And, of course, I could tell no one, not my closest (even fellow Christian) friends or family.

I couldn't bear it. I phoned Mark again just before the weekend to say that I had changed my mind and would be coming after all. I travelled down and went through with it. The relief at having done the 'right' thing, and at being at peace again with my God, far outweighed the soreness I felt, both during and after the event.

The absurdity of this rigmarole had not registered with me at all. However, I began to question it soon after this last beating. There was no single factor: I read a book that painted the picture of a very different kind of God to one that would want me to commit myself to the masochism I have just described. My close friends at university, although I did not discuss it with them, seemed to be surviving and developing as Christians without such a regime (as far as I knew). My readings of the Bible spoke of a different, more forgiving, God.

When I next went down to see him for a beating, I told Mark that I was not happy with this any longer, and that I was not going through with it this time. I thought that I might feel the guilt and fear again, but I did not. I was nervous, but I was clear enough about what I thought. Mark tried, unsuccessfully, to dissuade me from my decision.

I felt relief over the following weeks and months, but also doubt and anxiety. If I had made the right decision, how could I have felt the weight of conscience so powerfully only a few weeks previously? How could God have been 'commanding' me to do one thing one month, and for me to be sure that the same thing was not what He wanted the following month?

Other experiences changed my faith. In my final year at university–a few months after the Mark business–I became weary of the insular world that I had become part of. I read books, as part of my English Literature studies, which spoke of how people had developed different ways of making sense of the world. My evangelical faith would tell me that these ways were 'wrong' and I began not to be able to accept that.

I became more political. I left university and began work in a youth club, and then, a year later, in a probation hostel. I was still attending church, and would still have described myself as a Christian, but I think that I was merely holding on to the familiar.

Eventually, when I was 24, I knew that I could no longer keep going to church. I did not know what I believed, but I knew that it was not the faith that I had based my life around for so long. I saw this as progress, although I still worried, at times, that I was making a dreadful mistake. My family did not view it so positively. My parents, who had become increasingly involved in their local church life over the years, were deeply saddened. We spent many hours discussing the issue–what had happened? Why? They could not make sense of it. Simon seemed equally upset.

Ken, I am still unclear about what I believe. I do not have a faith that I can clearly define. In some ways I view everything that I have done over the past twenty-five years as attempts to work out what my beliefs and values are, what my 'faith' is. This, all this, being here with you, writing, talking, taking lines of flight, my dad, Petra, Rachel, Janice–this is all, this nomadic journey together, part of that quest.

I can begin to theorise what I've told you, but not now. Not yet. I'll stop now. Give you some space. I'll go and see if Hélène will talk with us too.

In the beginning was the Word, and the Word was with God, and the Word was God (St. John. chapter 1, verse 1)–July, 2007 (Ken)

I have turned your story over and over; again and again it reveals itself to me and surprises me with its clarity, its sense of loss, uncertainty and sadness. I have a powerful sense of what this all means to you and how it is still clearly affecting the life that you lead now. So much is unresolved.

I was going to go for a walk. The air is fantastic here; I love the warmth in that breeze. I haven't had chance to tell you but when you went to talk with Hélène at the other end of the tent I talked with two women who were close by me.

You noticed? Yes, I was deep in conversation.

I was going to introduce you to them; we were talking about belief, faith … it was uncanny … I kept thinking that you should have been there … they … they seemed to appear out of nowhere … I was going to introduce you to them … and now they've disappeared. I wanted to continue our conversation. All the time I have been talking with them, it's as if I have been talking with you as well … one of those women … aah, it doesn't matter ... hey, but what about these people? Weren't you talking? Don't you want to go back? Are you sure?

I was just wandering really; deep in thought, immersed in feeling, haecceity of night, stars, your words, spirit, soul, the thick pungent mint tea, all teasing my senses. Feeling secure and enjoying the pleasure of being lost. Suddenly they were beside me. I was initially surprised by their arrival but then by the feeling of comfort that I felt in their presence.

One was focused and earnest; she kept looking into my face as if she was searching for something, seeking, wanting to find. The other was slightly at a distance, a little behind the one who was engaging me: she was turned away, side on to our conversing and coupling. At first I thought that she was not paying attention, perhaps distracted by something in the distance that she was staring into but I noticed her responding to certain things that I said. She would smile, or briefly turn her gaze toward me, catching me in a glimpse, a tiny shred of eye contact. I began to sense that she was concentrating, concentrating hard on me. I began to perform myself to her whilst talking to her friend. This was the strangest alchemy. I wanted her attention and so I began to talk to her, not directly, but through my conversation with her friend. And I was sensitised by her responses to me: always in profile and then suddenly around, an urgent nod, a quiet knowing grin and then away again, seeming to be mesmerised by something out in the desert, under the sheltering sky[17]. I was unable to resist her seductive temptation and became drawn into sharing my secrets with her, wanting her to return words and gestures to me. As her friend began to ask me questions I was aware that her silence was captivating me.

The conversation is still present in me.

We began talking about being lost, about wandering in the world; a conversation that soon deepened and took on a spiritual turn. I was a little surprised when almost without introduction the more inquisitive of the two said:

"But what about the Bible … what about the wisdom that it contains? Does that impel you to believe?"

"No … I agree, it is a marvellous book, but I have this feeling that that is all it is: a book. I am taken by its stories; they have fascinated me throughout my life but increasingly I find I have a belief, a feeling, perhaps, that that is all they are. My mother used to read those stories to me. I used to attend Sunday School, pray, sing hymns and read the Bible. Many of the stories of the Bible are imprinted upon me and I suspect that they have helped me to form my values, my sense of self and the ideas of right or wrong that I might possess. But that is all. Perhaps there is a belief but there is no faith. I can feel those stories telling me things; this is embodied, so that when I think about the Good Samaritan my whole sense of self is urgent in wanting to be fair, in wanting to help and not to pass by on the other side. Who knows, maybe it is such a story that has encouraged me to be a socialist, an egalitarian, a person who will always fight for the under dog. These feelings energise my rebellion, I want to take on the men in grey suits, I want to fight the racist, the homophobic and the misogynist: I am happy to fight but this does not translate for me into any kind of belief or understanding of a higher order, a transcendental being, a god, or would you prefer me to say God?"

---

[17] This is an allusion to Paul Bowles' book, *The Sheltering Sky*, (Bowles, 2006) an atmospheric tale of displaced people wandering in the deserts of Morocco.

As I was talking I sensed in the other woman a smile, a flash of dark eyes, an almost imperceptible shuffle of feet and a hurried look away but my attention was captured again by the insistent questioning of her companion

"But are you not able to look around you and marvel in the wonders of the Creation ?... look at the depth of the sky tonight and the sharpness of the stars, feel the warmth rising out of the sand, taste the beautiful freshness of this water from the spring ..."

"Yes, yes ... I know what you are saying but I am unable to connect all of that beauty to the idea of a Creator. And it is not just about meaning, it is not some theological construct that I am challenging here. I remember studying this as a philosophy undergraduate many years ago: the ontological argument, the cosmological argument, the teleological argument! No, it is not about logic or the implausibility or a lack of understanding of a particular epistemological stance. I don't seem to be able to connect up with the metaphysical; so much of what I have read or heard seems to deal with the abstract, appealing to something that is beyond nature or the physical. For me it is more to do with intangibility, it is about immanence, it is about sense: I suppose it is about soul perhaps, or spirit, but then I begin to lose articulacies, my words begin to founder and I just want to smile or simply to be."

All the time that I was trying to explain this I was aware of my attention being drawn by the other woman's eyes, glancing my way for the briefest of moments and then turning away.

"Perhaps the Bible will help you to find those words and to share its wisdom with you."

"Yes ... I am happy with that! I can really imagine that happening, but I am afraid that it is not enough. It might be sufficient at a particular time of day or in a given place but it is only contingent, there is no necessity here. I am not grasping beyond anything but the moment in which the words might be uttered, the moment in which their effect is felt. You can probably guess that I live a long way from here, in a place called Cornwall. It is a land that is surrounded on three sides by wild, turbulent seas. Great sheer granite cliffs rise out of those thrashing seas, seeming to remain impervious to the relentless turmoil below. Those seas draw me in; I am captivated by the danger that always seems to be there. Powerful forces in those waters throw me around. I sense that I am powerless but within these thresholds of doubt and fear I find a place of existence. Moving my arms and legs is a kind of swimming but it is the waves and their incessant energy and surging force that move me, that fill me with awe and wrap my body in rolling, life-affirming embraces. There are times in these waters when I am with God. These times are beyond explanation. They are times of sense, hallucination, loss of gravity, laughter and sometimes tears. In these times I know myself perfectly but not at all."

You know, Jonathan, how I find myself becoming wound up in these things?! I was immersed in my subject, on a roll, when the slow, silent smile of the other woman caught my eye again and held my gaze for a few seconds: it seemed like an eternity. I don't know why but I had to look away.

I spoke:

"Here … this vast marvellous place: this great desert. Its seemingly never ending expanse of shifting sand beneath its sheltering sky could be like the sea that I have described as both holding and frightening me. I could imagine that kind of fearful, abandoned and very total absorption here in these undulating hills of sand. I sense that I could be lost here and in that sense I have a feeling that I could find a self that was close to God. But as I use this word I hesitate, I sense ambiguity, I feel uneasy about this usage and I know that it is to do with what God *means* in the culture from which I come. Here, with you, trying to connect with what you are saying to me, I am not talking about meanings and understandings I am talking about sense.

"Look, I would like you to meet my friend Jonathan. He's over there talking in that small group near to the tent entrance. He is very close to me and I know that he has a sense of God which is different to mine. We have shared many conversations. We write together, we have come upon this closeness through the writing that we share with each other. This has nurtured an intimacy between us, we talk in our writing about our 'between-the-twos', in which we refer to the spaces that our writing generates, a kind of shared ontology in which our being sparks liminality and ignites fires of truth telling, affection and inquiry. In our talking and writing together we are working with some of the things that you and I are talking about here."

It was funny, you know, I sensed hesitation in their faces. They were exchanging glances, appearing poised and tense, unsure of how to react. I started to move across the crowded souk, between groups of travellers, skirting tables, being careful not to knock drinks or to disturb conversations, slowly moving towards where you were sitting, facing in my direction, talking with animation and deep concern with a group of people. It was at that point that you saw me, rose out of your seat and moved toward me. If you remember, I waved to you, looked, and was surprised to find that my two companions had gone, completely disappeared!

It's all this talk about belief and spirituality. I feel so connected with what you have been saying on this journey; connected on that level of friendship, of being with you in the sensuality of the listening, hearing and embodied space of total absorbed attention. My attention is affect as I know your utterances are.

ENDING:

A FINAL BETWEEN-THE-TWO

WRITING SPACE THIRTEEN

WHERE ARE WE NOW?
(NOVEMBER-DECEMBER 2007)

Jonathan, November 3rd-14th 2007

We are near the end.

I am writing in time and space. I am now, here, at my desk, typing, hand-written drafts beside me. I am back to writing between the two of us, me to you, writing that will invite a response from you whenever I eventually click 'send'. This writing practice is where we started.

We are nearing an end. Not the end of all our writing, nor the end of us, but near the end of this.

I was at a family event in September, when Tessa's uncle, Hamish, a retired professor of history, asked after our writing. I had not seen him for eighteen months. I attempted to describe what you and I are doing:

"We are interested in subjectivity, in how we perform ourselves, and what it means to be 'me' and 'you' and 'us', how we understand these. We draw from Deleuze."

He was interested, but puzzled. He told me that he did not know of Deleuze.

I tried again: "We write. We are interested in writing, and how in writing to and with each other we construct ourselves."

This seemed to help, but as soon as I heard myself say the words I knew they weren't 'right'. I didn't *feel* them. He listened, thoughtfully. He is a kind and interesting man. Still mystified, he asked, with a glint,

"So, so…what is your thesis?"

I could not answer him. I could say neither what our 'thesis' was nor how we had 'tested' it nor what we had 'discovered'. I could have said, "Well, it depends upon what you mean by thesis", but I didn't. Luckily, we were joined by another member of the family, and Uncle Hamish and I laughed as I said "Let's come back to that, shall we?"

I was disappointed with myself. I wanted to be able to respond cogently, convincingly. Later, and feeling kinder to myself, I began to consider whether it might be that the questions that I was responding to did not fit. I asked myself, what question could Uncle Hamish have asked instead that I would have been able to respond to? I think that this would have been one: Jonathan, where are you, now, here, in this writing?

More recently, at the end of October, as my mother and I were out walking, slowly–it was the eve of her hip replacement–on a bright, warm autumn Saturday, she asked me, as she has done before, "How is the writing going? What are you and Ken writing about?" This second question–what is it about?–has been one over which I have stumbled in the past. However, this time, I became able to respond as I talked.

"It's going fine. We should finish soon. We're writing about... I'd say that we write to and with, each other about, well, I would say, friendship. Yes, friendship."

She was happy with this. I was too. It felt authentic. True.

We have used this word, friendship, in our writing[1]. We have talked about love, in Two Men Talking[2]. Recently, in our email correspondence, you have offered the phrase 'soul mates' to describe us, and I can embrace that. It carries the sense of ourselves, us, working–and becoming–both with and beyond our bodies ('soul/mates'). Now, nearing the end, it is friendship that makes most sense to me now. This journey has taken me into an experience of friendship, a friendship carved through writing: a writing-friendship. Of course, we have not been writing (only) *about* friendship, but we have been *doing* friendship. We have been becoming friendship.

I see our becoming-friendship, now, here, near this ending, as being not so much an outcome of these two years of writing together, but as being at our writing's methodological heart. I see this now.

Tillman-Healey (2003) proposes friendship as research methodology, where research echoes "the practices, the pace, the contexts, and the ethics of friendship" (p.734); and both friendship and love are acts of resistance (Calafell, 2007; hooks, 2001; Tillman-Healey, 2003). Stivale talks of the "folds of friendship", in relation to Deleuze's work with Parnet, Guattari, Derrida, Foucault and others (Stivale, 2000). Stivale refers in a later paper on Deleuze's work with Parnet to folds of friendship as a *practice*:

"As a result of this overlap and folding of thoughts and concepts shared by two interlocutors who are in fact a crowd, an in-between of thought comes to the fore through the folds of friendship, that is, through the resonances,

---

[1] e.g. pp.19, 147, 178
[2] p.164

differences, and repetitions available only within the intimacy of mediation." (Stivale, 2003, p.23)

We have explored and travelled together within, and using, different writing practices. We have sent each other writing that we have each responded to–me to you, you to me, and back–spinning off what the other has written, at times in fictional settings (the oasis of Alterity 3, the consulting room of Therapy), a practice that Deleuze and Parnet might recognise as the *pick-up method* (Deleuze & Parnet, 2002, p.8). We pick up on what passes between the two of us, following the varied lines that we are made up of (Deleuze & Parnet, 2002). As Cavarero writes concerning friendship between women:

> "The habitual side of feminine friendship consists in this reciprocal narrative exchange–continuous though interrupted, intense though diverting–of our own life-stories." (Cavarero, 2000, p.58)

I claim our femininity in this writing between us (Cixous, 1991)[3]: we are wo-men involved in a continuous narrative exchange where we seek to write our own and the other's stories. When we write–as I am doing now– to you in "this act of reciprocal narration" (Cavarero, 2000, p.63), it is in solitude, "(b)ut it is an extremely populous solitude. Populated not with dreams, phantasms or plans, but with encounters" (Deleuze & Parnet, 2002, p.5). Such encounters are not just with people, the 'mediators' or *intercesseurs* of our writing–you, me and the others who have accompanied us[4]–"but also movements, ideas, events, entities" (ibid, p.5). Our *intercesseurs* may have names, but a name "designates an effect, a zigzag, something which passes or happens between two things as though under a mutual difference" (ibid. p.5). This *zigzag,* Stivale writes, is an interchange that flows between us, outside us, and in another direction, "in short, a conversation" (Stivale, 2003, p.26).

In the folds of our friendship, in this reciprocal writing inquiry, in this zigzagging, we have worked at understanding you, me, us and 'other'. We have not always agreed: "Is that what friendship is, a harmony embracing even dissonance?" (Deleuze, 1995, p.162). We have batted writings back and forth about how we experience, reflect upon and theorise our

---

[3] In *Women Who Run with Wolves,* Clarissa Pinkola Estes talks of *hombre con pechos*: "You just know that this man is nurturing ... paradoxically they are strongly masculine and strongly feminine at the same time." (Estes, 1992, p.113). See Two Men Talking, pp.144-164

[4] See The Inhabitants of This Book, pp.25-33

encounters with each other, our companions, tribes and ancestors[5]. We have sought through this pick-up process to *think otherwise* (Deleuze & Parnet, 2002) about subjectivity, at times finding–as Stivale notes with regard to Deleuze and Parnet–that our (plural, crowded) voices merge and become indistinguishable, whilst at others they are noticeably 'you' and 'me'. Stivale notes the paradox that while Deleuze and Parnet move towards authorial imperceptibility there are distinctive, authorial voices. This does not reduce the impact–*puissance de vie*–that arises from the "proliferation of concepts and the collective assemblages into which these concepts enter" (Stivale, 2003, p.33). We have folded paradox into our writing-friendship: how we are, for example, both Cavarero's unique existents and a Deleuzian body-without-organs; Ken and Jonathan as well as Becoming-Ken-Jonathan; two separate bodies walking the planet and simultaneously a collective verb-in-process.

So, this is one place where I am now: working in, becoming in, the folds of our friendship. A haecceity. I have already moved on.

Where am I now? In being here, in writing to and with you now, I am, too, in all my friendships. I am re-storying them (White, 2000). They silently people this book. One of my oldest friends, Andrew, and I met at university. We were in the same college. We had, primarily, sport and faith in common. During our three years together, we developed the practice of leaving notes for each other on the college notice board. They were sometimes lengthy and reflected upon matters connected with our lives and faith. I looked forward to receiving his notes, excitedly finding them pinned to the notice board. I see this friendship, which is still alive, differently now. A writing-friendship.

We are near the end. I feel it. I feel heaviness as I write, my eyes aching. I want this writing finished but I do not want to end. I have taken too long to write this piece, staggering from one word to the next over many days, in broken times.

We are near the end.

It has often struck me how our writing has considered loss and mourning (Rachel, Petra and your dad, for example, in Alterities 1, 2 and 3 respectively). I have often worried, about my writing more generally, that I tend towards the maudlin. A work colleague once teased me that my writing was a 'dirge'. I am concerned that I have developed a "taste for mourning" (Derrida, 2003, p.110). I do not believe that I am indulging a taste for it here, but I take a risk.

---

[5] See The Inhabitants of This Book, pp.25-33

I have been haunted in recent weeks by a paragraph in Lather's new book where, writing about Derrida's take on mourning, she says:

> "(I)t is impossible mourning, unsuccessful mourning that is, in Derrida, the very promise of affirmation....Remaining true to the memory of the other is not about withdrawing affirmation but about being "always a bit lost" (Krell, 2000, p.20) to one another, a loss of presence at the heart of being." (Lather, 2007, p.107)

A loss of presence at the heart of being. We find affirmation in an object–a friendship–precisely as we know we must, at some stage, lose it (Derrida, 2003; Krell, 2000). In a sense, we never quite *have* it. It is always lost, or becoming lost.

I want to tell you this story about my Joe[6].

A few weeks ago he left home for university. I drove him there, just the two of us, the car laden with bags and boxes. The final item that he placed in the boot as we left early that Saturday morning was a poster, hurriedly removed from his bedroom wall. I think that he had taken one last glance around and, spotting it, impulsively took it down: his authentic post-Oscars 'One Flew Over the Cuckoo's Nest' publicity flyer. I had brought it home for him from a visit to Michigan, but he probably didn't bring it for sentimental reasons. He's not like that. It's simply a fine poster: one of the rare occasions when I chose a good present.

On the four hour drive to Norwich we listened in sequence to the cds that over recent years he has compiled for me in order to further my musical education. We sang along to The Ramones' version of 'Wonderful World', three different covers of Leonard Cohen's 'Hallelujah', and Jimmy Cliff's (not Johnny Nash's) 'I Can See Clearly Now'.

It's going to be a bright, bright, sunshiny day.

We settled him into his hall of residence by early that afternoon, with a fridge and cupboard healthily stocked after a trip to the local supermarket, and I left him talking to a handful of other young people, similarly anxious, similarly excited.

I drove home to his music again, empty boxes sliding as I rounded corners. It was late evening when I arrived home. I turned off the engine and cleared the car of water bottles and other detritus. Reaching across to the passenger door, feeling blind into its pocket, my fingers encountered

---

[6] The following writing about Joe also forms part of unpublished writing that we have undertaken within the writing group referred to in the footnote on page 205

the softness of leather. I picked up the object and held it in front of me in the dark. His wallet.

I phoned him immediately. He hadn't noticed that he was without it. I ranted. How was he going to pay for anything? How was he going to get into his halls without the card that the caretaker had given him barely four hours ago? How was he going to get by?

His new-found friends lent him cash and made sure he didn't get locked out. We sent him the wallet. It all worked out.

I wondered whether, unconsciously, he forgot his wallet in order to let something important remain. So as not, quite, to leave.

I am sleeping badly. Since he went I have, most nights, in the early hours, moved to sleep in his now empty bed lest my restlessness disturb Tessa. I think that this is a way of attempting to hold on to him. I am struggling to let him go.

I know that it is a healthy thing that he has gone. He will be back, too soon, and I shall tire of his mornings in bed, the scattering of his belongings, and the sheer size of him, his big, loping presence, the space he seems to occupy. I shall look forward to his returning to Norwich for the new term.

I know that it is right: that he should leave, that it is good to see him go and begin to find his way. It is what we have been expecting, what we have prepared him and ourselves for during our sometimes muddled attempts to raise him. His going is affirming.

I–we–never quite had Joe. I have been mourning him since he was born.

You have annotated a recent draft of this dissertation. I sent you my first draft of our third writing space[7]. You printed it, wrote on it, and sent it. A gift: your handwriting that, as I once commented to you (see Inquiring into Writing, p.75), seems to permit a certain vulnerability that you–we?–sometimes protect ourselves from when we type. The text that I had typed speaks about how you and I, amongst others, people this writing. Sloping underneath, at angles around my typed text, at the foot of the page, you have written:

> "You will become, you are becoming, our archivist. I will die before you and I will live for a while longer in the writing that you will continue to do. I say this with love, not arrogance. Our words write our heaven. No longer loss just its anticipation."

---

[7] The Inhabitants of This Book, pp.25-33

I had to pause as I copied into my notebook your handwritten comment. I had to look out of the window of the small Oxford café where I was writing. I wanted to deny your words. I told you, in my head, "You don't know this. It might be me that goes first. You can't be sure."

We know, whichever it will be, that one of us will die first. Derrida writes that friends are aware at the outset that one will survive the other, that friendship is formed on this very basis:

> "From the first moment, friends become, as a result of their situation, virtual survivors, actually virtual or virtually actual, which amounts to just about the same thing. Friends know this, and friendship breathes this knowledge, breathes it right up to expiration, right up to the last breath." (Derrida, 1989, p.171)

You have made this explicit about us. Maybe what we have been doing, throughout our work together, is giving to each other our words to carry; and, within–or between–our words, our souls. The practice of exchanging writing as attachments to emails, whilst it is a practical convenience, also symbolises a desire to escape, fleetingly, the concrete. For a moment, in the electronic ether, we fly. Then the other 'receives' us, and the text is printed and held. And, at the point where we feel we are ready to talk to others, we publish, in the hope that others will read us–our "remains" (Derrida, 2003, p.170)–and that we, Becoming-Ken-Jonathan, will continue to become in them. Our names, will survive us; they already survive us (Derrida, 1989).

There is another paradox that perhaps we have unknowingly explored. Derrida wrote, a year after Lyotard had died, that he felt charged with the impossible task of both creating an opportunity for his friend, and no one else, to speak whilst simultaneously not leaving him alone as he did so: "A double injunction then, contradictory and unforgiving. How to leave him alone without abandoning him?" (Derrida, 2003, p.225) Our writing is, perhaps, an attempt, pre-empting our corporeal deaths, to provide space for each to have a voice whilst not leaving the other alone. We have wondered–agonised, at times–about how we respond to each other's writing. We have not known how to honour each other. It has never felt enough. There is always some aspect of the other's writing that we have had to leave unacknowledged. We have given each other voice but each time we leave the other abandoned, and we mourn that.

We are close to the end. I am approaching the end of this, now, today, at 11.45pm on November 14th 2007, typing still, grabbing at spaces of time, desperate to find a way to finish, sheets of paper around me. And at this moment, I sense absence of (our) presence. I recognise that our writing with, to, for, and between each other is an impossibility (Cixous, 1994c). Yet, writing fills me with hope. I feel alive. We are alive. Our writing lives. There is affirmation at the very moment at which I mourn. In letting in death through our writing (Pelias, 2000) we find the pulse of becoming:

> "With one hand, suffering, living, putting your finger on pain, loss. But there is the other hand: the one that writes." (Cixous, 1991, p.8)

Where am I now? With one hand I mourn, with the other I write into the folds of our friendship. I am holding endless paradoxes: of being two and legion and one; of being men and not men and both and more; of being Ken and Jonathan and Becoming-Ken-Jonathan; and, and, and, and, and: the stammering of language itself (Deleuze & Parnet, 2002).

As I end, where am I now? I am writing, still writing, keeping on writing, however impossibly, to you.

Ken writing *with* Jonathan in a parallel between-the-two (13th November 2007)

> "I haven't finished my writing for us yet. I was over-optimistic! I am writing to the question "Where are we now?", a kind of reflective look at where this journey has taken me. It's a between-the-two, a piece of writing from me to you. I am finding it slow and difficult, but good. Hope to get it to you before too long."
> (Part of an e-mail from Jonathan to Ken, sent 12th November 2007)

I am wondering whether to respond to what you said in this e-mail to me that I received yesterday before I receive what you have to say about 'Where are we now?'.

I am here with windows.

My ever-present window on to the outside world. Today my view is one of greyness and gloom, winter seems heavy and sodden, the clouds are grey and unforgiving; I want to see a chink of light in the distant western sky but it is not there for me yet.

My window of optimism opened surprisingly this morning when the meeting that I had to attend fifty miles away was cancelled; suddenly 'our writing' began to niggle me. Time to write. What to say?

My window into our writing is a little stained. Rivulets of condensation cloud my vision; I have not written to us, with us, to you, from me, between-the-twos, for a long time.

Other windows have been closed, doors barred, liminality excised and possibilities constrained by the daily burden of marking, meetings and preparations. This is before the hard edge of crystal scratches the glazed surface of sadness that swells in my depths. Through this window I see freedom, laughter and liberty but somehow I am held back, left alone, peering through the damning opacity of this veiled transparency.

And yet the question 'Where are we now?' opens up something for me, catches are released, air breathes through the widening space, I begin to feel refreshed: I have something to say. Where *are* we now? So many places, such multiplicity, so many interconnections, we have traced paths in many different directions, traces between absence and presence, traces to which we go back, and scratch at, over-line or perhaps sometimes try to rub away. Our stories become us. Whatever *is* our between-the-two as we write today in response to this question 'Where are we now?', it will shift with our new hesitations, our nascent curiosities and itchy troublings. We have acknowledged this. Part of the abstract that we recently submitted to the next QI Conference (Gale & Wyatt, 2008a) makes this clear: we have come out! This is where we are now:

> "Over recent years we have been exploring writing through writing, understanding that in writing together we become less 'Ken' and 'Jonathan', and more a process, a Deleuzian between-the-two, a Becoming-Ken-Jonathan. We are a verb, not nouns."

The paradox that is inherent in this is of course so much fun. We have been foundational! We have established ourselves! *This* is where we are now! Where? Here. OK. Got it! No you haven't! No you haven't! 'This is where we are now' is of course a shifting sand. When Michael, Robert De Niro's character in *The Deer Hunter* (Cimino, 1975), levelled his sights on the lone deer, ready to blast it into eternity, then hesitated and said 'This is this' we all knew that 'this' was only a moment in the unravelling eternity that was the deer's and the character's shared destiny. As soon as those words were uttered, their referential moment, their phenomenological energy, began to dissolve. When I watched *The Deer Hunter* all those years ago and was absorbed by this powerful cinematic moment I had not read Deleuze and Guattari. Now I feel that we have a Deleuzian haecceity here. In that sacred, reverential moment the whole of De Niro's life, past, present, future, flashed before his eyes and entered his soul as, indeed, his soul entered the world that he 'saw' before him. And it feels to me that our becoming, in, through and with this writing is 'where we are now'. I referred earlier to Ron Pelias' inquiry into the performative nature of writing, 'What work does it do?'. It seems to me that Ron presents this question not in instrumentalist or functional terms; he is not asking about efficiency or effectiveness, rather he seems curious to know what these words are doing. If they are performative utterances what are they performing? What are the dialogics involved? Do these words evoke or charge our emotions? Do they resonate and connect with our experiences? Do they open spaces for reflexivity? And so on.

So this writing of ours seems to open up vast territories of the soul.

I am drawn to imagery of the desert in which we wandered and wondered, where we found travellers, other nomads, lost souls perhaps.

I am drawn to the connections that our words have made with each other and with others; how your writing about your dad has brought tears to my eyes, how your informal reading of 'Petra' so moved people at QI last year.

I am drawn to the traces and to the stories yet untold, I am drawn to envision the magnitude of this ever-growing, perpetually-morphing rhizome that both is us and which is being fed by us.

I am drawn to the journeying that we do; I am glad to be a nomad, inquiring, pushing in at bus queues, staring out the windows of the railway carriage, questioning, questioning, always troubling those edges with new thoughts and feelings.

I am drawn by the chance that this writing is giving me to escape, to take great arching lines of flight into stratospheres of love, passion and emotion: this chance will slowly, gradually be realised and right now I am enjoying the liminality of anticipation, envisioning the space in which I will grow and be born again. And again? And again…?

I am drawn to what this writing is doing for me now, in this very moment, as I write. I am drawn to write in a way that enters my soul as I stumble through my life experiences. Here I am making connections with the death of my marriage, with the love of my children, to the love in my heart: this "methodology of the heart" (Pelias, 2004) dissolves the binary relation between the writer and the writing. I sense myself, my doing, in the conjunction of the two; within me there also seems to be a 'between-the-two'. It is now partly what I strive for in my writing but it also what makes me come alive in the doing of the writing. So present, though perhaps not objectively visible in my writing, will be these things; my unhappiness and sometimes my joy. Often it is my tears that stain these pages but laughter is also there. As I write to you I bring to you the love of a woman or the passion of the sea, dances with my children and the vibrant rhythms of music. These things and many more are ever present in my writing to and with you. Sometimes you will see them and sometimes you won't, but they are always there and they are always a part of us, of the writing that becomes us. I know they are always there because I sense them; they are always dancing in my heart and energising my soul.

My skin tingles and my jaw aches. Cold sweat collects in the crevices of my body as I tease these words out to you. Remember it is you whom I am writing to; I am desperate to talk with you to give you these words. The energy that is driving me now is based upon desire, desire to write, to *give* to you, to get these words out, to *be* and *become* in the writing. In the clarity of this moment I sense body-without-organs; every organ in my body is alive to the writing, my writing and the writing that this writing together has become. I feel that I might be at a moment where I will stop.

Where are we now?

Where are we now? In response to Jonathan's. 21 November 2007

Where are we now?

This has become a correspondence within our correspondences, we are creating another 'minor literature' within our 'minor literature'! You have given this a stark temporal reference when you say: "We are near the end." What does this mean, "We are near the end"?

In many ways I hadn't or haven't thought about this and as I write this now I am feeling my way into this. Your question pushes me, encourages me to leave the world of Ken-becoming-through-the-writing that has become so dear to me in our writing between-the-twos. So I am thinking that endings are never complete, but my sense tells me that this writing draws to a close. So what is this sense? What are these senses? I feel excitement, awe, disbelief and perhaps a slight sense of mourning. We have shared so much when we have talked of loss but there is so much there: I have hardly begun. You see? My senses give me worlds of manifest incompletion. I write.

I write.

Where have I said, "This writing is me"? In these pure, crystal moments when I am lost in words, when my 'Becoming-Ken-Jonathan' energises me, when the line between my conscious existent self and my writing passion dissolves, when the noun becomes a verb, I can never envision endings. Being in this writing, being this writing: writing this being[8].

---

[8]I have struggled with this word. We have been using 'becoming' as and with Deleuze, that is what I have wanted and this has become our sharing. Today as I write these words 'being' or 'dasein', as in Heidegger, somehow seems more

My feeling self never wants this to end. When I begin to try to answer the question: 'Where are we now?' I cannot think of endings. Here now as I am writing these words my feeling is that this is this. This is what I do. This is where I become. So, I know we have to finish; I know that it has to have an ending but this has a strange incompleteness of meaning for me. I will always write to and in these between-the-twos. I have made this decision. Where are we now? The response is existential, it is being. However, it is also, as you say, temporal and spatial. You say "I am writing in time and space" and so then will I. I will try to give this summation; I will try to give this some closure. Logic, reason and rationality tell us that our book has to have an ending and whilst I express ambivalence about this here, I want to share in the wonderful celebrations that that signifies. So I am going to write to your question 'Where are we now?' In the words of Dr. Dre (BlackStreet, 1996), "No diggity, I gotta bag it up"

So here we go:

Last week it was Book Week in Phoebe's[9] school; a wonderful celebration of stories, of reading, writing, imagination and creativity shared by all the children and teachers. Phoebe was totally immersed in the whole thing, selling books at the Book Fair, helping in the library, dressing up in fancy dress, as Pippy Longstocking, along with all the other children and teachers as book characters. I felt pleased to be invited to read to Class 4, Phoebe's class. Phoebe assured me that the children were very excited about this and I then wondered with some concern, what could I read? After a good deal of deliberation I settled on a story called *William and The Perfect Child* from the Richmal Crompton collection *Sweet William*. In planning my reading I made some introductory notes; I felt that I wanted to contextualise the story for the children. This is what I prepared and was going to use as a prompt sheet for my introduction to their story. On the day I decided actually to read it in full and I told them it was my story about the story I wanted to read to them:

"When I was your age I used to live with my mum and dad in a tiny terraced cottage that had two little bedrooms, one living room and a scullery (which was what we would call a kitchen but it was only about the size of a large cupboard!) That was it! We didn't have a toilet indoors,

---

appropriate to my feeling, my sense of self. This very writing, this footnote, is, of course, a becoming, a new line of flight, refusing me the will to end this writing. I am so influenced by you in this: there always seems to be a great soulfulness in your writing, your acute awareness of mortality and your poetry of loss always draws me.

[9] Ken's daughter, now aged 11

so if we needed to go to the loo we used to have to go out the front door (which opened right onto the street) then walk down the street to the end of the cottage and up some stone steps to a little yard at the back of the cottage and into the tiny brick toilet. It was often very cold and wet to go there in the winter and it was also a bit scary in the dark because it had no electric light, so we used either a candle or a torch to light our way.

When I look back on my childhood life at that time (which was in the 1950's, just after the Second World War) my little family was quite poor, but I never knew that we were because my experiences there were happy ones and I never seemed to lack anything in my life. My pleasures were probably similar to yours. I remember having lots of toys, although nothing electronic or digital of the kind that you have today. When I was 11 my parents bought a TV and that was really something, it had a tiny little black and white screen and only one channel! I lived near a park so I also had a great place to play with all my friends. But the biggest pleasure in my life at that time was reading. I couldn't stop reading: whether it was books, comics or magazines, I seemed to spend a very large part of my free time reading. For me at that time reading provided an entry into a magical world, a world where my mind could wander wherever it wanted, a world where my imagination could run riot. It is still the same for me now even though sometimes the books that I read are ones that I have to read for my job. There was one writer whose books I used to read then and whose writing I still enjoy now. So when Reuben and Phoebe go to bed they often listen to tapes of this writer and when we all go out in the car on family trips, these stories are the ones that we play the most as we go on our journeys. I think that they are lovely stories. Why are they lovely? Well mainly because they make me laugh. When I was reading these stories lying on my bed in the little cottage that I told you about, that was what I used to do. Laugh! Out loud! There is something else about these stories that I realise now as I have grown older and that is that they have taught me things, they have helped me to think and feel about the world in certain ways and they have taught me words, lovely words that are part of the language that I use today. I have learned so much from these stories in many different ways and think that this shows that learning can be fun. These stories were written over 60 years ago, before I was born, so some of these words and phrases might seem unusual to you, so when I have finished reading the story you might want to ask me about them and we can talk about what you think they mean.

The author of these stories is called Richmal Crompton and they are all about a little boy, about your age, called William. These stories have brought joy to my life and I am going to read one of them to you now."

This seems important. I had forgotten this. Perhaps I had blocked it out. In writing these notes for the children the circumstances of my early life with my mum and dad came flooding back. Mostly my memories were of the happiness that was there; I am glowing as I think, again, about those times now. But the circumstances! The tiny space we lived in. The damp. The front door opening out onto Race Hill, a really busy road into the town. And the outside toilet. I think about that now and I shudder. What was that like? Getting up in the night or the early morning to use a bucket which I guess my mum would then empty in the morning: out the front door, down the busy street, up the back steps and into the little brick toilet. What is this to do with writing? My writing? I can't begin to enter the psychology of this remembering but I am writing this now because it seems to have some connection with these early memories of reading, of words, of the piles of books and comics in my tiny little room that I would voraciously devour whenever I had the chance.

Writing? Where are you now?

I have here in this office, my space, writing which I have never thought to refer to before. Diaries. At a guess there are about twenty scruffy, cardboard covered notebooks of various sizes containing neat, sometimes scribbled, hand-writings, drawings, notes and reflections on and of my life.

Here is the very first entry, dated Saturday 2nd January 1965, when I was 17 years old:

"Went down around town, club, café, etc. Same again in afternoon, poor ol' Den had his haircut. Shade of Blues dance at St. Stephens. Went out with Sandra Griffiths."

Here is the last, a poem, dated 17th November 2007:

"Mad moments of irresponsible love.
The gush of words, apropos of nothing,
the whimsical purchase
and the flying fist in the face

Turning back with feet to go,
an impetuous bet on outside chances.
Jumping from the edge when all is lost.
Baring your knee caps at dinner.

Life can be … what the fuck,
But so rarely is …
Often only is when:

> Off your guard
> When drunk perhaps
> When ravaged by lost love
> Or intoxicated by love
> that is newly found

The drugged ennui
of the dead albatross,
the rotting corpse
hanging around your neck.
You carry it publicly
not proud,
but resolute.
Others see you and …
Pass by on the other side
Pass by on the other side

Crucifixion,
pain of nails,
acceptance of lot.
Humility and conservatism,
concocts a muddy cocktail, potent and heavy with loss.
Its effects so powerfully leaden, weighing down
the extravagance of chance
and the serendipity of choice.

Sun setting … is it set?
Sunset … is it darkness?
What *is* that darkness?"

Writing! In here, in this book, inspired by the work that we do together, is my writing, book-ended by these two pieces. Where are we now? This writing has given me confidence. I reflect back upon when we started to write together. What brought us together was our awareness of our different writing styles; we have written about this. I realise that my writing then, as we tentatively began writing together, was for me a line of flight, a way of escape, a first step on a nomadic journeying, an expression of a desire to write. In what way I didn't know, but in a way that I think and feel that I am finding now. Our writing styles and what we write about continue to be different, but look at how the differences have changed: I feel so happy to have put to one side that 'academic' writing that I started off doing, those long wordy sentences and all those erudite citations. I feel so happy that Jane[10] ticked me off for this when she marked my assignment for the first unit on the EdD programme. That pulled me up straight. It made me think and, with your help, swung open a door that continues to swing, perhaps a little unhinged, as I continue with this writing today.

You talk so tenderly about your conversation with Tessa's Uncle Hamish, the difficulty of talking with others about what it is we do and what this is all about. "I attempted to describe what you and I are doing ... I tried again ... as soon as I heard myself say the words I knew they weren't 'right' ... I couldn't answer him ... I was disappointed with myself." We have encountered this before and still, now, I too am unsure what to say when confronted with situations like this. In part this destabilises me. It takes me back to the place where I was before, lacking confidence about my writing, trying to adopt a style of writing that was not my own, knocking humbly, cap in hand, at the barred door of the academy. But now growing, in much greater part, I am saying: I can do it! I can do it my way! Look what we do and have done together! Look at the people we have met on this journey: people we like and people who like us and what we do.

About ten days ago, I was busy at work, rushing to the photo-copier room, making final preparations for my lesson that evening. Copies of the Times Higher Education Supplement (THES) littered the table next to the door of the room; a banner headline caught my eye: "Exclusions from RAE see steep rise". I read on:

"Dramatic increases in the proportion of academics excluded from the research assessment exercise were confirmed by a number of universities this week ... amid speculation that more academics than ever before could be branded 'research inactive' and left out of the exercise." (Corbyn, 2007a)

Looking further into the paper, another headline, "What a waste: 2008's rejects vent dismay" (Corbyn, 2007b), leads into a proliferation of quotations about the experiences of academics whose efforts to be included in the exercise and to be deemed 'research active', were unsuccessful. The article made harrowing reading. I had recently read Andrew Sparkes' paper that presented "the embodied struggle of an academic at a university that is permeated by an audit culture" (Sparkes, 2007, p.521) and in powerfully engaging with the narrative style of the paper found both empathy and anger being evoked in me as I read through

---

[10] Jane Speedy

its content. Over the next few days the coincidence of these two readings seemed to prompt me in mulling these things over, encouraging me reflect upon my own experiences, and provoking thoughts that had not been manifest before.

About a year ago, when my own faculty began its preparations for the Research Assessment Exercise (RAE), I duly submitted my four best publications (three in *Qualitative Inquiry* and one in *Teaching in Higher Education*) and in due course received indications that my submissions would be three-star rated. Over the ensuing period personnel responsible for RAE decision-making in the faculty changed and on 4 September 2007 I received an e-mail that included the following passage:

> "None of these were considered submissable with reference to the requirements set out in the RAE definition of research (attached) and the Education sub-panel's statement (see paras 3 and 25-29 of the attached pdf file). Looking again at the reviews of your papers, it seems that problems they had in common were their lack of focus on education and the difficulty of seeing them as reports of investigative research in terms of the RAE definition and the sub-panel's criteria."

Surprisingly, perhaps, on reflection, I didn't feel particularly fazed by this; the e-mail was submerged beneath the frenetic business of the new academic year and a plethora of associated tasks. I forgot about it for nearly two months until I read the THES article and the Sparkes paper, just two weeks ago. When I wrote to you about this, your e-mail response on 12th November was immediate and direct:

> "I read this email last night, and scrolled down to read your colleague's comments. It stopped me in my tracks - I'd been doing our writing at the time. I couldn't do any more. I felt angry, and sad, then defiant. On both yours and my behalf. How dare they! Followed by 'am I bothered?' I write for us and for people who appreciate what we're doing, so the rest can all sod off!"

When I mentioned it to Jane[11], she responded, on the 13th November, in a similarly forthright manner:

> "Oh God, Ken that's terrible ...your QI articles would have been given a 3 star rating here and aspired to...(3 is one from top)."

---

[11] Jane Speedy

What am I saying here? What does this have to do with our writing? Where are we now?

I was so taken by the emotion in your response when you said: "I write for us and for people who appreciate what we're doing, so the rest can all sod off!" I have thought about this in relation to Tessa's Uncle Hamish and in relation to other people we like and respect and with whom we would like to share our work. As far as the RAE is concerned I totally agree with you. I will probably lose some research hours on my timetable as a result of being deemed 'research inactive' but even though it has finally made me feel a little disappointed, I think that I will be able to live with that. I am really thinking about your question "Where are we now?". I have already responded to you in what you might call a 'Ken-ning' kind of way; fast, spontaneous and phenomenological with a logic of sense to the fore. For me, this question flicks all those switches. I only begin to think about the spatial or temporal objectification of this question when I am pushed. As so often happens, your writing to me, with me, about me, pushes me to re-write, to feel differently and to re-position myself. That is what I have been trying to do in these last few lines. I have tried to stand back from myself, to be reflective, to answer your question because we need to tidy up the ending to this shared work together. I am not that good at it but I have tried not to resist!

Can I go back home now?!

EPILOGUE

Writing Space Fourteen

Return to QI

It's the 25th International Congress of Qualitative Inquiry, University of Illinois, Urbana-Champaign, USA. May, 2029.

Two men walk slowly along a concrete walkway to the right of the long quadrangle of grass behind the imposing Illini Union Building. In the Spring sunshine, they feel good (still) to be alive. The taller man, perhaps 70, stoops slightly as he walks, feeling in his joints the effects of a jog earlier the previous evening; the other, a few years older in his mid-80s, wears his gray hair long. His T shirt reveals tanned arms covered in a mat of hair; soft, silver fur.

On the quadrangle, groups of students occupy the space in clusters, some lying in the sun around piles of bags and books, others throwing ball, and still more chasing frisbees. The two men pay them no attention. They are absorbed in conversation as they prepare for the presentation they are giving in a few moments' time. The smaller man is saying, "…but it's the story that counts…", which the lanky one interrupts–"yes, but it's the lines of flight it traces in the nomos of smooth space, the deterritorialisation…"–but the rest of his sentence is lost amongst shouts to "Catch it!". A young man leaps to clutch the disc in front of them, tumbling spectacularly to the ground, and laughs. He gets up, undamaged by the fall onto the path, and saunters away.

The two men enter the brown brick building just off the quad and negotiate their route to an obscure, battered classroom. Its chairs have wooden 'desks' that lift and drop to allow students to rest their books and write. There are four other presenters there, waiting, and, by the time the session starts, eight people are scattered haphazardly in the audience.

When it is their turn, the men stand, though it takes a while.

"Thank you for coming," the tanned one says. "I'm Ken Gale and this is Jonathan Wyatt. We're both retired, me from the University of Plymouth and Jonathan from the University of Oxford in the UK. We're pleased to be back here–it's been a while for both of us."

Wyatt picks up the cue:

"We've kept writing during this time. We've been writing together for a long time now. Today we wish to share something of what we've been writing recently."

They begin.

A middle-aged woman in the audience, who has come to this session to hear one of the other presenters, searches through the thick, red, black and white conference prospectus to remind herself of the title of Gale and Wyatt's paper. She finds it:

"Two Men Going On and On: An Inquiry into Writing and Friendship in Our Silver Years."

REFERENCES

Allen, W. (1984). The Purple Rose of Cairo. J. Rolins & C. H. Joffe (Producer). USA: Orion.

Althusser, L. (2001). *Lenin and philosophy and other essays* (B. Brewster, Trans.) New York: Monthly Review Press

Atkinson, P., & Coffey, A. (2003). Revisiting the relationship between participant observation and interviewing. In J. Gubrium & J. Holstein (Eds.), *Post modern interviewing* (pp. 109-122). Thousand Oaks, CA: Sage.

Atkinson, P., & Silverman, D. (1997). Kundera's immortality: the interview society and the invention of self. *Qualitative Inquiry, 3*(3), 304-325.

Austin, J. L. (1962). *How to do things with words.* Oxford: Clarendon Press.

Bachelard, G. (1969). *The poetics of space* (M. Jolas, Trans. 1958). Boston: Beacon.

BACP. (2007). *Ethical framework for good practice in counselling and psychotherapy* (2002). Rugby: British Association for Counselling and Psychotherapy.

Bakhtin, M. (1981). *The dialogic imagination* Austin: University of Texas Press.

Bauman, Z. (1991). *Modernity and ambivalence* Cambridge, MA: Polity Press.

Beineix, J. C. (1986). Betty Blue. C. Ossard (Producer): Gaumont/ Constellation/Cargofilms.

Berry, C. (1958). Reelin' and Rockin' L. Chess & P. Chess (Producer). Chicago: Chess.

Boal, A. (1979). *Theatre of the oppressed.* London: Pluto.

Bion, W. (1961). *Experiences in groups.* London: Routledge.

BlackStreet. (1996). *No Diggity*: Interscope Records.

Bollas, C. (1987). *The shadow of the object: Psychoanalysis of the unthought known.* London: Free Association Books.

Bolter, J. D. (2001). *Writing Space: Computers, Hypertext and the Remediation of Print* (2nd ed. 1991). Mahwah, NJ: Lawrence Erlbaum Associates.

Bolter, J. D., Joyce, M., Smith, J. B., & Bernstein, M. (2001). Storyspace. Watertown, MA: Eastgate Systems.

Bond, T. (2004). *Ethical guidelines for researching counselling and psychotherapy*. Rugby: BACP.

Bond, T., & Mifsud, D. (2005). Investigating cultural differences: A methodological pilot of narrative inquiry using creative dialogue, *British Association of Counselling and Psychotherapy Research Conference*. Nottingham, United Kingdom.

Bourdieu, P., & Passeron, J. C. (1977). *Reproduction in education, society and culture*. London Sage.

Bowers, M. (2004). *Magic(al) realism: The new critical idiom*. London: Routledge.

Bowles, P. (2006). *The sheltering sky* (1949). London: Penguin.

Braidotti, R. (1994). *Nomadic subjects*. New York: Columbia University Press.

Buber, M. (1937). *I and Thou*. (Original publication 1923). Edinburgh: FT Clark.

Budick, S., & Iser, W. (Eds.). (1987). *Languages of the unsayable: The play of negativity in literature and literary theory*. Stanford, CA: Stanford University Press.

Butler, J. (2004a). *Precarious life: The powers of mourning and violence*. London: Verso.

—. (2004b). *Undoing gender* Abingdon, UK: Routledge.

—. (2006). *Gender trouble* (Original publication 1990). Abingdon, UK: Routledge.

Calafell, B. M. (2007). Mentoring and love: An open letter. *Cultural Studies <=> Critical Methodologies, 7*(4), 425-441.

Cavallaro, D. (2000). *Cyberpunk and cyberculture*. London: Athlone Press.

Cavarero, A. (2000). *Relating narratives: Storytelling and selfhood*. (P. A. Kottman, Trans. 1997). Abingdon: Routledge.

Cimino, M. (1975). The Deerhunter. B. Spikings & M. Deeley & M. Cimino & J. Peverall (Producer). USA.

Cixous, H. (1991). Coming to writing. In D. Jenson (Ed.), *Coming to writing and other essays*. Cambridge, MS: Harvard University Press.

—. (1994a). The newly-born woman. In S. Sellers (Ed.), *The Hélène Cixous reader*. London: Routledge.

—. (1994b). Three steps on the ladder of writing. In S. Sellers (Ed.), *The Hélène Cixous reader* (pp. 199-205). London: Routledge.

—. (1994c). (With) or the art of innocence. In S. Sellers (Ed.), *The Helene Cixous Reader*. London Routledge.

—. (2005). *Stigmata* (1998). London: Routledge.

Clough, P. (2002). *Narratives and fictions in educational research.* Oxford: Oxford University Press.

Coles, R. (1989). *The call of stories.* Boston: Houghton Miflin.

Corbyn, Z. (2007a, November 2nd). Exclusions from RAE see steep rise. *Times Higher Education Supplement.*

—. (2007b, November 2nd). What a waste: 2008's rejects vent dismay. *Times Higher Education Supplement.*

Crapanzano, V. (1992). *Hermes' dilemma and Hamlet's desire: On the epistemology of interpretation.* Cambridge, MA: Harvard University Press.

Davies, B., & Gannon, S. (Eds.). (2006). *Doing collective biography.* Buckingham: Open University Press.

Davis, C. (2004). *After poststructuralism: Reading, stories and theory.* London: Routledge.

de Beauvoir, S. (1978). *The second sex.* Harmondsworth Penguin.

Deleuze, G. (1986). *Cinema 1: The movement-image* (H. Tomlinson & B. Habberjam, Trans.) Minneapolis: University of Minnesota Press.

—. (1990). *The logic of sense* (M. Lester, Trans. 1969). New York: Columbia University Press.

—. (1993). *The fold: Leibniz and the Baroque.* London: Continuum.

—. (1994). He stuttered. In C. Boundas & D. Olkowsky (Eds.), *Gilles Deleuze and the theater of philosophy* (pp. 23-33). London: Routledge.

—. (1995). *Negotiations (1972-1990).* (M. Joughin, Trans.) New York: Columbia University Press.

—. (1997). Desire and pleasure. In A. Davidson (Ed.), *Foucault and his interlocutors* (pp. 183-192). Chicago: University of Chicago Press.

—. (2004). *Francis Bacon: The logic of sensation.* London Continuum.

Deleuze, G., & Guattari, F. (1986). *Kafka: Toward a minor literature.* Minneapolis: University of Minnesota Press.

Deleuze, G., & Guattari, F. (1994). *What is philosophy?* London: Verso.

Deleuze, G., & Guattari, F. (2004a). *Anti-Oedipus: Capitalism and schizophrenia* (R. Hurley & M. Seem & H. Lane, Trans. 1984). London: Continuum.

Deleuze, G., & Guattari, F. (2004b). *A thousand plateaus* (B. Massumi, Trans. 1980). London: Continuum.

Deleuze, G., & Parnet, C. (2002). *Dialogues II* (H. Tomlinson, Trans. 2006 ed. 1977). London: Continuum.

Derrida, J. (1976). *Of grammatology.* Baltimore: Johns Hopkins University Press.

—. (1978). *Writing and difference.* London Routledge.

—. (1989). *Memoires for Paul de Man* (C. Lindsay & J. Culler & E. Cadava & P. Kamuf, Trans). New York: Columbia University Press.

—. (2003). *The work of mourning*. Chicago and London: The University of Chicago Press.

Denzin, N. (2003). Reading and writing performance. *Qualitative Research, 4*(3), 243-268.

Due, R. (2007). *Deleuze*. Cambridge Polity Press.

Ellis, C. (2007). Telling secrets, revealing lives: Relational ethics in research with intimate others. *Qualitative Inquiry, 13*(1), 3-29.

Ellis, C., & Berger, L. (2003). Their story/my story/our story: Including the researcher's experience in interview research. In L. J. Gubrium & J. Holstein (Eds.), *Postmodern interviewing* (pp. 157-186). Thousand Oaks, CA: Sage.

Ely, M., Vinz, R., Downing, M., & Anzul, M. (2001). *On writing qualitative research:Living by words*. London: Routledge Falmer.

Estes, C. P. (1992). *Women who run with wolves*. London: Rider.

Etherington, K. (2004). *Becoming a reflexive researcher*. London: Jessica Kingsley.

Faris, W. (2004). *Ordinary enchantment: Magical realism and the remystifation of narrative*. Nashville, TN: Vanderbilt University Press.

Ficacci, L. (2003). *Bacon*. Los Angeles: Taschen.

Field, N. (Ed.). (2005). *Ten Lectures on Psychotherapy and Spirituality*. London: Karnac.

Fontana, A., & Frey, J. (2000). The interview: from structural questions to negotiated text. In N. Denzin & Y. Lincoln (Eds.), *Handbook of qualitative research* (2nd ed.). Thousand Oaks: Sage.

Foucault, M. (1986). Of other spaces. *Diacritics, 16*(1), 22-27.

—. (1998a). Different spaces. In J. Faubion (Ed.), *Aesthetics: the essential works, 2* (pp. 175-185). London: Allen Lane.

—. (1998b). *The history of sexuality volume 1: The will to knowledge*. London: Penguin.

—. (2002). *The archaeology of knowledge* (A. M. Sheridan Smith, Trans. 1969). London: Routledge.

—. (1998). Mythical time, historical time and the narrative fabric of the self. *Narrative Inquiry, 8*(1), 27-50.

Gadamer, H.-G. (1980). The universality of the hermeneutical problem. In J. Bleicher (Ed.), *Contemporary hermeneutics: Hermeneutics as method, philosophy and critique* (pp.128-140). London: Routledge and Kegan Paul.

Gale, K. (2007). Teacher Education in the University: Working with Policy, Practice and Deleuze. *Teaching in Higher Education, 12*(4), 471-483.

Gale, K., Pelias, R., Russell, L., Spry, T., & Wyatt, J. (2008). Five ways of caring: The complexity of a loving performance, *4th International Congress of Qualitative Inquiry*. University of Illinois at Urbana-Champaign.

Gale, K., & Wyatt, J. (2006). Inquiring into writing: An interactive interview. *Qualitative Inquiry, 12*(6), 1117-1134.

Gale, K., & Wyatt, J. (2007a). Two men talking. *3rd International Congress of Qualitative Inquiry*. University of Illinois at Urbana-Champaign.

Gale, K., & Wyatt, J. (2007b). Writing the incalculable: A second interactive inquiry. *Qualitative Inquiry, 13*(6), 787-807.

Gale, K., & Wyatt, J. (2008a). Two men talking two: Therapy - A story, *4th International Congress of Qualitative Inquiry*. University of Illinois at Urbana-Champaign.

Gale, K. J., & Wyatt, J. (2008b). Becoming men, becoming-men? A collective biography. *International Review of Qualitative Research, 1*(2), 235-254.

Gale, K., & Wyatt, J. (2008c). Two men talking. *International Review of Qualitative Research, 1*(3), 361-379.

Gannon, S. (2006). Writing into the space of the 'other', *2nd International Congress of Qualitative Inquiry*. University of Illinois at Urbana-Champaign

Gibson, W. (1984). *Neuromancer*. London: Collins.

Goffman, E. (1959). *The presentation of the self in everyday life* (New York: Doubleday

Gonick, M., & Hladki, J. (2005). Who are the participants? Rethinking representational practices and writing with heterotopic possibility in qualitative inquiry. *International Journal of Qualitative Studies in Education, 18*(3), 285-304.

Goodchild, P. (1996). *Deleuze and Guattari: An introduction to the politics of desire*. London: Sage.

Grosz, E. (1994). A thousand tiny sexes: Feminism and rhizomatics. In C. V. Boundas & D. Olkowski (Eds.), *Gilles Deleuze and the theater of philosophy* (pp. 187-210). New York: Routledge.

Gubrium, J., & Holstein, J. (Eds.). (2003). *Postmodern interviewing*. London Sage.

Harvey, P. J. (2000). Stories from the City, Stories from the Sea. P. J. Harvey & R. Ellis & M. Harvey (Producer). New York: Island Records.

Haug, F., Andersen, S., Bunz-Elffeding, A., Hauser, K., Lang, U., Laudan, M., Ludemann, M., Meir, U., Nemitz, B., Niehoff, E., Prinz, R., Rathzel, N., Scheu, M., & Thomas, C. (Eds.). (1999). *Female sexualisation: A collective work of memory.* London: Verso.

Heaney, S. (1966). *Death of a naturalist.* London: Faber.

Heidegger, M. (1962). *Being and time.* London: Blackwell.

Hillman, J. (1984). *Inter Views.* New York: Harper.

—. (1992). *Re-visioning psychology.* New York: Harper Perennial.

hooks, b. (1994). *Teaching to transgress: Education as the practice of freedom.* London: Routledge.

—. (2001). *All about love: New visions.* New York: Perennial.

Irigaray, L. (1985). *This sex which is not one.* (C. Martin, Trans). New York: Cornell University Press.

Jarvinen, M. (2000). The biographical illusion: Constructing meaning in qualitative interviews. *Qualitative Inquiry, 6*(3), 370-391.

Joyce, M. (1987). afternoon, a story. Watertown, MA: Eastgate Systems.

Kerouac, J. (1976). *On the road* (Originally published in 1955). London: Penguin.

Kesey, K. (2005). *One flew over the cuckoo's nest* (Originally published in 1962). London: Penguin.

Klein, J. (2005). What happens between people. In N. Field (Ed.), *Ten Lectures on Psychotherapy and Spirituality.* London: Karnac.

Klein, M. (1984). Notes on some schizoid mechanisms. In R. Money-Kyrle & B. Joseph & E. O'Shaughnessy & H. Segal (Eds.), *The writings of Melanie Klein.Vol III.* London: The Hogarth Press.

Kolb, D. (1994). Socrates in the labyrinth. Watertown, MA: Eastgate Systems.

Krell, D. (2000). *The purest of bastards: Works of mourning, art, and affirmation inthe thought of Jacques Derrida* (University Park: Pennsylvania State University Press.

Kristeva, J. (2002). Word, Dialogue and Novel. In T. Moi (Ed.), *The Kristeva Reader.* Oxford: Blackwell.

Kvale, S. (1996). *Inter Views: an introduction to qualitative research writing.* Thousand Oaks: Sage

Lather, P. (2007). *Getting lost: Feminist efforts towards a double(d) science.* Albany: State University of New York.

Lee, K. V. (2005). Neuroticism: end of a doctoral dissertation. *Qualitative Inquiry, 11*(6), 933-938.

Lyotard, J.-F. (1984). *The postmodern condition: A report on knowledge.* Manchester: Manchester University Press.

MacIntyre, A. (1982). *After virtue: a study in moral theory.* London Duckworth.

Macksey, R., & Donato, E. (Eds.). (1970). *The structuralist controversy: The languages of criticism and the sciences of man* London: Johns Hopkins University Press.

MacLure, M. (2003). *Discourse in educational and social research.* Buckingham, UK: Open University Press.

Mann, C., & Stewart, F. (2003). Internet interviewing. In J. Gubrium & J. Holstein (Eds.), *Postmodern Interviewing.* Thousand Oaks: Sage.

Massumi, B. (1987). Translator's foreword: Pleasures of philosophy (B. Massumi, Trans.). In G. Deleuze & F. Guattari (Eds.), *A thousand plateaus: Capitalism and schizophrenia.* Minneapolis: University of Minnesota Press.

McLaren, P. (1997). *Revolutionary multiculturalism: Pedagogies of dissent for the new millennium.* Boulder, Colorado Westview.

Melly, G. (1974). *Revolt into style: Pop arts in Britain* (1970). London: Penguin.

Merleau-Ponty, M. (1962). *The phenomenology of perception* (London Routledge and Kegan Paul.

Monk, R. (1991). *Ludwig Wittgenstein: The study of genius.* London: Vintage.

Moreno, J. L. (1946). *Psychodrama: Vol 1.* Beacon, NY: Beacon House.

Morgan, W. (2000). Electronic tools for dismantling the master's house: poststructuralist feminist research and hypertext poetics. In E. A. St. Pierre & W. S. Pillow (Eds.), *Working the ruins: Feminist poststructural theory and methods in education* (pp. 130-149). London: Routledge.

Moulthorp, S. (1992). Victory Garden. Watertown, MA: Eastgate Systems.

Mulvey, L. (1975). Visual pleasure and narrative cinema screen *Screen, 16* (3), 6-18.

Myerhoff, B. (1982). Life history among the elderly: Performance, visibility and re-membering. In J. Ruby (Ed.), *A crack in the mirror: Reflexive perspectives in anthropology.* Philadelphia: University of Pennsylvania Press.

Ogden, T. (1986). *The matrix of the mind: Object relations theory and the psychoanalytic dialogue.* Northvale, NJ: Jason Aronson.

—. (1994). The analytic third: Working with intersubjective clinical facts. *International Journal of Psychoanalysis*(75), 883-900.

Pelias, R. (1999). *Writing Performance: Poeticising the Researcher's Body*. Carbondale and Edwardsville: Southern Illinois University Press.

—. (2000). Always dying: living between *Da* and *Fort*. *Qualitative Inquiry, 6*(2), 229-237.

—. (2004). *A methodology of the heart: Evoking academic and daily life*. Oxford: AltaMira Press.

—. (2005). Performative writing as scholarship: an apology, an argument, an anecdote. *Cultural Studies <=> Critical Methodologies, 5*(4), 415-424.

—. (2007). Performative writing workshop, *3rd International Congress of Qualitative Inquiry*. University of Illinois at Urbana-Champaign.

Plant, S. (1999). *Writing on drugs*. London: Faber and Faber.

Rajchman, J. (2000). *The Deleuze Connections*. London: The MIT Press

Reynolds, S. (1998). *Energy Flash*. London Picador.

Rhodes, C. (2000). Ghostwriting research: positioning the researcher in the interview text. *Qualitative Inquiry, 6*(4), 511-525.

Richardson, L. (1992). The consequences of poetic representation: Writing the other, writing the self. In C. Ellis & M. Flaherty (Eds.), *Investigating subjectivity: Research on lived experience* (pp. 125-137). Thousand Oaks, CA: Sage.

—. (1997a). *Fields of Play (Constructing an Academic Life)*. New Brunswick: Rutgers University Press.

—. (1997b). Poetic representation. In J. Flood & S. Brice Heath & D. Lapp (Eds.), *Handbook of research for literacy educators through communicative and visual arts* (pp. 232-238). New York: Simon and Shuster.

—. (2000a). Introduction – Assessing alternative modes of qualitative and ethnographic research: how do we judge? Who judges? *Qualitative Inquiry, 6*(2), 251-252.

—. (2000b). Skirting a pleated text: De-disciplining an academic life. In E. A. St. Pierre & W. S. Pillow (Eds.), *Working the ruins: Feminist poststructural theory and methods in education* (pp. 153-163). London: Routledge.

—. (2001). Getting personal: writing-stories. *Qualitative Studies in Education, 14*(1), 33-38.

—. (2003). Poetic Representation of Interviews. In J. Gubrium & J. Holstein (Eds.), *Postmodern Interviewing* (pp. 187-201). London Sage

—. (2007). *Last writes: A daybook for a dying friend*. Walnut Creek, CA: Left Coast.

Richardson, L., & St Pierre, E. (2005). Writing: A method of inquiry In N. Denzin & Y. Lincoln (Eds.), *Handbook of Qualitative Research* (3rd ed., pp. 959-978). London: Sage

Robinson, W., & Rogers, R. (1964). The Way You Do the Things You Do. W. Robinson (Producer): Gordy (Motown).

Rogers, A., Casey, M., Ekert, J., Holland, J., Nakkula, V., & Sheinburg, N. (1999). An interpretive poetics of languages of the unsayable. In R. Josseloson & A. Lieblich (Eds.), *Making meaning of narratives: The narrative study of lives, Vol. 6* (pp. 77-106). London: Sage.

Sartre, J.-P. (1973). *Existentialism and humanism* (London Methuen.

Scott, R. (1979). Alien. W. Hill & G. Carroll & D. Giler (Producer). USA: TCF/Brandywine.

Sellers, S. (Ed.). (1994). *The Helene Cixous reader.* London: Routledge.

—. (Ed.). (2004). *The writing notebooks of Hélène Cixous.* London: Continuum.

Smith, B., & Sparkes, A. C. (2008). Contrasting perspectives on narrating selves and identities: an invitation to dialogue. *Qualitative Research, 8*(1), 5-35.

Sparkes, A. C. (2007). Embodiment, academics, and the audit culture: A story seeking consideration. *Qualitative Research, 7*(4), 521-550.

Speedy, J., (with Thompson, G., & others) (2004). Living a more peopled life: definitional ceremony as inquiry into therapy outcomes *International Journal of Narrative Therapy and Community Work*(3), 43-53.

—. (2005). Failing to come to terms with things: a multi-storied conversation about poststructuralist ideas and narrative practices in response to some of life's failures. *Counselling and Psychotherapy Research.*

—. (2008). *Narrative inquiry and psychotherapy.* Basingstoke: Palgrave Macmillan.

St. Pierre, E. A. (1997). Circling the text: nomadic writing practices. *Qualitative Inquiry, 3*(4), 403-417.

—. (2000). Nomadic inquiry in the smooth spaces of the field: A preface. In E. A. St. Pierre & W. S. Pillow (Eds.), *Working the ruins: Feminist poststructural theory and methods in education* (pp. 258-283). London: —. (2004). Deleuzian concepts for education: the subject undone. *Educational Philosophy and Theory, 36*(3), 283-296.

Stivale, C. J. (2000). The folds of friendship - Derrida - Deleuze - Foucault. *Angelaki: Journal of Theoretical Humanities, 5*(2), 3-15.

—. (2003). Deleuze/Parnet in "Dialogues": the folds of post-identity. *The Journal of the Midwest Modern Language Association, 36*(1), 25-37.

Tamboukou, M., & Ball, S. (2002). Nomadic Subjects, young black women in the UK. *Discourse: Studies in the Cultural Politics of Education 23*(3).

Tillman-Healey, L. M. (2003). Friendship as method. *Qualitative Inquiry, 9*(5), 729-749.

Torfing, J. (1999). *New theories of discourse.* London: Blackwell.

Townshend, P. (1978). Who are you? G. Johns (Producer): Polydor.

Tuckman, B. W. (1965). Developmental sequence in small groups. *Psychological Bulletin, 63*, 384-399.

Vygotsky, L. (1962). *Thought and language.* Cambridge, Mass.: MIT Press.

White, M. (1995). *Reauthoring lives: Interviews and essays.* Adelaide: Dulwich Centre Publications

—. (2000). *Reflections on narrative practice: Essays and interviews* (Adelaide: Dulwich Centre Publications.

—. (2000). *Reflections on Narrative Practice: Essays and Interviews.* Adelaide: Dulwich Centre Publications.

Wittgenstein, L. (2001). *Philosophical investigations.* 3rd ed. Oxford: Blackwell.

Winnicott, D. (1958). *Collected papers: Through paedatrics to psychoanalysis.* London: Hogarth Press.

Winterson, J. (1993). *Written on the body* (Originally published in 1991). London: Vintage.

Wyatt, J. (2001). *Confronting the Almighty God: How do psychodynamic counsellors respond to clients' expressions of religious faith?* Unpublished MEd dissertation, Oxford Brookes University with the Isis Centre, Oxford.

—. (2005a). A Gentle Going? An autoethnographic short story *Qualitative Inquiry, 11*(5), 724-732.

—. (2005b). The telling of a tale: A gentle going? An autoethnographic short story, *1st International Congress of Qualitative Inquiry.* University of Illinois at Urbana-Champaign.

—. (2006). Psychic distance, consent and other ethical issues: Reflections on the writing of "A Gentle Going?" *Qualitative Inquiry 12*(4), 813-818.

—. (2008). No longer loss: Autoethnographic stammering. *Qualitative Inquiry, 14*(6), 955-967.

Zembylas, M. (2007). Risks and pleasures: a Deleuzo-Guattarian pedagogy of desire in education. *British Education Research Journal, 33*(3), 331-347.

Žižek, S. (1989). *The sublime object of ideology.* London: Verso.

INDEX